WHEN I FELL

WHEN I FELL

How I Rerouted My Life and
Found Strength in a Severed Spine

MICHAEL MURPHY

NEW YORK

LONDON • NASHVILLE • MELBOURNE • VANCOUVER

WHEN I FELL
How I Rerouted My Life and Found Strength in a Severed Spine

Published in New York, New York, by Morgan James Publishing. Morgan James is a trademark of Morgan James, LLC. www.MorganJamesPublishing.com

ISBN 978-1-63195-250-0 paperback
ISBN 978-1-63195-251-7 eBook
Library of Congress Control Number: 2020910202

Cover Design by:
Rachel Lopez
www.r2cdesign.com

Morgan James is a proud partner of Habitat for Humanity Peninsula and Greater Williamsburg. Partners in building since 2006.

Get involved today! Visit
www.MorganJamesBuilds.com

DEDICATION

For Mom and Dad—who raised me right,
loved me lots, and never missed a game.

For my family—who are all so weird and wonderful.

And for Casey—who inspires me to be better every day.
I Love You to The Moon and Back

TABLE OF CONTENTS

Those who hope in the Lord
will renew their strength.
They will soar on wings like eagles;
They will run and not grow weary.
They will walk and not grow faint.
Isaiah 40:31

"While tragedy can be a cruel teacher, it can also lead you to understand
a truth and beauty that is much greater than yourself, as long as you
refuse to quit...Even when you're feeling weak, alone, outmanned, or
out-gunned, as long as you are breathing, then you are still in the game.
Mark Zupan, Paralympian, Wheelchair Rugby, Quadriplegic
Gimp (2006)

"So, our responsibility is not simply shielding those we
care for from adversity but preparing them to meet it well."
Aimee Mullins, Paralympian, Sprinter, Double Amputee
"The Opportunity of Adversity" (TED, 2010)

Prologue
THE STARTING GATE

February, 2017. In The Rockies with the NSCD. Winter Park, CO.

Winter Park Resort sat small below me at the bottom of the slope, a cluster of buildings and parking lots in a narrow valley between two towering snow-capped ranges running parallel like a pair of great walls.

I paused to catch my breath before my next run and let my eyes wander where they wanted. I found myself smiling beneath my facemask, admiring a view I still could not quite believe was real.

All of Winter Park was quiet and still under a blanket of fresh fallen snow. Gathered in valleys, gorges, and crevices, the blanket of white was deepest. Higher up the mountainsides, evergreen pines covered every rocky range, an army of frozen sentinels, their still-green needles dusted with winter.

Higher still, above the tree lines, the rolling, rocky crags and peaks looked cold and windy, as they always did, even on a sunny, "blue bird," Colorado day like today.

I watched a gust of wind trace one of the bare peaks. Above the tree-line it moved free as the waves at sea, beyond the reach of the piney sentinels. A huge wash of new powder rose from the ground and swirled in the sky, dancing in the wind. It was strikingly beautiful. The landscape looked as formidable and uninviting as it did gorgeous.

Sitting in the starting gate atop the slalom course, strapped in good and tight to my brand new monoski, it was my turn "on course."

1

My eyes narrowed-in on the task before me: the zig-zag line of red and blue gates set up for the day's training session.

— — — — —

In February of 2017, I arrived at the National Sports Center for the Disabled (NSCD) in Winter Park and began training with their Competition Team. It was a critical step on the road toward my life's greatest, loftiest goal: Beijing 2022.

The NSCD is one of the largest outdoor therapeutic recreation and adaptive sports agencies in the world. Their mission, since 1970, has been to enable the human spirit through recreation and sports, whether it's skiing in winter or whitewater rafting and horseback riding in summer.

Additionally, the program boasts a very serious and highly competitive racing program through their "Comp Center." Ski racers of every level—paraplegics, amputees, visually impaired—come to Winter Park to be trained by some of the top coaches in the business.

Some fly in from the U.K., Chile, Japan, and New Zealand to train beside members of the U.S. Team gearing up for World Cup competitions or the next Winter Paralympics.

The ski training is serious, the instruction is world-class, and the camaraderie of the group is as sincere and genuine as that found among the community of handcyclists on the Paralyzed Veterans of America Racing team, who took me under their wing in 2008.

It was to this alpine ski team that I joined in February, 2017. When I did, I ceased being a recreational monoskier and dove headfirst into the world of competitive ski racing.

Three days a week, from sun-up on Tuesdays to afternoons on Thursdays, I spent time away from my new wife, Casey, our German Shepherd, Gunner, and our new Denver home to stay in Winter Park and do what was necessary to learn about ski racing and being a racer.

Week after week, my skiing improved, I asked a thousand questions, watched how the Paralympians did it, learned from my coaches, grew comfortable with gate-training and found a new passion that bordered on obsession as I learned the differences between free skiing and race training as well as the subtle nuances between Slalom (SL) and Giant Slalom (GS), Super G (SG) and Downhill (DH).

— — — — —

I watched as the racer before me attacked the turns and cleared the course. Halfway down he disappeared up and over a knoll at the foot of the slope. I concentrated on the gates. I chose my first line and planned my attack, replaying the latest tips given to me by my coach, Scott, after my last run.

Chest up, head up. Turn earlier, edge to edge. Eyes downhill. Breathe.

The radio on my coach's shoulder crackled beside me. "Course clear," the voice said.

Scott was quick to reply. "K. Murphy in the gate."

Behind me came another voice. "Go get it, Murph!"

I knew the voice well. Everyone did. It was the unmistakable Serbian accent of a new friend, with a similar spinal injury as mine, who I was trying to emulate.

I embraced his words and used the encouragement as fuel. He was the Paralympian, after all. If I wanted to go to Beijing in five years' time, listening to every word this guy said would surely help.

I lined up evenly in the gate between the posts. With the tip of my ski sitting over the edge, I started thinking...

You can be him. You can. You can. It starts here. If he can do it, you can do it. Why not me...? 2022. 2022...

I was so honed-in that I missed my cue. Through a salt-and-pepper beard, Scott called out again with extra emphasis and sarcasm in his voice.

In a flash, the picture in my head vanished and the big imaginary "Team USA" logo on my chest disappeared. In its place is a smile...and a burning determination, a relentless tenacity. I pushed off and found my line.

As I attacked the first gate, the last word from Coach Scott in the starting gate echoes in my head—its significance in my heart. A command. A starting gun. A simple call-to-action.

"Murphy... GO!"

Chapter 1

LIFE 2.0

April 22, 2007. Randolph-Macon College. Ashland, VA.

Gravity introduced me to the earth and my spine exploded. Tiny shards of bone tore through my back like shrapnel from a grenade. The cord within never stood a chance.

I tried moving my legs, my knees. I wanted to get up, badly. To resume the night. Have another drink. Go back to the way things were. I wanted my legs to move.

What happened to me would puzzle most, but I put the pieces together quickly, long before the doctor, clad in coat of white, knelt beside my bed and leveled with me.

When your legs refuse to budge it's an odd feeling. An inexplicable, unfamiliar void. A nothingness where there once existed…everything. Youth and vitality, strength and life, vim and vigor—all of it gone, all of it numb.

The reality of my situation was sobering. I was blind to what would happen next and what my future could hold. But in my inebriated state of confusion, and despite the questions and uncertainties swirling about my head, I knew one thing…

Oh, crap.

Just then, reality clocked me in the jaw like a prize-fighter to an underdog. There was nothing I could do. I rested my head, slow and sullen, contemplating how both the evening and my life had taken such an abrupt turn and veered off course.

Gazing up at a tapestry of diamonds dotting the sky, a tough worn footpath beneath me cradled my broken body yet gave none of the comfort, or answers, I was seeking. I had found myself on the ground, seconds after innocently enjoying the end to another Saturday night at Randolph-Macon College.

─ ─ ─ ─ ─

When I relive the accident, my mind conjures up a blurry, disjointed collage of snapshots. Fast-moving images from accident to ambulance to ICU. From the moment I fell to when paramedics sedated me on the gurney, what happened is, oddly, both clear and cloudy.

The shock trauma of such a viciously powerful event undoubtedly played a role in this strange clarity while my brain repressed—smartly—some of the more cringe-worthy moments.

The brain has an amazing way of saving ourselves from a lifetime of memories we otherwise might choose to forget. For me, it was the half-second of free-fall. What I call the Black.

Having said that, though, I'd still be stupid and naïve to think my BAC levels didn't have a hand in the rolling fog that disrupted my memories. After all, it was Saturday night in college…I *was* 21…and, I should add, it was 80's Night.

Yes. I was drunk. I'm fine with that.

Despite this, my mind functioned relatively clearly after coming to—at least until the drugs took effect in the ambulance. I took my experience as an obvious matter of fact.

I was conscious. Cognizant. Aware of what had physically happened to me and the truth about my future that took form in the Black—the precise moment of my life's rerouting. I knew because paralysis is no stranger to our Murphy-Gardner clan.

Seconds after the Black released me, after I first felt the invisible cement locked around my legs, things happened fast. I saw hurried movements, vague shapes in my peripheries, mysterious silhouetted bodies framed in moonlight rushing to my side. Their voices quivered with worry.

What happened? Why…why am I here?

My mind jumped from question to question, looking for answers to the unknowns.

Who's there? What's going on?

I realized the figures weren't apparitions, but the friends I was with, 80's outfits and all.

I lifted my head, looked down. Once more I tried to stand. This futile attempt was quickly met with a volley of commands.

"Don't move, don't move!" One voice instructed, anxious yet assertive.

"S-stay still." Stammered another. "Just…just lie down. L-Lie down!"

"Yeah. Yeah. P-put your head down, just put it down!"

But my head was down.

After the second attempt to pull myself up failed, the thing I knew from the start was fully confirmed. Again, nothing. Again, I knew. *Paige…* Resigned to a fate known only to me, I found hollow respite on the unforgiving earth. I had no further intentions of moving.

But everyone continued to try and help, using words of comfort with calming touches to keep me safe and still. From what I heard later, I don't blame them…

After I hit the ground, I remember sitting up quickly, thinking I was indestructible.

As the story goes, this otherwise impossible act of sitting up despite sudden onset paralysis was followed by a look of confusion that then turned to one of cold discomfort and dead-pan uncertainty before my eyes glazed over into a sobering stare—the kind that comes only from knowing something terrible or true. Then, slowly, I laid back down.

It was at this point the Black let go and clarity ensued.

Now they were helping. Preventing me from further action after my multiple attempts to turn back time.

"Yeah, just be still, Mike," instructed a fourth faceless figure crouching like the rest at my side. Two others silently placed soft hands on my chest and shoulders. Perhaps they didn't know what to say or what to do.

For those who did speak, the discernible panic clinging to their words spoke more than the words themselves: Concern. Fear. Ironically, it was I who was calm, not them. The commands continued.

"Stay still!"

"Don't move! Stay down!"

"Don't panic…"

I'm not, you are, I thought, as I struggled to breathe steadily. I was no longer trying to decipher the surrounding alarm when another voice spoke, a new voice, this time behind me.

"Don't move, buddy, just stay down" it said.

The words came low and close to my right ear in a hushed, less-panicky tone than the rest, as if the very words themselves would heal me. It was the only familiar voice.

Nick Jones.

Nick Jones was one of my closest friends and the wing-man you wanted. He was a year older, a linebacker. We'd gotten to know each other well during my first football preseason three years earlier.

Nick was there on the roof when I fell.

"Stay still, buddy. The ambulance is on its way. They're on their way."

An amb—What?!

Mention of an ambulance scared me until I realized it was my ticket to safety.

As this reality further set in, other thoughts struck me. I was in a fragile state emotionally and at one point—I'm not positive why—I became more mad than scared.

I noticed a lack of pain as well, thankfully. Shock was keeping it at bay, but she arrived later, in full force. The main struggle now, though, shortness of breath.

Each was labored and small. Shallow and wheezy beneath ribs I later learned were cracked. It was so troublesome I had to fight, literally, for air.

As I focused on moving from one breath to the next, the paramedics arrived.

Chapter 2

AWAKE: A NEW SCIENCE OF SURVIVAL

"Even in the face of unthinkable tragedy,
possibilities for growth are waiting for you." [1]
—Tedeschi and Moore, *The PTG Workbook*

It was not my dream to partake in the Paralympics. Nor was it a dream to be at a national trial for the Paralympics, or on a mountainside in the Rockies training with Paralympians. I had, however, dreamt of becoming a Marine. It had been what I wanted to do after college, and I was living my life with a military mindset, determined to serve.

Until, that is, I severed my spine, started over, suffered a ton, and then found passion, purpose and strength from my irreparably rerouted life. A life that now includes one chair, two less legs, and four shiny wheels.

For twenty-one years of my life, the Olympics was a phenomenon that rolled around every two and four years where medals were won and for seventeen days the red, white, and blue of The United States were the only colors that mattered. It was a celebration at the highest level of the two things in my life that have held center stage the longest: sports and competition.

The Olympics were anything and everything except of course a dream or possibility—let alone a feasible reality.

<<>>

Posttraumatic Growth, or PTG, is a growing scientific phenomenon based on empirical studies and hard data that was first coined in the early 1990s by pioneering psychologist Richard G. Tedeschi and Lawrence G. Calhoun from The University of North Carolina at Charlotte. They define PTG as "positive change experienced as a result of the struggle with a major life crisis or a traumatic event."[2]

Despite coining the phrase, Tedeschi and Calhoun openly admit that, as a concept, the idea of humans experiencing change—often in "radically positive ways"—via life challenges is hardly new.

"The theme is present in ancient spiritual and religious traditions, literature, and philosophy," they note. However, in terms of what is new, is the "systemic study of this phenomena by psychologists, social workers, counselors, and scholars in other traditions of clinical practice and scientific investigation."[3]

Since the expansion of this academic field, scholars have picked up on the work that Tedeschi and Calhoun have launched venturing off in countless directions and debates that have led to even more perspectives and new takes as academics continue to push toward new PTG horizons.

Demands for new studies, fresh approaches, and practical, measurable in-clinic use is a common final thought found in the conclusions of many published studies that have tackled this subject.

Although still a novel concept, the field remains open for interpretation and is far from finished. In fact, PTG's recent exponential growth compared to its birth in the 90s is indicative of the social and cultural times we now live in—PTG is more relevant than ever.

Our collective curiosity of adversity and dealing with challenge, as well as our relatively recent acceptance, interest, and mainstream out-in-the-real-world inclusion of people with physical and mental disabilities, has helped to assure this relevancy.

It is this, that, as of late, has pushed the conversation surrounding PTG. Humanity's innate curiosity simply makes us wonder, and ask questions.

When we hear of or see someone who has experienced some life challenge, we want to know what happened, what they went through. And then, if that were not enough, we want to know how.

In light of these developments, the academic community has continued their efforts to make sense of this, taking up new, untouched territories whose origins Tedeschi and Calhoun set in motion.

Tedeschi and Calhoun found that PTG typically occurs in five areas: Awareness, Warrior Spirit, Attachment, Knowledge of Self, and Ecstasy. The result of which is a conscious state of improved living, a renaissance—literally a "rebirth"—following your own personal Dark Ages due to your trauma.

1. AWARENESS—of new opportunities and new possibilities that were not present before.
2. WARRIOR SPIRIT—an increased sense of one's own strength. "I got through that, so I can get through anything!"
3. ATTACHMENT—closer relationships with certain people and often a connection with others who have experienced similar challenges/ traumas.
4. KNOWLEDGE OF SELF—greater appreciation for one's life and living in general.
5. ECSTASY—Spiritual or religious awakening, or a deepening of one's spiritual lives.

Think of this conscious state as the new you—a you who is completely and utterly AWAKE. Tedeschi and Calhoun estimates that as many as 30 to 70—and in some instances even 90—percent of survivors experience at least one of the five aspects of PTG.[4] So just remember—science is on your side.

In other words, you will grow. In some manner, inside or out. I promise.

I know. I've lived it. When the academic field of PTG was just barely over ten years young in 2007, I was beginning my own journey in discovering growth after trauma.

My story is proof that the science of Posttraumatic Growth is not only sound, but available for all to learn when the trying times of trauma rock our existence and reroute our lives.

— — — —

1.6 seconds. That's how long it takes to fall two stories. That's how long it took for my life to change.

When I fell off the roof, tiny shards of bone tore through my spine on impact like grenade shrapnel, shattering my vertebrae as I slammed into the ground. Two seconds changed my life, putting me permanently in a wheelchair.

Now, well over a decade later, I have changed…by putting that wheelchair to work, emboldened by the surprising strength found in my severed spine.

Every person falls. But then what?

That's the question I intend to answer with this first book. It is about my story—a "memoir message," if you will, of being abled, disabled, then empowered—of a growth I'm grateful for by way of circumstances, acceptance and aid on all fronts.

This book will combine the story of my recovery and the years of paraplegic prep work ahead of it with the science of resilience to teach you how to attack your adversities and hit home runs when life throws you curves.

At the very least, though, the book will introduce you to PTG and point you towards helpful resources if you need more answers or you're simply still curious about this fascinating concept of internal and external conquest.

My life's path has taught me many things. I know what it's like to run, and I know what it's like to wish to run. I've suffered. I've succeeded. I'm lucky to be alive and getting here wasn't easy. Recovery was misery, but I fought through to independence and discovered my true purpose and potential through my most fortunate misfortune.

I can still remember lying on the ground knowingly thinking that my life had changed forever.

The good news though is that I was right.

Chapter 3

OF GOOD STOCK

Home. McLean, VA.

Whether you've known him for years or minutes, it's not hard to tell that Frank Murphy III is, to borrow a phrase he often uses, a "tapped down" individual. Much of who my father is—his conduct, demeanor, how he goes about things—is because of his time in the military.

Where the shirt, belt buckle, and fly align perfectly down the middle in the Gig Line of the military uniforms he has always told me about, Dad lives by a similar code and it is a philosophy he has tried ceaselessly to impart on us kids.

Even after his service, Dad has lived by the mantras of do things the right way, pay attention to detail, follow instructions, and, as he always reminds me, when you do something "don't half-ass it."

He got this from his father, my Grandad. "He was a very stoic type of man," Dad often says when recollecting. "Very imposing. Six-five, about two-thirty to two hundred forty pounds."

Grandad was raised by his parents, attended Catholic University in D.C. and earned a degree in Civil Engineering. However, when the U.S. entered World War II, as Dad says, "they tossed him in the water."

Underwater Demolition.

My Grandad—Frank Murphy Jr.—was a SEAL before SEALs were SEALs.

My Grandmother, Margaret, by comparison, was a mouse, flirting a few inches past five feet with heels. She was small but quite feisty and played competitive sports in high school and college. "And as you well know, Son," Dad would say to me, "Your Grandmother was a *pisser!*"

Together they made a formidable force, a duo for couples to emulate and admire.

And together they imprinted their morals and mantras onto my Dad, before such were truly being drilled into him in the 60's, when he enlisted in the Army and later became an officer and then Officer Candidate School Drill Instructor.

It is this approach to living and harkening proper do-right ethics that has since shaped and affected me.

Dad has also been a jock his whole life.

He was a standout in basketball, but tennis was his game. As he says, he missed "the big money by four years" and when he went to Florida Southern, he became the best player in the SEC (Southeastern Conference) and continued competitive play for nearly two more decades. Later, after meeting Mom, he describes how "he was a ringer back at Congressional with Mom and her friends in doubles tournaments."

Finally, Dad is also a businessman.

After World War II, Granddad went into the building and construction business where Dad often tagged along, getting first-hand experience at a young age.

Eventually he got into the business himself by running a construction company. When he sold it, Dad next decided to go into broadcasting. His Dad's best friend was in it already and encouraged him to take the leap.

After running two radio stations in Frederick, Maryland, in the 70s Dad moved over to Mutual Broadcasting System, at the time the largest in the country. At some point, when audiences declined, Dad called a man whom he describes as "the smartest guy I've ever met" and talked to him about doing a show. That man was Dick Clark.

During that time Dad was also the radio producer for Notre Dame football games.

At one point, during his Mutual Broadcasting days, Dad hired a guy to host the midnight radio slot and, despite hitting the waves during the graveyard shift, his ratings went through the roof. Not surprising when the DJ your Dad hired was Larry King. When Frank IV was born in 1979, it was DJ Larry K who announced his arrival to the nation live on air.

Shortly after hiring Larry King, together, Dad, two other Mutual executives, and Dick Clark took the syndicated radio network business by storm with the formation of The United Stations Radio Networks, back in the heyday of Casey Casum and his *American Top 40* show.

As one of the company's Senior Executives, Dad traveled a lot. The company was a powerhouse and the legendary Dick Clark became a friend of the family.

But then, after too much time away from the family, Dad got out. "Dick Clark couldn't believe it," Dad told me.

And then there is Teri Gardner, Mom.

It's from her that I got my creative mind, my better-than-average cooking skills, my outgoing personality, my humor, my Faith, and, let's not forget, my phenomenal calves.

Before she gave me those calves, and long before she ever became my mom, Teri Gardner became the first-born of four to another dynamic duo, Betty and Joe—our Mommom and Poppy.

Long and lean, Poppy stood six-three with kind eyes, a sincere smile, chiseled jaw and an unquestionable handsomeness that put him on a Clint Eastwood-level.

For all Poppy's hilarity, and his inclination for goofiness, it was the beautiful Betty Gardner who became his voice of reason, business partner, and an irreplaceable cornerstone of our family.

Like Poppy, Mommom showered her children and grandchildren with warmth and love. And, also like Poppy, she, too, graced us with a particular set of skills.

Whereas Poppy's engineering background sent him retreating to his toolbox—marvelously disguised as the trunk of his car—to fetch WD-40 and duct tape when a broken something needed tinkering, it was needle and thread that Mommom called on. Very rarely did Mommom come across a garment that refused to bend to her nimble-fingered will.

With Poppy in the Navy, the family moved often which included a four-year stretch in Colorado Springs, where my Mom's sister Paige was born. Ultimately, the family packed up and moved to Northern Virginia.

Mom attended McLean High School and went to The University of South Carolina. Her first job out of college was working as a secretary for a construction company. There she met Dad, her boss. In 1978 they were married.

For as long as I can remember Mom has wielded a keen eye for interior design and fashion, using this knack to buy nicely coordinating clothes and decorating the house to a professional degree. Outside, every spring, her green thumb and great taste creates astonishing gardens around the house with *Home*

& Garden-esque flower beds that light up the yard. The woman knows what looks good, and she's funny.

Mom knows how to unravel a joke and tell a good story to a room of people, with perfect timing and cadence. She also possesses an unflinching faith with God. And when it comes to food…just ask anyone—Mom is a kitchen magician.

Chapter 4

SIBLING DICHOTOMY

The 90s. Home. McLean, VA

"**M**eredith is like your Grandmother," Dad said, "Unbelievably competitive." A picture of Grandmother and Meredith came to mind. Grandmother was tending the flag as I lined up a putt, Meredith sprinting through defenders cradling a lacrosse stick. Dad was right. Both were unassumingly tiny, deceptively feisty, athletic, and competitive.

"And you know your sister," Dad continued. "What an animal on the athletic field!"

He wasn't exaggerating. Meredith was ferocious. During her sophomore season at Trinity College she broke her back, had an operation, and returned to compete the next two years.

"And no one is more competitive than your brother. I mean, you have to sort of separate him from everybody else." Uh, hello? What about me? I thought reflexively as Dad spoke proudly of his kids. "No one is more competitive than your brother, except maybe you."

Thaaat's better!

"So," he said next. "My God! You're three of the most competitive people I know!"

My brother, Frank Murphy IV, was born August 13, 1979, arriving on Mom's birthday with exactly one minute to spare. In January 1984, Meredith joined the family and less than two years later I rounded out the bundle.

17

I would be remiss, however, if I did not mention my wonderful half-sister, Melanie, from my Dad's previous marriage.

Gentle-hearted, compassionate, and charitable, Melanie is all-around incredible. Without question, these attributes and more influenced me as I grew up because Melanie was another moral compass in my life to emulate. Most notably, Melanie's love of animals comes to mind and her deep devotion to her playful Boxers. Melanie is one of the kindest people you will ever meet.

In countless ways, I grew up fortunate and blessed. To have both a brother and two sisters, and to experience the dichotomy of growing up with, at minimum, one of each is undoubtedly one of those blessings that made for a special way to go about life.

(Melanie was 18 when my parents married so of course I didn't grow up with her.)

Growing up the youngest in this sibling dichotomy of course came with its fair share of challenges and privileges, but there's no question, being the "baby" has affected me entirely for the better.

Being six years younger than Frank, to him, I wasn't fun or cool, I was pesky and annoying. Naturally, we fought and bickered, but not always.

At North Myrtle Beach each summer, Frank taught me how to take a wave and body surf, cause trouble with water balloon launchers on a well-covered ocean-front balcony, and how to talk to girls and flirt. (Hint: Ask questions. Let them talk.)

When it came to baseball it was Frank—together with Dad, of course—who was instrumental in my upbringing and development on the diamond.

I looked up to Frank. As a baseball player and athlete, I wanted to be just like him. Swing and hit like him, throw and field grounders like him, break my glove in, stand, run, wear my hat like him.

From his days in the Majors in Little League, playing for Naval Air, to his stand-out seasons in high school and then short stint at Lynchburg College, I watched close and worked hard to emulate Frank's game. Frank had a gritty, hard-working competitive approach to baseball. He played it well with quick hands, a soft touch, and light feet.

Luckily, Frank wanted the same for me, and took the time to help make that happen.

Whether it was long toss out front in the cul-de-sac, tee work out back, grounders after practice in high school or letting me join a practice when I was only half his team's age—Frank made sure I followed his footsteps.

It was his quick feet that carried Frank into The Potomac School history books with his single season stolen base record of 25/25 during his senior year in 1998.

The record-breaking third base now hangs in my parent's basement beside an article commemorating the achievement.

Because of our age differences, while growing up, I was naturally closer with Meredith. Once we matured into adulthood, however, the three of us became tight like never-before.

Until then, though, Meredith was my partner-in-crime. Together our imaginations ran wild.

Being the younger brother, I was often subjected to the whimsical fantasies of my big sister and her best friend, Alexa. Most notably the two different make-believe marriages to two different brides they concocted during separate vacations at Myrtle Beach.

The second I remember more clearly. I was maybe 7 at the time and Meredith and Alexa hatched a plan for me to wed Alexa's little sister, Abigail, herself a few years younger than me.

Abigail had a wedding gown and vail, and me a nice jacket. I pretended to hate the whole thing—even though I secretly loved the attention. With our families in attendance vows and I Do's were exchanged following a processional with music and programs.

Chapter 5

TREE TRUNKS HERE BEFORE ME

"This does not happen immediately or easily, and rarely by itself. We need to actively work toward positive change, and we need the right tools and support in order to transform a bad break into a breakthrough."[5]
—Dr. Michaela Haas, *Bouncing Forward*

Early-May, 2007. MCV/VCU Medical Hospital. Richmond, VA.

The therapy room at the end of the hall bustled like it usually did at peak morning hours. Physical and occupational therapists moved about purposefully helping patients. Nurses, doctors, and family members added to the din, making it feel more crowded than it was.

Distractions surrounded, but on this day my mind was focused.

As I positioned my chair beside the therapy table, my family looking on, I was more concerned with my objective than anything else. This was one of my first in-patient therapy sessions with real meaning. I was back at Square One.

Achieving a New Normal means starting at the basics, and on this day, my task was to sit up, put on shoes. Nothing more. Just two ordinary tasks.

I still had not mastered transfers, so Gregg helped me with the move. My primary PT, Gregg, was a towering figurine with a big heart and kind smile that matched his imposing frame. Using an assisted transfer move I had become familiar with, Gregg scooped me up and easily placed me on the padded blue table.

As instructed, I held myself up while Gregg took my ankles and swung my feet onto the table. Then, he held me and lowered my broken body until I was on my back.

The Shell made it awkward to lay completely flat, but I smiled at the welcome relief the position had on my throbbing back. Gregg gave me a few seconds to enjoy myself.

After some words with my parents he turned, looked down, and said, "Okay. Now get up."

Nothing else; zero instructions. It was a test to guage what I could and could not do, which, for the most part, was "Very little" and "A lot," respectively.

"Okay!" I responded cheerfully.

Then I went to work on the puzzle of sitting up, lacing up.

Dr. McKinley and his under-study happened to then drop by. They stood around the big square table with my therapists and family, watching as I sought the solution. With everyone hovering over, I felt like an experimental lab rat.

I worked tirelessly, nonetheless, on my objective.

But my Shell made everything a hundred times harder, not to mention my lack of abdominal muscles. I was lucky to have my top two remaining, but those alone couldn't get me sitting, even without the Shell, which kept my torso rigid to promote healing. Bending at the stomach was out of the question.

After flopping around for a bit, arms flailing, struggling like a caught fish on a dock, it dawned on me that I had to get my arms beneath my body at my sides to get up on my elbows. From there it would be a simple tricep extension and I would be sitting.

Through trial and error, and still more floundering, I next determined that rolling onto my sides would allow me to work my hands and arms into position. By the time I got to my elbows, I was surprised at how physically exhausted I was.

I had struggled for what seemed like hours, but I had a goal to achieve. All eyes were on me. It was going to take something much more than being tired to deter me from reaching this first milestone to recovery.

When I finally pushed off my elbows and sat up, my family burst into cheers and Gregg slapped me light-heartedly on the back. I slumped forward, relieved, more tired than ever, and rested my chin on the top rim of my Shell to catch my breath. But only for a second. My mission was only half complete.

Staring at my lap, I moved my gaze down and scanned the motionless set of legs before me…

Thanks to so many grueling in-season and off-season workouts from Potomac to the NCAA, my legs became the tree-trunks before me here on the therapy mat—each one still, un-feeling objects with an odd sense of detachment.

For now, my legs looked like they did before my spine exploded, but I knew they would gradually wither as atrophy set in. Like a Death Eater from Harry Potter, this inevitability would methodically suck the life from every muscle south of my injury until little was left.

A grim prospect that quietly haunted the dark corners of my mind.

There was nothing I could do about that now, though, so I blocked out the sudden flood of memories, choking back the negativity.

Sitting on the therapy table, recovered from my efforts, I could only go forward here at the start of my second life. Nostalgia would not help me complete Step 2 of my task.

I focused, took a breath, and walked my hands towards my shoes as I worked out a plan for the simpler task of putting them on. Once that was done, there were more cheers, and then it hit me.

This was it. It was now time to take control of the hand I'd been dealt—to actively work towards positive change and transform the reality of my own bad break. Rehab had truly begun.

— — — —

After growing up watching her grandfather create a fulfilled, successful life, despite being afflicted with polio as a child, Dr. Michaela Haas was inspired to discover how people emerge from their pain wiser for the experience.

In 2015 she published her discoveries and *Bouncing Forward: The Art and Science of Cultivating Resilience* became the latest addition to a rapidly growing field.

Dr. Haas' goal was "to find out what protects us and those around us from unnecessary suffering; to discover strategies to intervene when life's trajectory goes ballistic; to help the healing. And not only to heal, but to use the crisis as a launching pad for a new beginning."[6]

Like Tedeschi, Calhoun and other professionals in this field, Dr. Haas conducted interviews with survivors and "thrivers" from all walks of life who experienced and witnessed a broad spectrum of traumas to help readers in the real world.

As a result, she identified certain factors that help survivors "face life's perils and pitfalls:" Our upbringing, personal genetics, available resources, social skills, and our perceived purpose in life.

Dr. Haas then concluded that "acceptance, openness, flexibility, optimism, patience, mindfulness, empathy, compassion, resourcefulness, determination, courage, [and] forgiveness" are the most important resilient mindset characteristics to turn bad breaks into breakthroughs.[7]

The theory of posttraumatic growth is simple; implementation, however, is not.

Taking it from theory to reality comes with time, willingness, open-mindedness, and adaptability. No doctor can prescribe it. No psychiatrist can magically manifest it.

It's not an outcome that one arrives at wholly on their own.

And yet it takes them, and them alone, to make the decision that will allow themselves to begin the journey of turning PTG from theory to reality—their reality.

When an event throws you off course and reroutes the path you thought you were comfortably walking, recognize that you're facing a challenge. And challenges—in terms of how you cope—means choices. You can control it, or it can control you.

When you actively take responsibility for the way you respond and recover to the life-changing ramifications of your trauma or adversity or even a setback, you put yourself in the best possible position to grow.

Dr. Haas alluded to this theory in her *Introduction*, one that I've consciously kept in mind:

"A growth mindset not only fortifies us in challenging times, but the same qualities and skills help us in our everyday lives as well."[8]

Chapter 6

THE SUMMERLEAS SCHOOL

The Mid-90s. Northern VA and Rapidan, VA.

I grew up twenty-minutes outside Washington, D.C. Although I was a "city boy," some of my fondest memories are of the country variety.

I was nine or ten and away at Camp Friendship one summer with my cousin Duane when we got word that our grandparents had bought a farm.

Summerleas is ninety-minutes outside Northern Virginia on four hundred acres of rolling farmland in Culpeper, some of the best the Old Dominion (Virginia) has to offer. It is a short drive to the smaller country town of Orange and even shorter to tiny old Rapidan, named for the river passing through.

In the years to come I would learn much about our own mid-19th century farm; its fields and streams, thick woods, its slave-holding history, and what it means to exist in the rural Virginia countryside, where underfoot its iconic red clay dirt earned a reputation for staining whatever clothing it touched with reckless abandon.

I learned to love this red clay and missed it whenever I went back home—for Summerleas instilled in me a side so opposite to that of my suburban, non-camouflage-wearing McLean life that the contrast is almost cliché.

Farm life involved, demanded more like, getting in trouble, causing mischief, and running amuck in ways suburbia could not offer. And it required a partner in crime to do so. My cousin Duane happily joined me in this.

Duane lived in Centerville, by Bull Run Park. Together, no matter where we were, we always seemed to cause trouble and then get in trouble.

The trouble we found, at least the most severe and memorable, was often somewhere in North Myrtle Beach during our annual two-week August vacation. Otherwise it was the farm. We were always on the go, always doing something, even if it was not the smartest or the safest thing. Often both.

As Duane was the older one, naturally I followed Duane's lead, emulating him as best I could. Like his dad, Uncle Paul, Duane has always been an outdoorsman, with a strong love of guns, dirt bikes, and hunting, and so by association, I grew up sharing these passions.

Before the commitments of sports in high school, weekends were spent mostly at Summerleas with Duane and family. The objective was always to get dirty, rustle up said mischief and eat, sleep, and breathe ATVs and four-wheelers.

We got to know every inch of the farm and met these objectives handily. Without our coveted John Deere Gator this would have been much harder. Between me, Duane, Meredith and whoever else was around, we would pile into our little green 4x4 truck and cruise across the property dawn to dusk.

Before the Gator, our sole means of exploration was another, albeit lesser, John Deere—from their lawn mower line. It could carry a driver and two small passengers and was good enough for slow trips down the long gravel driveway, but little else outside grass cutting. The arrival of the Gator revolutionized farm weekends.

We crisscrossed fields at speeds that made the mower jealous as we explored forests, hauled project materials around in the flat-bed, and blazed trails where the bush and brush grew thick along creek beds and by the pond. We put more miles on that thing than we knew what to do with.

As we got older, we needed something more. Something grittier, with more muscle. Duane and I knew precisely what.

Having our own four-wheeler had long been a pipe-dream. Blame it on *Dirt Wheels* and *ATV Action,* our favorite ATV magazines. When a new edition hit the racks at Sheetz it was Christmas morning. We read and re-read every inch and kept up on latest brands and models to see which could escape the nastiest mud pits.

"Okay…" One of us would prompt. "Your dream four-wheeler…?"

Duane's answers were professional.

"I'd go with the Honda over so-and-so because of X, Y, and Z, with at least a 450cc engine. At least. It would obviously have the LCD digital monitor, push-thumb handlebar shifting, cargo racks front and back and front grill guard—

with the winch. Just in case. A lift-kit, too, to jack it up a few inches… Then a mean set of tires with huge ass treads!"

Then Duane would pause, flip through a magazine, and point out the exact set. "These, right here. Need wheel spacers too, to make them fit. The whole thing would be a couple inches wider, but it'll be good for stability…. But then you'd need mud flaps, obviously."

Our answers were almost always the same, and our dream ATV always resembled a mud pit monster, huge, powerful, and gnarly.

Eventually we couldn't take it anymore. With the Gator aging, we needed an ATV.

Duane and I started raising money to chip away at the staggering price tag. We got some help from our grandparents, sure, and our parents pitched in come Christmas and birthdays, but we still put in work the hard way.

Whenever Northern Virginia got snow, we grabbed our shovels and scoured the neighborhoods before the plows. We knocked on door after door with bright smiling eyes and told whoever answered our story and what we were doing. You would be surprised at how many people happily shelled out fifty bucks in exchange for a shoveled driveway.

Our work paid off around 1997-98. We had enough money for the red 350cc Honda Foreman we had been eyeing.

Finally, one Summerleas Saturday we called the dealership in town and watched as our once-upon-a-time dream showed up on a trailer an hour later.

Life on the farm changed post-Foreman. It opened a world of possibilities. We could explore new places, ride trails the Gator couldn't, go faster and ride farther and longer.

Mudding became our favorite year-round pastime. Armed with disposable cameras, we spent weekends wearing out old crossings and hunting new ones. The creeks and streams changed with the weather, drying up one day, soppy and muddy the next. It was always a surprise.

Winter made for the best pictures once snow turned every bog and bottom into a mudders' paradise with heavy boot-sucking muck begging to be chewed through to which we bundled up tight and happily obliged.

The solemn white snow with violent splatters of mud and earth contrasted beautifully.

When not mudding we spent hours tinkering. The old three-car garage was perfect for this, a virtual warehouse of old junk.

There was a huge worktable along the right wall forever littered with this and that, tools, tin cans, storage containers and boxes for stuff you did not know you needed until you did.

We used this dusty cache to put things together to outfit whatever schemes we were into that weekend. Like the time we built a raft out of scratch for no other purpose than floating from one side of the pond to the other.

And when we ran out of ideas and got bored all over again, we resorted to fumbling about with tools and picking through the cob-webbed boxes that time forgot, seeing what goodies lay within.

Summerleas is also where the military side of me went through its nascent phase—I just did not know it at the time.

Summerleas is where I learned about guns, hunting, and camouflage, shot my first dove, tagged my first deer, and became hooked on dirt bikes. It is where my love of the outdoors took root and blossomed.

I spent nearly every possible weekend there, Friday afternoon to Sunday evening. There is a reason I wanted the outdoors so badly when I could not have it while hospital-bound facing a life of paralysis:

It was ingrained in me.

Chapter 7

ACADEMICALLY UN-SMART

The Mid-90s. The Potomac School. McLean, VA.

The Potomac School sits on a plot of land across from CIA Headquarters at Langley, Virginia, and is home to some of the best and brightest with a nationally renowned curriculum.

Before paralysis, my toughest challenge was this place.

School was an on-going headache that plagued me Pre-Kindergarten through 12th grade.

Grade to grade, surrounded by exceptional classmates who excelled across the board, I lagged. Math stumped me. English confused me. Science escaped me. It took forever to complete assignments. I was always the one handing in work or tests long after others had finished as I muddled through the weeds of learning. I read at a slower pace, and I felt embarrassed when I spoke up incorrectly or stumbled over "reading comprehension" sections.

When a teacher handed back papers or quizzes, no one ever had as much red ink as me. I was always quick to flip the sheets over or cover grades and corrections with well-placed forearms and a hunched-over back, silently wishing that this was a poster project or poem hand-back, something where my creative side could have flourished instead of yet another math test or English essay.

But they knew. They all knew.

In a school of 850 students, it's no secret how everyone stacks up intellectually and athletically. Academically, I rarely had anything to show, so I felt I had something to prove.

It began in Mrs. Hein's first grade class, 1992-1993, during a reading lesson.

Our class of eighteen was busy with reading workbooks, most of the kids sitting on the rug with Mrs. Hein and her famously long blonde bunned-up hair. She led the group, surrounded by the Reading Rabbits, the fastest readers. It was a group you wanted to be in—and I was not part of it.

Instead, I sat with two others off to the side at separate tables where we received special attention from the beloved Language Arts lady who floated from class to class.

With every uproar of laughter or audible semblance of yet another speedy job-well-done, I would glance up from my work, see the Reading Rabbits, and get struck with a painful sense of inferiority, thinking I was less intelligent than those who so easily conquered Potomac's curriculums.

Second and third grade had its moments, sure, but things really got bad in Middle School, where my lacking was exposed, and I felt more ostracized than ever.

It got worse in 6th grade.

I labored through the typical line-up of subjects, hitting setbacks at every turn. Like the Reading Rabbits episode, this 6th grade scar also involved reading.

Phillip Pullman's *The Golden Compass* was popular that year and several in class had read it. I can still remember how painful and belittling it was when another classmate, graced with the gift of speed-read, was visibly shocked at the glacial pace at which I had progressed through it. "You're only *that* far?!" He mocked. Before I could answer, he walked away.

However, when it came to posters, projects, poetry, and writing I never walked away. That was my thing. (Thanks, Mom!)

In Lower School, Ms. Swope, the eccentric, fun-loving Potomac mainstay who ran the art room, dubbed me "The King." I wore it like a badge of honor.

My knack for creativity sprouted at an early age, and Ms. Swope picked up on it. As the years went on, it was this talent that became a redeeming saving grace amidst the rigorous workloads thrown at me.

In 4th grade it was Egypt, 5th ancient Greece and in 6th it was Medieval Times. If it involved markers, colored pencils or construction paper and "have at it" guidelines—I crushed it.

Of my most memorable "crushed" projects was a poem about a grape.

It was part of our ancient Greece and Rome studies in 5th grade. We had learned about "Ode to…" poems where a single object or person is paid homage through poetry then illustrated in ancient Greek style with meander patterns in the margins and drawings to go with the poem's subject.

"Ode to grape…" it opened. I used an exhaustive number of similes and metaphors to depict the grape's shape, shiny exterior, taste, and overall versatility of the food. I added colorful vines up the side and bunches of purple grapes on each line to fill space—and to me it was just another poem.

But when the lady from The Admissions Department walked in one day, without a family on her arm, and Ms. Parsons tapped my shoulder motioning me outside, I became confused, even nervous.

My unease turned to elation when she brought up my poem, which she had gotten wind of. And when she asked permission to have *Ode to Grape* set behind glass to display in her Admissions hallway for all to see, I couldn't agree faster as I grinned uncontrollably and swelled with pride.

Until major renovations, *Ode to Grape* hung proudly in the halls of Potomac's Middle School wing. For passersby it was just a poem about fruit by some 5th grader. But for me, it was proof of my untapped potential.

I never did finish *The Golden Compass*.

— — — —

At recess I subconsciously took my academic short fallings out on my Middle School uniform.

My khaki pants and shorts always needed Dad's special grass-stain-removal technique on Friday afternoons, even a few Mondays, too.

When the weather kept my long-sleeve, school-issued navy-blue turtlenecks and sweaters in the drawer, my collection of rough, plain white, short-sleeved Polos quickly turned dingy and took on unpleasant shades of off-yellow.

My brown school shoes took the brunt of it, though. They barely lasted the year, let alone a semester. Not even the strongest adhesive could stop the toes from coming undone or the soles from breaking free from the leather, thanks to the way I attacked recess.

Because recess was my escape from academics—and that meant sports.

When teams were picked, I was never last or even in the middle. If I wasn't one of the captains, I was always one of the first draftees. I was tenacious and competitive to begin with, but I routinely ramped it up during heated games of soccer and two-hand-touch. And despite lagging behind my friends academically these brainiacs were still that: friends.

I got along with everyone and had no trouble befriending classmates or seamlessly crossing between cliques.

Even though I was a happy social butterfly at Potomac I still felt I had something more to prove, especially on days where tests or quizzes were handed back. Recess, then, was the easiest place for me to go nuts with genuine friends.

It was also the easiest place to use as a proving ground to deliberately showcase my physical worth and hide—albeit temporarily—my intellectual blunders. Sometimes this energy led to a last second victory. Sometimes grass stains or screwed up shoes. And sometimes it led to trouble when I played too rough.

Chapter 8

THE CARBON COPY DECEPTION

The Late-90s. The Potomac School. McLean, VA.

With nowhere to hide, my shortcomings promptly went on display after entering Intermediate School (I.S.), Potomac's separate stepping-stone wing for 7th and 8th grade.

By the middle of 8th grade I was drowning. Potomac's famed academics were taking their toll and with each failed quiz, terrible test, and missed homework assignment awaiting me at the end of too many days was something I regularly dreaded: An Academic Notice.

Different from a Discipline Notice, Academic Notices were school-related, small pink slips for the student's parents, bearing good news or bad. They had to be signed that night, the carbon copy returned pronto.

I always received these dreaded pink slips at the end of the day when homeroom lined up to shake hands with our advisor, Ms. Stein. I never knew exactly what they said, but I had a hunch, so I always lingered at the back of the line—so others wouldn't see me getting yet *another* notice.

It's not like they were all bad. I got good ones, too. These I promptly delivered to Mom and Dad.

More than not, though, I was anything but prompt. I put these bad ones off out of shame, often waiting until morning before school to get the signature. I never had the courage to do it the night before.

Eventually, schoolwork slipped to such an extent that Academic Notices began rolling in at an alarming rate. Suddenly, I had English, Spanish, Science, and Math teachers all expecting me to return signed copies by next class—

So, I cooked up a plan—one to simultaneously meet the "next day delivery" policy and save Mom and Dad the burden of giving me another lecture about school.

All I had to do was save an old notice, good or bad, place it over the newest slip, grab a sturdy pencil, ensure the coast was clear, shut my door, return to desk, sit, concentrate, commence firm tracing, and…voila! A faint imprint of Mom's signature.

Next, the tricky part: tracing it in pen. Too many stops and starts could leave a rigid, timid-looking signature awkwardly scribbled that might lead to my undoing. A close look could have exposed the chicanery.

But practice makes perfect. And practice I did, many, many times, until I felt ready for the real thing. It never failed.

A couple years later, while moving across the hall to my brother's old room, I stumbled upon the long-lost evidence of this great charade.

Rummaging through drawers, I found a massive wad of crumpled paper shoved to the back of one of the dressers. It had to have been years since the white and yellow carbon copies had seen the light of day. I wasn't even sure what they were at first.

I reached in, pulled out a handful to examine, and before I finished unraveling the first slip, it clicked. Laughter overcame me. I read through them and was hit by a flood of 8th grade memories.

Finding the notices was tangible evidence of how far I had come and the academic adversity I managed to escape.

I stood back from the pile of papers scattered on the bed, took it in, remembered, and gave myself a well-deserved pat on the back for not only the sheer size of my swindle, but also the level of untarnished success of my carbon copy deception. Neither teachers nor parents ever found out.

Despite my ruse, I couldn't hide from report cards. No trickery would get me out of those. I still had to face a daunting hydra that breathed fire from three nasty heads: homework, tests, quizzes.

And when it came time to do battle with all three, regularly…well… It wasn't pretty.

Not only did my parents become concerned, the school did too. Things were getting worse, something had to be done… The heads of the I.S. were simply unsure if I would be able to make the transition to high school. A meeting was called.

— — — — —

I walked somberly into the office.

After exchanging less-than enthusiastic greetings with Mr. Sheerin, the I.S. Head, and my advisor, Ms. Stein, we took our seats on a sofa, Mom, Dad, and I. Ms. Stein pulled over a chair and sat beside Mr. Sheerin, across from the couch. The coffee table separated us like the Berlin Wall.

I was silent with a belly full of knots and breathed in the tension-filled air hanging over the room. I knew nothing good could come of this meeting. Fidgety and fearful, I plunged my hands into my pockets. Inside, my left hand found the only distraction available: my trusty four-colored pen.

Mr. Sheerin opened alongside Ms. Stein. They laid out the reason for being there, leaving no stone unturned regarding my extremely sub-par classroom performance, which had spiraled out of control as incompletes and failing grades became the norm.

During the opening monologue, I found myself digging the pad of my thumb into the pen tip, harder and harder. I didn't care how much it hurt. Swirling it against my thumb kept my mind distracted. My only escape from this uncomfortable mess I had put myself in.

Still, as much as I leaned on this hidden pocket crutch, it hardly whisked me away from the reality I was facing. The fact of the matter was that I was bad at school.

I dug my thumb down harder yet felt nothing. I was numb all over.

Later, when the meeting was over, I looked down at my hand… My thumb was raw and throbbing. The whole thing smeared with blue ink.

Chapter 9

THE SMALL STUFF

1999. The Potomac School. 8th Grade. McLean, VA.

The meeting concluded after what felt like an eternity, made worse by the happy sounds of the other students enjoying the freedom of break before next bell.

And while my parents and Mr. Sheerin and Ms. Stein knew I could do better, they wondered if I would by year's end, and then keep it up as a 9th grader. They wanted what was best for me. And at that time, what was best for me, they worried, might not be at Potomac.

The thought of going to another school filled me with dread and twisted my stomach tight. The prospect was terrifying. Humiliating. I dug my thumb yet again onto the pen, wondering what my parents were thinking.

Far and away it was one of the most uncomfortable twenty-minutes of my life. I was mortified. I wanted to flee to some dark corner and go full-ostrich, my head hidden in the sand.

Then it was over with hard promises from Mom, Dad, and I to follow the game-plan we had laid out and to show real signs of progress. Meaning, frequent meetings with teachers and new tactics to stay organized and on task. We shook on it like a sacred vow.

The bell rang. The start of "BBS"—Band, Bells, and Strings—spared me from any further uncomfortable conversation.

Never did I look forward to Bells so much than I did that day. I darted up the stairs with a spring in my step, elated that the meeting was behind me. Sure, the departing "We'll discuss all this later" from Mom and Dad was heavy and foreboding, but at least I was free.

— — — — —

It was a science test, under the tutelage of the always-popular, way-too-likeable Mr. Peery, in which change started to show.

Tall and lanky, hair cropped short and red—Mr. Peery was the type of teacher every school needs. A teacher who knows how to successfully coach multiple sports and who runs an excited classroom by sparking interest and effort in even the most dispassionate of students out of his own passion and personality.

In Mr. Peery's case science was his thing. As much as I neither hated nor loved the subject, Mr. Peery made class fun and I wanted to be there. Not that that translated into good grades.

The test landed on the desk looking like it was bleeding. It was riddled in red ink. I covered it fast, embarrassed. After class, Mr. Peery brought me aside to set up a one-on-one to go over it.

This was my turning point.

Today I'm a speaker. I use sayings and slogans as call-to-actions according to the audience in front of me. There is one I use often because of how it has shaped me and how it has helped me through tough times. Its universal meaning is something we can all relate to—and it was first given to me as a listless 8th grader sinking in his studies.

"You get what I mean?" he asked, sitting back in his chair, not a trace of condescension in his voice.

I looked at the test and marveled silently at the volume of red. I thought about his advice a moment longer. I nodded slowly. "Yeah…" It came out more hesitantly than I'd wanted. I repeated it, stronger this time. "Yeah. Yeah, I do. I definitely get what you mean."

Mr. Peery smiled, happy I caught his drift. Leaning forward, he continued, studied page three, then broke the silence. I leaned in and studied the same, waiting for his next move.

After scanning the third set of questions I'd botched, he sat up, nodded, and tapped the sheet with his pen. "It's clear you've got a pretty good grasp of the material," he stated reassuringly. "You're just making a ton of little mistakes that are adding up. A point here, a point there…"

He flipped through the test and indicated the stream of deductions that brought me to his cramped office stuffed with texts, paper piles, and sagging shelves laden with books and binders. "See? A few here. Some here. Two here, one there and so on."

I nodded, mouth shut, then reiterated his point, partly to show him I understood, partly to bring us closer to finishing up. "So, I just need to focus… on the little things."

"Exactly. You need to sweat the small stuff. Pay attention to the big picture, the overall stuff, that's fine. Do that. But don't ignore the details. The details comprise the big picture. Don't just brush it aside. Don't pretend like it doesn't matter. It does. You have to worry about the details. You have to sweat the small stuff."

"I have to sweat the small stuff."

"Exactly. You have to sweat the small stuff." He glanced at the clock and closed the test, bringing this surprisingly productive and eye-opening meeting to a close.

I stood and shook his hand and looked him in the eye to give him a sincere thank-you.

He did the same and buoyed my spirits with an encouraging reminder of my grasp on the material, and how I could rid myself of those pesky one- and two-point deductions. "All you have to do is—"

And in unison we said, "—Sweat the small stuff."

Sweat. The Small Stuff.

Chapter 10

THE ART OF THE TRANSFER

"Those who try to put their lives back together exactly as they were remain fractured and vulnerable."
—Dr. Stephen Joseph, *What Doesn't Kill Us*

May, 2007. MCV/VCU Medical Hospital. Richmond, VA.

"It's all about the weight-shift, really." Gregg added, putting a bow on his introduction on The Art of the Transfer. "The concept's simple. You just have to go for it. Commit fully to the movement, and remember to account for a few details, and *boom!* That's it!"

If the magnitude and importance of this first major lesson of mine hadn't hit home, Gregg made sure of it.

"Again. Transfers. They're *absolutely* paramount. Without transfers, you're stuck. You can't get in your chair or out. You can't get on the commode or off. You can't get in and out of the shower, your car. And you certainly can't be independent."

To regain independence, mastering the transfer is an absolute for paraplegics. Transfers are how you do pretty much everything.

There is a lot to learn, do, and master to go from accident to independence and transfers are one of the first steps for an SCI patient's bag o' tricks. They are both necessary and difficult, requiring upper body strength, precision and

38

patience for mastery, and mastery for independence. And independence for a life.

This is the essence of occupational therapy (OT), the day-to-day things to live, whereas the strength and functional component comes from physical therapy (PT), whether you're in-patient or out.

Transferring began week one at the big blue padded therapy table during early PT with Gregg. Sitting beside me on the table he had run through his opening spiel about why learn transfers and how they are done. Demonstrating, he returned to what he considered the crux of it all: weight shift.

"Your body can be used as a fulcrum," he explained, "which will allow you to do things and move parts of your body that no longer move."

He sat flat on the edge of the table, squared his feet on the floor, and placed his hands on the table at his side and pushed up. Gregg was tall, towering, and quite friendly. "If I lift myself like this…and want to scoot to the left, I can only do it if I shift my weight. Watch what happens when I throw my head to the right…"

Slow and deliberate, he did so, demonstrating the basic principle of the action. His butt hovering just off the table, he threw his head to the side and pushed with his arms. His head went one way, butt the other. "See what happened there?"

I nodded slowly, watching his every move with laser focus.

He continued, "Your head and eyes are the key ingredient for the weight shift to make the fulcrum work and the transfer possible. Whichever way you want your lower half to go your head goes opposite.

"Shift weight…eyes…fulcrum…head goes the opposite. Got it."

"Good. Now let's get you on here. We'll start simple and work on going back and forth on the table, so you can get comfortable with the technique."

"Sounds good to me."

I unlocked my brakes and positioned my chair perpendicular to the table and locked them again. Gregg looped his therapy belt around my waist and synched it tight.

Gregg used the belt to do a chair-to-table transfer for me, since I hadn't yet graduated to the transfer board. That would take weeks to get to. I was as green as they come so transfers were 110% in the hands of my therapists.

As instructed, I scooted to the edge of my seat. Gregg moved to stand in front and looked down. "You want to watch your feet as well. Even though you can't feel it, your feet and legs still hold and take weight. If they're back beneath you and you lean forward, you could easily fall flat on your face."

"Ahh yes, good call. Wouldn't want that."

"Watch the *placement* of the feet, too. Other than falling, the last thing you want during transfers is to have your body and legs going one way while your feet don't and get left behind. You could easily break an ankle. And then you'd really be up Shit's Creek, paddle free." He gave me another look and cocked a brow.

I responded with a look of my own. "Yikes."

"Yeah." Gregg proceeded.

Leaning over me, he grasped the belt firmly at the back by my kidneys. I got a face full of shoulder as he readied himself. Then, slowly at first, Gregg rocked me, gradually building that other important factor: momentum.

Then, with surprising ease, he hauled me up and over and placed me soundly on the mat, my feet planted squarely on the tile. Gregg let go and stood. He exhaled, happy with the landing.

Away from my wheelchair I was instantly struck by a sense of exposure and vulnerability with nothing around to hold myself up. I grabbed fast at the table's edge for balance, all reflex, and held tight.

As soon as I felt comfortable, I explored the boundaries of my new body with tiny weightshifts and flirted with disaster using increased leans as my ability-barometer. I learned by doing and failing.

"Okay, you got yourself?"

"Yup," I said with assurance.

He stood back. "Start with this. From right there, just try lifting yourself up off the mat so you can gauge your balance and get used to that." He crossed his arms and watched as I followed orders. I could sense his focus and knew he was locked on with that analytical PT eye of his.

It took me a few sessions before I could confidently scoot left and right. After nailing down the theory of it, I now had to put in the hours.

Over time, millimeters became centimeters, and inches became more inches, taking me from one end of the table to the other faster and faster, each time with less single scoots. My confidence and capabilities grew to the point where I could casually lift my body up and throw my head and torso one way with enough force and momentum so that my ass would clear the table, shift opposite my head and land far enough over where inches then became a foot or more per scoot.

"Well done! Well done, indeed." Gregg said approvingly. "I think you're ready for the transfer board."

The transfer board was used to span the gap between a wheelchair and your transfer landing zone or vice versa. A bridge.

Gregg showed me how it was used and identified things to be careful of before we got into it. "Whether you're in your chair or sitting on the side of the bed, always make sure the board is placed so that enough of each end rests solidly in place. You wouldn't want it to slip off halfway across mid-scoot."

"Makes sense. Noted."

"Getting it in place is pretty straightforward, too. Just lean far enough over one way to free up the weight on your butt so you or someone else can wedge the board under a cheek. Watch your clothing. You can easily catch shorts or pants under the board. Keep an eye on that before you scoot or you'll get snagged."

"Also noted. Got it."

We started with the table, going back and forth from chair to table to chair before moving on to more practical stuff like hospital beds. From there, again, it was a matter of practice.

Seeing signs of progress in something as important as transfers was a huge boost in morale—boosts that became instrumental in helping to manage all the stressful newness of my situation.

Little daily victories like these led to a certain clarity of my mind and a constantly replenished reserve of motivation so I could stay focused on controlling my so-called uncontrollable diagnosis.

— — — — —

Dr. Stephen Joseph, once a child of Belfast who witnessed Ireland's political violence firsthand, is a passionate proponent of taking responsibility for one's own recovery and growth.

After two decades of study, practice, and research "devoted to understanding the effects of adversity on our psychological system"[10] *What Doesn't Kill Us: The New Psychology of Posttraumatic Growth* (2011) is the culmination of his work, a piece that has been instrumental in advancing the academia surrounding PTG.[11]

As part of his "paths to posttraumatic growth," Dr. Joseph argues there are two ways, positive and negative, that people cope.

"Approach-oriented coping" is about facing up to and accepting what has happened, dealing with feelings, and actively managing or changing tough situations in different ways.

"Avoidance-oriented coping" is a stick-your-head-in-the-sand approach to ignore the sticky situation and the emotions that come with it.[12]

Feel free to…avoid…that approach.

Instead, opt for what Dr. Joseph advocates for: task-focused coping and emotion-focused coping.[13] Attacking your adversity by proactively addressing the physical and practical problems (task) as well as the mental problems (emotion).

When it comes to task-focused coping, working tirelessly to learn transfers and being able to get in and out of my wheelchair is about as practical and physical a problem as it gets when reality involves figuring out how to be human and do all the human things.

Yes, doing PT and being at scheduled sessions was mandatory. Bodily, I had to be there; we all had to be there. Each person's mind, however, is a free spirit, immune to the schedules printed and taped on the back of our chairs, and it showed. Not everyone took to these sessions quite so proactively.

My existence had been shattered so severely that there was no going back. I knew that. I would never be my old self. But I could certainly start creating my new, slightly more metallic self.

In doing so, I unknowingly acted out what Dr. Joseph highlights as the guiding principle underlying his book: how "focusing on, understanding, and deliberately taking control of what we do in our thoughts and actions can enable us to move forward in life following adversity."[14]

I didn't have power over much, but I had the power to do at least that—to make the conscious decision to build something new from the broken, severed pieces of me leftover...

Something new and beautiful.

Chapter 11

CLOSET SMART

1999. The Potomac School. 8th Grade. McLean, VA.

The words imparted by Mr. Peery worked. So did the meeting. The last thing I wanted to do was transfer and start over.

I made concerted efforts to meet teachers regularly to go over tests and homework, work out material that tripped me up, and created new habits to begin assignments earlier.

But, something was still missing.

One evening, after yet another Academic Notice for a D- History test, Mom knocked lightly on my bedroom door. I'd secluded myself upstairs after showing her the notice. She'd helped me study and knew I knew the material. It was a test I'd prepared for and seeing that red-penned 62 tore me up like never before.

Mom entered and quietly sat beside me at the foot of my bed. I had tears in my eyes.

We spoke about the game-plan and, as we talked things through, I pulled myself together once Mom helped me discover the missing piece. She then used an analogy that clicked to further unmask my real academic antagonist.

My friend Robbie had recently taught me how to juggle using three balls. I'd gotten pretty good and could even do a few cool tricks. Mom related it to school.

"It's just like juggling." She explained. "You can't just focus on one ball or the rest will fall. Equal energy and attention must be given to all three, or four or five, so they all stay in the air."

It made sense because it was true. I'd show spurts of success, glimmers of hope, but not across the board. I was scatter-brained, unorganized, and, therefore, unprepared and ineffective at homework and study time. I could juggle tennis balls and hacky sacks—but not school.

By far the most impactful thing Mom did for me academically, after the juggling talk, was to buy me a giant desk calendar, with big blank squares for every day of the month. This cured me of one of the biggest reasons for my foibles: organization.

Again, I had none. I had zero systems for staying coordinated and on-the-ball. No wonder I missed so many assignments and constantly turned in late homework. I filled the calendar with every assignment with due-dates highlighted for easy viewing. After that, juggling classes was no longer the Herculean task it had once been. I was sweating the small stuff and evenly juggling my priorities.

Help also came in other places—like in the bedroom next door.

There, a selfless older sister took time out of her homework-filled evenings to throw me a lifeline where my parents couldn't.

With two more years of Spanish under her belt, Meredith's room became my private tutoring center. She helped me with conjugations, translating, and showed me how to memorize using vocab flashcards. Soon my understanding took shape, but more importantly my knowing how to study it.

Outside help only took me so far in un-sinking myself. The rest was up to me. And that's where the words of Mr. Peery took root, permanently. *Sweat the Small Stuff.* He told me to buy into this simple motto and I did.

And through a deeply concerted effort and lots of juggling… I showed them I was capable—and that I *could* handle it.

Chapter 12

WHEN FATE INTERVENES

August, 2000. The Potomac School. Preseason football. McLean, VA.

In the darkened room Coach Hoehn hit pause, bringing the afternoon film session to a halt.

Coach Hoehn was a Southern-speaking football brain. He demanded perfection. And he always had a dip spit bottle at the ready. He also happened to transform Potomac football with his genius.

Hoehn created an offensive scheme so impressive that it drew praise from Hall of Famer Howie Long when we faced St. Anne's-Belfield, from Charlottesville, led by son Chris Long, a future NFL standout.

"Rory!" He barked sternly. The room snapped still. Others around me, in back, sat tall and bright-eyed, no longer sleepy thanks to a single word from the man wielding a laser pointer running film. He turned to the senior running back indicating an egregious gaff on screen. "Rory! You stupid?!"

"Yes, Sir!"

The response knee-jerk, military-like in timeliness and tone. He stared focused at the projection and Hoehn stared at him, with daggers.

I saw Hoehn eye Rory a second longer. Rory was an old family friend; our moms were dearly close and as a freshman, I looked up to his size and strength on the field.

Coach Hoehn turned back to the screen to analyze the mistake and capitalize on a teachable moment…but not before issuing his characteristic calling-card for effect.

Half-turned, Hoehn finished his glare and, in a deliberate, measured manner, raised a plastic Pepsi bottle to his bottom lip. A brown substance oozed inside. Hoehn added to the slop, squirting a glob of tobacco spittle out between pursed lips.

The sound was heard in the back and for some reason I was transfixed. I watched it slide down the bottle in nauseating fashion.

Film continued and Hoehn resumed his analysis of the varsity. At length, he broke his train of thought and glanced at his dog in the corner; a regular during preseason two-a-days. Not skipping a beat, he addressed the issue of the dog in true Coach Hoehn fashion by calling on his designated errand boy: the team's lowest-string quarterback.

"Locey! My dog looks like he needs to take a shit. Be quick about it!"

The room burst into laughter at this unexpected demand so nonchalantly delivered by our coach.

Brent Locey, a six-foot-four born athlete who could chuck a pigskin a quarter mile, joined our class as a 4th grader. Reluctant, Locey stood to do the deed and was promptly met by greater applause and hilarity.

The rowdiness followed Locey obediently to the back entrance, much like the very dog trailing dutifully at his heels. He shoved the door open. Sunlight flooded the room and Locey disappeared outside, shaking his head.

Hoehn gave an abrupt final *Ha,* spat out a glob, and clicked play.

This was freshman year football at its core: me in the back watching how the older guys did it, while a dip-spitting, football brain ran the show on his own terms. As hard and intimidating as those two-a-days were, I loved it.

Our coaches were incredible, the juniors and seniors big and mean, and our group of freshmen, plus most sophomores, was stacked with depth and talent, with guys like Locey at quarterback and Mike Fischer (now one of my closest friends) playing Wide Receiver and Defensive Back. Fischer was the only 9th grader to play in Varsity games, but both he and Locey were big and gifted for their age.

Together they would later stand-out on the basketball court, helping Potomac's Varsity become a championship powerhouse alongside another freshman friend and classmate of mine—Peter Prowitt. Big, goofy, and smart,

Prowitt dominated the lanes at a towering six foot ten before taking his talents to Paolo Alto as a Stanford Cardinal.

High school football was the source of some of my greatest excitement and anticipation heading into 9th grade. It lived up to the hype and as September rolled around, I continued to look forward to a fun season. Little did I know that fate was about to intervene and foil my plans.

God was about to send me my first set of wheels.

— — — — —

In life things don't always go as planned.

That's obvious; everyone knows that. But why? How come "things don't always go as planned" is such a common phrase? Aren't we largely in control of our own ship, steering it generally where we want it to go with plans and hopes and dreams?

After all, each of us is taking our own life's paths, each more varied and unique than the next. Surely, we have a good amount of control over what we do and the things around journeying these paths, right? …*Right??*

We may think we have control, but we don't. At least not a lot. There are so many untouchable, uncontrollable forces at work in our daily lives that dictate the course of these "paths" at a far greater rate than we could ever dream of. Forces like traffic, weather, the opinions and actions of others.

And though we're forced to live with them—these uncontrollable variables—how we do so and how we deal with these and the forces of fate is up to us.

When you find yourself suddenly sidelined you have two paths to choose: You either adopt the right attitude, or you don't. You either throw in with the proper effort or you don't. Attitude and Effort. The right path or the wrong.

What path do you choose? What path *will* you choose?

Chapter 13

SIDELINED

September, 2000. Pre-op. Fairfax Hospital. Fairfax, VA.

I read the paperwork again to be sure, this time to Mom, sitting beside my hospital bed. My surgery was minutes away and she vowed to stay as long as possible.

"Uhh...yeah." I said. "So, this isn't right. Look..." I showed her the glaring mistake that you would not think possible for something as serious as an operation.

Mom read it and let out a "Huh!" of disbelief.

"How can they get that wrong?"

"Ya got me!" She said, equally perplexed. "Wait. Look...Good thing for that next part. That could have been reeeaal bad."

I read further. It asked the patient to state which part of the body is being operated on and, if it's an arm or leg, to then state which one is not being operated on. But that wasn't all. The form required the patient to physically write "yes" on their body at the spot being operated on, and "no" on its counterpart.

"Ha! I actually have to write on my leg, so they don't screw up?"

"I guess that explains the permanent marker."

"Guess so." I leaned forward and in big thick letters wrote "YES" on my left thigh and "NO!!!!" on the right.

I looked down at my legs again and considered the markings on my thighs.

"Hmm… Yeah." I said to myself, as if settling an important matter. I grabbed the marker, bent forward, and drew huge circles around the Yes and No just as the nurse returned to retrieve me.

She was cheerful. "All set?"

I glanced up, "Ummm…" and then hurriedly drew a few more circles and an extra exclamation mark for good measure, *just* to be sure. I leaned back, examined my work. "Yup. All set!"

"Go get 'em, son!" Added Dad.

"We'll be right here when you wake up…" Said Mom. And the happy nurse cheerfully rolled me from the curtained room towards another down the hall. "…I promise."

Minutes later, in a bustling space full of sterile machines, with sterile people in sterile outfits, I'm told to "just relax" by the anesthesiologist. I could only hear her. Brilliant lamps shone from above, hypnotically capturing my stare. A clear mask materialized above attached to the end of an arm that broke my trance. I blinked, cleared my eyes.

"Now I want you to take deep breaths and count backwards from ten… Ok, ready?" She didn't wait for an answer and lowered the mask before my meaningless nod. "Just relax. Remember, deeeeep breaths." I again nodded, meaninglessly. "Gooood." She pressed the mask firmly to my face.

I began a muffled countdown and took long drawn inhales. "Ten. Nine." Two numbers in and the first signs of anesthesia hit. After that it happened fast, just another breath or two. "Eight… Se…seven… Siii—"

I was out before five.

— — — — —

Up until then, things had been going well in my first month of high school football. I was thrilled once preseason wrapped up when August turned to September, bringing with it the start of the school year. I meshed well with my classmates, showed a good work ethic on and off the field, impressed a couple coaches, and fell into good graces with the upperclassmen.

I was slotted at fullback and linebacker and got time on as many special teams as they could put me. I was in my element—excited to finally be playing high school football.

My excitement was short-lived as I'd soon exchange the gridiron for a gurney.

On September 14th, 2000, the very day God chose to send me my first set of wheels, I was filled with this very excitement as I got ready to suit up for our next showdown. Catholic High School. Their place.

On a typical play in a tight game, everything changed in a flash.

From my spot at middle linebacker, after the center hiked the ball and the play broke left, I'd reacted quickly. Our Panther D had swarmed and both teams collided in the trenches.

In the melee, a far larger teammate had lost his footing and I saw him slip beside me as our paths converged towards the Cardinal's ball-carrier. Momentum sent him tumbling—and all two-hundred-fifty pounds of him rolled up the side of my left leg, buckling me in my tracks.

Bright, searing pain radiated at my knee and I collapsed in a heap. I writhed in agony. A whistle blew. Trainers and coaches sprinted over.

When they got me up, I was carried to the sidelines draped between teammates. The walk seemed forever. I couldn't touch the ground at all with my left foot—let alone a single toe—it hurt so bad. Seeing this, Dad immediately knew something was seriously wrong. The trainers agreed. The hospital couldn't wait.

— — — — —

"I'm sorry." The doctor said. "There won't be any more football this year."

The little hope I had clung to slipped away with that one little answer and that one little x-ray being held to the light. Hope of good news, of buckling up again this season. But hope was gone.

The plans I had and the mental map to get there were dashed across the tile floor at his words, shattering into a million pieces, blanketing the room like broken glass, as I found myself facing the mysterious unknown that remained: a winding way and an uncertain future.

I fought back tears, but not from pain. The doctor translated the x-ray and spoke frankly about the next steps. Dad paid more attention than I did. "See this line here and here?" He pointed to a spot above my left knee cap. "That's the break, at the very bottom of the femur…"

I listened but didn't hear. My mind was elsewhere, on the fact that I wouldn't be able to put on shoulder pads or run or tackle anyone for another year. I finally gave the x-ray a sidelong glance when I heard "something something surgery" and "something something screws."

What a way to start high school. I thought. *At least I'll get that cast I always wanted, and crutches that everyone will want to try…Oh! And sympathy points from girls! Can't forget those!*

But the cast full of signatures never came, nor the crutches for everyone to try.

The "cast" was something altogether unfamiliar, with Velcro straps and hinges, and not a single strip of plaster in sight with cool colors to choose from. And the crutches…well they weren't crutches at all.

Instead, they gave me a chair—with wheels on it; two big ones in back, small ones up front. I was wrong about the cast and crutches, but as I later discovered upon returning to school, I got one thing right: those sympathy points. But that came later.

Before I could get that weird looking cast, before I could move about in that clunky, standard-issued wheelchair, and before I could cash-in those sympathy points, I would have to go under the knife and take home a few supplies from the hardware store.

— — — — —

I awoke to Ginger Ale and crushed ice.

Someone placed it in my hand and guided it to my mouth. I gulped it down like it was the last liquid on Earth. Confused and still half-out of it, I couldn't talk let alone form words. I resorted to mumbles and babbles to request another Ginger Ale and ice, then another, and another—but I was cut off after three.

"Not too fast, hold on. They said you need to wake up a bit more."

The voice was close and familiar. Mom. Then slowly but surely, I emerged further from the anesthesia.

Clarity returned, but I still had to stay overnight. Though it sucked to not go home, I looked on the bright side when a nurse handed me a clicker and told me I have complete control of the Morphine drip hanging at the end of the IV poking from my hand.

"If you're in pain just click the button." She instructed. "You'll get a small dose each time."

I marveled at the awesome power in my hand and pretended to wildly click the remote like a madman.

The nurse laughed and said, "Well, I mean, not complete control. It's set to a time limit, about 15 or 20 minutes, I think. After that—go crazy!"

"Oh, don't worry." I gave it two quick test clicks. One was enough, but I gave it a couple more for good measure. I couldn't help it. I was drunk with power.

I spent the rest of the evening watching as much television as my heart desired, trying my best to relax and fight pain. Clickers rarely left my hand. One thumb worked the Morphine, the other the TV. They were decent distractions from the discomfort, but not entirely.

Constant knocks at the door also helped. Nurses and doctors came and poked at my leg, replaced my Morphine and checked vitals. My parents stayed close and Frank and Meredith visited a bit as did Mommom and Poppy.

Altogether it was enough to manage and get me to bedtime. But no further.

That's when the side effects kicked in, the ones no one bothered to warn me about.

It started small, a tiny flicker of flame you can't snuff out, until, left unchecked, the un-itchable itch spread like wildfire in the quiet midnight hours, when the hospital was silent and still.

What began as simple scratching ended in something closer to feverish clawing across my entire body. I couldn't scratch hard or fast enough, and I sure as heck couldn't fall asleep. There was nothing I could do.

I eventually tried TV, but even that distraction failed.

Morning refused to rise. My flesh radiated red and raw. My knee throbbed. And sleep teased me. It was one of the longest nights of my life. So far.

Chapter 14

NO SHORTAGE OF PERKS

Fall, 2000. The Potomac School. 9ᵗʰ Grade. McLean, VA.

I left the hospital with a new cast and a heavy wheelchair, homecare instructions, a rehab appointment, and one handicap parking placard that twinkled in my hand like Charlie Bucket's golden ticket.

If I had to go back to school in a wheelchair, miss football, and the annual freshman class trip to Natural Bridge down near Roanoke, it was a boost knowing I would at least have really good parking.

Returning to school felt like a gigantic rewind where I had to start 9ᵗʰ grade over again.

Besides the annual First Day of School picture by the post, this was one of the most nerve racking first days of my Potomac career. Starting Middle School was one thing. Entering I.S. another. But day one as a freshman was momentous with a different and new set of butterflies swirling in my stomach, even as I tried to convince myself that my Murphy reputation as sibling number three in these halls should've made for a smooth transition.

It started at the end of our driveway where two brick lamp posts stood constant sentry.

For as long as we were at Potomac, Mom always made us stand at the posts in our uniforms and backpacks on the first day of school. For years it was all three of us until three became two and two became one with each graduating sibling. At some five-feet tall the posts used to tower over me, but with each September photo shoot, the square lamp posts slowly grew smaller beside me.

Some shoots went smoother, more cordial than others. Most did not.

What's become a running joke is Mom's camera three-count, or lack of.

Rather than snapping the picture after three or one, Mom had a tendency to draw those three seconds out longer than necessary or interrupted the countdown entirely to move us closer together, reposition an arm, a stance, or request toothier smiles.

Nevertheless, the entire First Day of School series was one of those traditions that's hard to appreciate in the moment. The pictures always turned out beautifully and later made for a special surprise at each of our graduation parties when Mom presented her poster-sized collage of Frank's, Meredith's, then Michael's First Day photos.

In 2000, my First Day photo as an awkward fourteen-year-old freshman wasn't my best. But at the time, I wasn't worried about that. I was more concerned about the start of high school.

Meredith drove us to school after posing out front (Frank now graduated and gone) and as we walked from the parking lot to the Upper School building, I found myself more excited than nervous.

I was "Meredith's little brother" and the older kids knew who I was. I had an "in" with the upperclassmen. I'd also grown up playing youth soccer, basketball, and little league with a lot of the guys a grade older. I even got along well with the older guys on the football team because of this past and my sibling connections.

Entering high school then was far more familiar and exciting than scary—despite still harboring sheepish, out-of-my-comfort-zone gut feelings, which remained amidst the exhilaration caused by that Murphy reputation.

The social aspect of this new phase was something I could handle and even enjoyed as an awkward fourteen-year-old. The academic side considerably rockier.

Despite all the excitement of being in high school, I soon faced academic issues that once haunted me before. I had turned things around by the end of 8th grade to save me from getting kicked out, but my efforts were merely a stay of execution.

– – – – –

I started physical therapy sometime in the middle of September, a few days after getting home from the hospital following the September 14th femur fiasco. The school year had barely begun—it still had that fresh, new semester smell to it and already I was facing extra, unexpected challenges.

For a couple evenings each week, the objective was clear: return to full function, flexibility, and strength as quickly as possible.

Nights doing PT were grueling, painful, and yes, even fun. My therapist put me on a typical schedule for a broken leg, starting slow and steady before picking up the pace as I healed. They always made sure to mix things up, too, to keep workouts interesting.

Rehab isn't exactly something people bee-line to with bells on. It is a necessary pill that goes down rough. A stale program where every session is the same and predictable makes that pill harder to swallow. Therapists, like mine, are aware of this and purposefully incorporate new techniques to keep you guessing and make the suck, suck less.

On top of that, almost by rule, physical and occupational therapists bring a uniquely appealing brand of personality to the job to further stave off staleness. They know how to have good conversations, keep things light, and work in timely jokes. When they are demanding hard work be done—work that is tough and painful—this helps make patients smile.

I was no different.

I didn't mind the hard work and I looked forward to hanging out with my therapists on rehab nights. I often smiled during balance work standing on one leg and found myself distracted by laughter in the middle of a strength exercise, or flexibility sessions meant to bend my knee more, which really hurt.

I was surprised at how fast time flew riding the leg bike thanks to our conversations, some deep and powerful, others shallow and silly, each engaging. It made things easier and I worked harder as a result, leading to a quicker recovery.

Positive progress was great, but all in all it was still hard to believe at times that this was how my high school years had started.

When you're fourteen, summer winding down and about to enter high school, your mind starts racing with the what-ifs, how-do-I-'s, and all combinations of mysteries and unknowns that come with the anticipation of 9th grade.

You try and see yourself in that role ahead of time. Try to imagine what will happen, who you'll become, which upperclassmen (if any) might tease and intimidate you like they do on TV and in movies. You grow nervous and more excited, emotions mixing constantly, as day one nears, and you can't help but picture all the different scenarios, teachers and classmates, tests and papers, cafeteria food and cliques, all of it.

What you don't picture is you in a wheelchair.

«‹›»

Life as a broken-legged, wheelchair-bound freshman was different, unusual. But there was no shortage of perks.

Like the parking, but also… special elevator access. Only faculty and staff had permission to use it, but I now came and went as I pleased, floors one to three, a second golden ticket.

And since I often "needed help," I was allowed a "helper." My classmates picked up on this fast.

Not two weeks in people were practically clawing over each other to be the first in line to ask if I "needed any help." Sometimes I needed more help than others, so naturally I had to have an entire retinue when push came to shove. And shove they did, crowding round my wheelchair in the elevator.

Of course, though, more times than not, that first pick went to those doe-eyed coeds, which brings me to perk point four: sympathy.

Break a leg and wind up in a wheelchair…in high school…and you'll never lack for attention in the halls or run out of sympathy from girls. If they don't want to ride the elevator with you or carry your tray at lunch or push you around when you're perfectly capable doing so yourself, then it's your lap they'll want to sit on.

Again, I cashed in on this bad boy.

On the flip side, the wheelchair had two major downsides: missing the class trip to Natural Bridge and no football.

Natural Bridge was like Potomac's 7th grade Caroline Furnace retreat. The mission was class cohesion and camaraderie. The trips eased the transitions into 7th and 9th grade through faculty organized team building exercises, nature hikes, competitions, and games to foster bonding. For new students, they helped tremendously in finding their circle of friends.

It was also a time of rampant flirting. And for those at Natural Bridge, it was when the Homecoming formal date thing was hashed out. At least that's what I gathered later…because me and my wheelchair missed it.

I had to find out about it all from Potomac's notorious gossip hotline.

Then there was football.

Sure, not having to endure practices was nice, but it wasn't long until my routine of self-administered rehab in the weight room got old. I had no problem with the upper body workouts I could do in my wheelchair, but the flexibility sessions grew tedious.

I had orders to do hyper-extension exercises to counter the work I did bending my knee normally to improve range of motion. I had to prop my leg on a bench (both at home and in the gym) then put soft ankle weights on my straightened leg for increased lengths of time. The weights forced my knee down, in the direction knees do not typically bend.

At times it was painful, others merely uncomfortable—but it was always boring.

I stared out at practice each afternoon watching from the windows, wishing I could be back in pads, hoping I could be part of the painful suck of football practice.

I wanted to complain about coaches and gripe about drills alongside my team, who had gone on without me, complaining like they were supposed to one minute and going berserk over a full-contact Oklahoma Drill the next.

Standing there at my new position on the sideline, crippled as I was with not a pad on me, was torture. It would take four months to heal, just in time for baseball, but right then I wanted so desperately to suit up and stick it to someone full contact. To tackle and be tackled.

But I couldn't. And that sucked.

Chapter 15

THE RUDE AWAKENINGS OF SCI ED.

"The frightening and confusing aftermath of trauma, where fundamental assumptions are severely challenged, can be fertile ground for unexpected outcomes."[15]

—Tedeschi and Calhoun, "PTG: Conceptual
Foundations and Empirical Evidence"

May, 2007. MCV/VCU Medical Hospital. Richmond, VA.

Our instructor stood up and pulled over an easel with a large writing pad and adjusted it for all to see. I sat opposite her in the circle and leaned forward curiously, trying to see, while she momentarily blocked this new center-of-attention, flipping the first sheet up and over the back before sitting down.

Sheet two had a pre-written message, a title, I realized. When I re-read it, I suddenly registered their full meaning and now saw the four bold words like some flashing fluorescent Vegas strip sign. I read the title a third time to make certain.

At that, I swallowed a meaty knot in my throat proportionate to the staggering reality of my situation, which in recent days had slowly become clearer. Especially now, thanks to the four words on the easel and what lay ahead, right now and for all the coming tomorrows.

The Vegas sign on the board made me realize walking, or a lack thereof, was only a small part to being paralyzed. I read the title of today's discussion yet again and prepared myself for the day's uncomfortable, and even awkward, conversation.

"Bowel and Bladder Control" it read.

"Bowel and bladder control? On day one?!" I wanted to blurt out. *"Couldn't I start with something less...daunting, like 'How to Pop Wheelies' or 'Putting on Pants'?"*

But I didn't. I sucked it up and paid attention.

Together with PT and OT, my weekly schedule included this: an education class and group sessions to help with adjustment. "But really, how bad could it be?" I'd asked myself when I received my rehab itinerary. Well, according to the day one topic—quite.

When the visual aids in her bag made their debut, it got disturbingly worse.

The reality of my situation, and all I was up against, was a tough pill to swallow on my very first day. Until I entered the Spinal Cord Injury (SCI) Education class, going to the bathroom was something I never really considered.

When the instructor began introducing what's (infamously) known as the "Bowel Program," the ensuing reality-check hit me like a sucker-punch in the dark.

Holding the room's attention, the woman hunched over as she reached into a bag and dug around. With a quiet "Ah-ha," she stood and, like grade-school Show and Tell, held out the object for all to see. It was the top third of a plastic two-liter soda bottle. The bottom had been carefully cut off. What remained before us, when turned upside-down, was a rudimentary model of the lower large intestines.

With the rest of my classmates, who likely wanted to be there as much as they craved daily root canals, I watched her introduce and then demonstrate something called "digital stimulation."

I cringed hearing her throw around this medical euphemism, saying it so nonchalantly as if it was no big deal. But it was. The writing was officially on the wall.

After a word or two, she proceeded with a casual demonstration of this so-called "digital stimulation," as if she were teaching kindergartners to tie a shoelace.

Holding the plastic ass in front of her with one hand, she extended her index finger on the other and plunged it unceremoniously into the mouth of the up-ended bottle, giving instructions in a slow and clear voice for all to follow.

"…after 15 to 20 minutes or so, suppositories will help loosen the sphincter muscles, making the Bowel Program much easier. But digital stimulation…like this…will help get things moving and induce results."

She looked around the room, nodding slowly, one hand holding the faux-anus, the other below, with pointer-finger deeply inserted acting out a job it was never—I repeat—NEVER meant to do.

She nodded once more and continued.

"At this point, to stimulate bowel movement, you work your finger around in a circular motion…like so." She was too upbeat, I concluded. "You'll do this for about 60 seconds at a time in intervals…" She paused again and surveyed the circle for lost faces or confusion, which I found amusing.

Finding none, she continued. "But eventually down the road, each of you will develop slightly different techniques that will work better for you than it might for others."

Oh. Lovely.

SCI Education met in a bigger, more open auxiliary room than the main therapy center beside it. I'd been nervous earlier as I made my way to class and entered the double-doors. Inside I had found the instructor off to the side preparing her things while a dozen or more patients moved their wheelchairs about to find a place forming a wide circle.

I had already met a few of them, but most were new faces. Their stays here overlapped one another, and all varied according to injury and self-motivation. Some had manual chairs while others sat in power chairs; typically, your quads. We all came from different places, had different backgrounds, and ranged from too young to too old.

Moments before the visual aids, the session had begun with introductions to welcome newcomers like me. We went around and said a bit about ourselves. I listened closely and watched as the wheelchair-wielding patients stated name, age, and how they got injured, followed by an interesting personal fact for levity.

Most spinal injuries result from one of three events: gun shot, car crash, falling. Halfway around the room we had all three categories covered.

I was curious to hear their stories. I learned about the car crash that crushed one mother's neck; the night where one inner-city kid was caught in a drive-by shooting crossfire; and the stabbing that put another in our group in his wheelchair forever.

No one, it seemed, was exempt from a spinal cord injury.

There was one thing I knew for sure, though, despite our mental and physical differences. In this new world of SCIs, wheelchairs, and paralysis...I was definitely not alone.

Scanning the room, I saw most were watching closely, taking mental notes, while the blank stares of others in the circle made me think they were present only bodily.

One guy across the circle looked like he could care less. For a minute or two I watched this gunshot victim from the corner of my eye. He worked tirelessly at his legs, adjusting and readjusting them on and off his foot plate as if their very presence plagued him incessantly. Later, I got to know him and then this odd behavior made sense. From dawn to dusk, dusk to dawn, he had to helplessly endure a ceaseless burning sensation consuming his lower half. I felt for him.

While there was nothing I or the doctors could do, I learned another thing from him. Despite identical injuries to our T-9 vertebrae, the nature of our paralysis was like that of our personal backgrounds—shockingly different.

He experienced a painful burning side-effect in his legs, whereas I felt nothing.

Paraplegia, they say, is like a bunch of grapes thrown against a wall. They all hit the same wall, but each grape is distinctly different in damage. His legs burned and mine didn't. And yet, here we were, both T-9 Complete Paras.

Tragedy had rerouted our separate paths and delivered us to a hospital in Richmond, Virginia, where our two roads met.

Paralysis was our great equalizer. What each of us did next going forward, however, was up to us.

Starting over... It's about as rude of an awakening one can have. Except, maybe, for when you get blindsided in your new class with the wonders of the Bowel Program.

— — — — —

The aftermath of trauma is frightening and confusing.

But, what is trauma?

In their 2016 step-by-step manual *The Posttraumatic Growth Workbook: Coming Through Trauma Wiser, Stronger, and More Resilient,* psychologists Richard Tedeschi and Bret Moore identified trauma as "the onset of physical disability, terminal illness, divorce, bereavement, natural and man-made disasters, rape, sexual abuse, combat, or the onset of a child's serious illness or disability."[16]

What comes after isn't set in stone, but they offer ideas. "The average person is flooded with different emotions, struggling to make sense of what happened and trying to find ways to make things 'normal' again."[17]

Survivors typically battle strong—often negative—emotions in addition to unwanted and intrusive thoughts directly related to the trauma. "This is a normal and expected part of the healing process…"[18]

Growth is not a direct result of trauma; it doesn't just happen. It's the individual's struggle with the new reality wrought by that trauma that is crucial in determining the extent to which PTG occurs.

This "what happens next" is no picnic. Nor is it universal. Differences in culture, geography, religion, social status and upbringing make sure of that. Nevertheless, human to human, it's typical for beliefs and assumptions about existence to be challenged.

Assuming I was young and safe and that it "couldn't happen to me" was challenged.

Assuming I'd go through college and walk at graduation was challenged.

Assuming I'd enter the military and do my part was challenged.

And learning to make sense of it was no picnic.

Having bathroom realities demonstrated by a stranger was *no* picnic.

It was frightening, and confusing—and part of the process.

Whether your definition of trauma aligns with the one above—or it doesn't, and you find yourself trivializing a different adversity that suddenly seems mundane or silly—understand that comparing one person's struggle to another isn't necessary, or useful.

All degrees of annoying adversities need to be attacked, big or small, and the concepts surrounding PTG can be scaled to whichever degree suits your circumstance.

Each setback, roadblock, and hiccup that rears its ugly head presents its owner with a set of challenges.

And challenges require choices.

Chapter 16

WHAT IF I HAD SMALL FRIENDS?

Fall, 2000. The Potomac School. McLean, VA.

With the start of high school, I experienced significant developments in my social life that had ripple effects years down the road leaving me and my parents to playfully return to that on-going question after my wheelchair became permanent:

"What if I had small friends?"

Life around a small high school made it simple to hang out with a large group of friends. I became good friends and more-than-casual acquaintances with people from different sports and backgrounds. I got to know people I had known for years but never really knew because of a shared free block, a similar lunch schedule, a class, or an extra-curricular activity.

And with this, I became close with a select group of guys, largely thanks to football.

Football was the nucleus that brought the guys together who I still consider my closest crew. It consists of friendships that endured beyond the sprawling grounds of Potomac, crossing state lines when we all left for college, and then failing to fizzle out when we graduated and entered the real world.

How these guys stepped up to support me after my accident and how they still support me is a testament to who they are, their character, and the way they conduct themselves in life.

When Chris McNerney, largest and second oldest of five, came to Potomac in 7th grade, he earned a nickname that coaches, teachers, and parents would ultimately use because of one simple reason: the dude's got a massive dome. Massive. I mean, it's huge.

Thus, "Fathead" joined the vernacular surrounding this future real-world adult roommate of mine.

Like Fathead, Mike Fischer, the standout freshman playing varsity football, transferred in that same year, coming from nearby Vienna, Virginia. But, before Fischer became a Panther, my first impression of him was one of contempt and jealousy for completely sane reasons. Simply, the man stole all the best dancing partners at cotillion.

Fischer was tall, good looking, clearly athletic and because he came from another school, he had mystery about him. Naturally, jealous of him, I disliked him from the start. And then he came to Potomac. In the years that followed, Fish and I became classmates, acquaintances, teammates, and, with high school football, great friends.

Michael Amann and I were Lifers, entering Potomac in Pre-Kindergarten. And like Fish, he had his own thing that annoyed me—correctly so—from the start: he would not share the stilts.

At recess, Amann always got to the green stilts in Pre-K before I could. They were nothing more than two up-ended plastic cups with strings to hold, but they made you taller than everyone else. He had them. I wanted them.

David Brady, from Old Town, Alexandria, had a profound influence on a specific aspect of my life. Not only did Brady introduce me to punk music and "emo" bands, but along with becoming one of our football teams' biggest fans, leading a raucous cheering section from atop a hill overlooking our field, he is responsible for introducing me to guitar.

This fact might seem trivial on the surface, but I assure you, this new development during my teen years would have a long-lasting impact.

Chapter 17

SOPHOMORE SHENANIGANS

Fall, 2001. The Potomac School. McLean, VA.

Despite making it out of 9th grade academically alive, the concerns from the I.S. heads proved nothing short of warranted with the start of 10th grade.

The sage advice passed down from Mr. Peery got me through 8th and carried me on up to the high school. *Sweat the small stuff.* A mantra I used to keep afloat and hold me up like an injured athlete hanging on a trainer as he limps off the field to the sideline with, say, a cracked thigh bone.

By minding the details, I escaped I.S. and then squeaked by 9th.

At some point, however, the trainer stopped carrying me and I forgot about the details once I became a sophomore. The mantra's meaning faded and before I knew it, I had somehow completely abandoned my science teacher's advice, forgetting all about the small stuff. I was soon back to my old habits: falling short. This led to me digging my own academic grave-like hole.

The reason for this huge hole I dug myself into is not hard to find.

Aside from my preference for sports over school, featuring an interest in the latter that became almost entirely absent by my sixteenth birthday, another prime culprit for this regression is social.

My academic hole was the price I paid for weekends filled with house parties where my status as an underclassman with a senior-ranking older sister, wielding both popularity and athletic prowess, granted me VIP access to the coolest, most exclusive social circles come Friday and Saturday nights. I was no longer sheepish or outside my comfort zone.

Fathead and Amann had parties here and there as did Fischer and I. I a sophomore and Meredith a senior together we hosted several blowouts in the 2001-2002 school year that still get talked about.

Our most epic party was when the "party at Murphy's house" rumor spread to the point of reeling in crowds from larger nearby schools.

The numbers skyrocketed. Our basement filled to the brim fast and from there the individual stories from each of us spice up the regaling tales from that night—which only got better and funnier after Meredith and I were forced to play bouncer. We soon had to turn away hordes of unfamiliar faces, each claiming some unknown connection with a friend of a friend inside, hoping to get past our basement back door.

And then came the cops.

For some reason I chose to join a group up on the roof to investigate rumors of the fuzz. The window to my bedroom was perfect for this. It leads out onto a flat section above the family room, which carries over and above the kitchen, connecting to a more precarious section atop the house with a far steeper, yet walkable, pitch. It was a few degrees shy of deathly-dangerous; suitable to climb, if your shoes had enough grip and you kept feet and hands on the roof.

Staying true to technique for a safe window exit and climb across the roof, I joined the party already stealthily peering over the top ridge. Moving cautious and slow I did the same and had a clear view of the cul-de-sac fronting our house below.

It was typically dark and deserted at this hour, but the constant coming and goings of cars and people, along with the obvious high school party-like sounds emanating from within led some unknown party-pooper to pick up the phone...

It was the only explanation for why the dark, deserted lot was now occupied and bright.

"Ahhh, CRAP!" I blurted. Quickly, I beat a hasty retreat from the lookout and moved light and swift back across the roof. I was clumsy climbing through the narrow window but gathered myself and sprinted to the basement.

I wasn't sure what to do or how to avoid jail, but I had to warn everybody, get them to shut-up for two minutes, and find my sister. She was older, smarter, wiser. Surely, she'd know what to do about twin cruisers parked side-by-side out front with high beams flooding our property.

Patient, they sat there, ready to pounce at the first sign of underaged movement...

"Dude! I remember it so clearly," I said looking back years later, adding my two cents to the nostalgia.

Come Monday stories had spread like crazy. Everyone was talking. Those who were there bragged about it, those who were not pretended to.

"I ran downstairs…" I continued. *"It was crazy looking out over the basement. It was literally filled to the brim, wall to wall…"*

I looked around at the faces of my friends. Each new retelling, whenever it popped back up, came with reliving, and it was always like the first, with just as much excitement and laughs among a group of old friends.

"…I just kept yelling 'Shut up, shut up! Shhhh! COPS! Shut. Up!"

"Dude, yes! That's when the cops showed up at the back door. Downstairs, right?"

As always, the next jumped in, triggering dominos. We all had our own stories and took turns rounding out the tale.

— — — —

I became a sinking ship destined to hit rock-bottom barely a month into 10th grade.

It happened so quick and dragged me so deep that even Mr. Thomas gave me a slim-to-zero chance of clawing my way out. I was in such dire straits across the board that even before Thanksgiving break 2001, I feared that all hope of passing grades by summer were already out the window. It seemed not even the sagest of slogans nor catchiest mantra could raise my ship and save me.

There was no question now. The I.S. heads sitting across that coffee table had been right: Potomac was too hard.

Unless it involved being creative, as in my earlier days, I wasn't interested and it showed in my grades—a result of late homework, failed tests, and lackadaisical effort across the board.

With all my struggles in the classroom, I at least had a contact sport to fall back on now that my femur was fully healed. Still, I was back to my old ways. I'd forgotten how to juggle, and the balls were dropping.

Each student is assigned an advisor from the Upper School faculty. For me and all my academic shortcomings, my advisor was also a pretty important figure in this corner.

Mr. Thomas was a mainstay in the language department. He taught Spanish for years before I arrived in 2000 and has since risen high in Potomac's faculty ranks. He knew Frank and Meredith well, too, which helped foster a relationship between he and I that would ultimately prove critical.

Mr. Thomas kept me on track.

When I had issues, frustrations or missteps, Mr. Thomas guided me to a solution. We met often to ensure that I stayed in line and continued sweating all the small stuff. He encouraged me to schedule similar meetings with my teachers, especially ones I had trouble with, which was usually all of them.

It was Mr. Thomas who showed me how to re-build and re-discover the intellectual ladder that I eventually used to climb up from my self-dug hole and find success.

Chapter 18

THE CHILL FACTOR

Fall, 2002. The Potomac School. McLean, VA.

I love music.

While I was big into The Beatles in middle school and 90's rap as a pre-teen, the start of high school was a musical milestone.

During my musical-milestone, I looked for artists and albums that could pump me up in the weight room, before pitching, and always before football games. Enter: hard rock metal, with scorching guitar riffs, dynamic vocals, and adrenaline-inducing double-bass pedals.

During fall of junior year, a new type entered the picture.

Our tight end was having a party one Saturday when Brady happened upon an acoustic guitar. I had wanted to learn to play for a while, so when Brady first plucked at it and adjusted the tuning knobs, I found myself planted right beside him, fixated on his fingers.

I befriended Brady in 4th grade and we have been close ever since. It was our shared interest in guitar and emo that kept us close.

I bobbed my head, eyes locked on his fingers, wondering how he did it. They danced fret to fret and I forgot all about the party. Brady was working the strings, forming chords with his left, strumming a grunge-emo rhythm with his right. Green Day's *Brain Stew* had us hypnotized.

He stopped. "Wanna try?" He held out the guitar like a peace offering.

I hesitated then excitedly jumped at the chance. "Uhh...sure! What do I do?"

Brady showed me what a power chord was, how simple it is to learn, and how bands like Green Day used it in almost every song. My fingers weren't nearly as deft and agile as his. He had to physically place each one in the correct position.

"Put your pointer…here." He instructed. "Leave the middle free. Place your ring and pinky…here, without touching any other strings. Make sure you push them down hard, too, so you get a clean sound."

"Okay. Got it."

The wire strings dug uncomfortably into the pads of my fingertips. I had what you would call "Linebacker hands" with cuts and scrapes from not wearing gloves, ever. I liked my Linebacker hands. They looked tough, and I felt tough.

But acoustic guitar strings were entirely different. I had zero calluses to ward off the wire strings from digging into the flesh.

I ignored it. And then I completely forgot it when I strummed my first strum and basked in the clean crisp sound I had made. I smiled and looked at Brady for approval.

"Nice!" He said. "Now do this…"

Brady demonstrated how to slide up to the next fret then another while keeping the Power Chord position, which was tough.

"Okay," he said, leaning in close across from me. "Now do two quick strums…" *Duh-Duh.* "K. Now go up and do two more." *Duh-Duh.* "Now go to…here and strum two more." I did. *Duh-Duh.*

The notes got lower. Alone, they sounded like any old insignificant power chord…together they were iconic. In that order with that steady, two-strum staccato rhythm, they formed my first song on guitar.

I must have played the beginning of Brain Stew a hundred times that night.

Chapter 19

TINY ORNAMENTS

December, 2002. Christmas morning. McLean, VA.

I bounded down the stairs and into the living room, looking for that one gift topping my list.

As the presents under the tree dwindled, I was grateful and happy with what I had…but I couldn't shake the empty longing for the one thing that was not there. Mom then handed Meredith and I each a small wrapped gift.

It was about the size of an ornament and, upon opening, I saw that it was just that: an ornament. I held it up and feigned excitement as I pretended to strum the tiny black and white electric Pacifica. Across the room, Meredith was doing the same with a tan "wood" colored acoustic.

I guess I got a guitar after all, I thought. I gave a sincere 'Thank you,' set the ornament aside, and fumbled through my other gifts. I was too busy with an Xbox game to notice Mom.

There in the doorway stood Mom with her hands behind her back. She fought back a subtle grin. I spotted a twinkle in her eyes as she brought her arm forward and held up her hands.

The tiny ornaments had come to life.

In one hand a tan acoustic guitar that she held out towards Meredith before turning to me with the other. My jaw dropped as I stared at the sleek black and white Yamaha Pacifica, glinting gloriously in the morning light. Meredith and I promptly freaked out.

Accepting it cautiously so as not to hurt my new Precious, I then set it across my lap and played the only song I knew…a punk song, about brains and stew. It didn't matter that it was unplugged and quiet, it was beautiful.

All I need now is—

"You can't truly play an electric guitar without—" Mom reached down behind the couch. "—this. Right?" And she held up the small amp that would complete the bond between me and my guitar.

— — — — —

During weekends at the farm, Uncle Paul would teach me and Duane different chords and notes and show us riffs and other iconic intros from the most classic songs in Rock.

Using Google to find more sophisticated chords to my favorite songs, I learned about tabs—instructions with numbers and lines corresponding to frets and strings. Sheet music really, but without the little notes dotting the treble and bass clefs.

I spent countless hours at the computer studying tabs on sites like Ultimate-GuitarTabs.com—anything that had the easiest and most accurate instructions for the Metallica or Dispatch song stuck in my head, the two bands that occupied my playlist at ages 17 and 18.

I taught Meredith a thing or two as well, but she was not nearly as hooked and eventually I went from simply borrowing her acoustic to boldly laying claim after she left it behind when she returned to Connecticut to resume freshman year at Trinity College.

Playing became one of my favorite pastimes—particularly alone in my room.

Going back and forth from acoustic to electric I wailed away as best I could, surrounded by pages and pages of printed tabs for entire songs and whole albums.

I was okay, not good, and far from anything sniffing great, but I was obsessed, in my element, and once I developed those calluses, I danced freely over the strings and frets pain-free.

As much as I progressed in those last couple years of high school, it was later, as a freshman in college, that I really started to improve and get closer to something better than good—even if "great" was still never in my cards.

College, though, is where I met two friends on my hall who showed me more than any online tab could. If I thought I was somewhat good, these guys were somewhat great. Jamming with them turned guitar from a pastime into a passion.

Then, when those inevitable dark days followed my fall, guitar became an outlet. A therapeutic escape from reality.

But first, before all this, I had to get to college. No. Scratch that. First, I had to find a college, and then somehow convince Admissions to let me in.

Chapter 20

THE SHATTERED VASE

"Those who accept the breakage and build themselves anew become more resilient and open to new ways of living."[19]
—Dr. Joseph, *What Doesn't Kill Us*

May, 2007. MCV/VCU Medical Hospital. Richmond, VA.

Busting up my spinal cord sent my internal system through the ringer. When it came out the other side, it was just as confused and in need of rehab as I was. The whole thing was in a state of shock, the doctors described.

"It'll take time for things to get back to normal. Right now it's confused and not sure which way is up or down."

Think of it as being woken up suddenly from a bottomless REM sleep or impromptu nap.

You're startled, a bit confused, even scared maybe. You're unsure of what's going on, where you are, how you got there. Your vision is blurred. You rub at your eyes, but they are slow to recover. You can only feel around guessing at what is what.

Only after enough time has passed can you then escape the confusion and start the trek home to normalcy—whether it's the confusing three-and-a-half seconds after waking from a dream or something longer and far more unsettling.

Life post-spinal is unsettling.

You don't know what's what. You find you have been plucked clean from your old life and discarded someplace foreign where your body struggles to function in a state of shock.

Your internal system is completely FUBAR with haywire temp-regulations the least of your concerns. Communications and controls from brain to body have been hijacked and operate inexplicably. Mixed-signals are sent back and forth in similar screwy fashion, stopping abruptly at the walled impasse of the injury site.

The consequences of this impenetrable wall are devastating. There is virtually no control. Anything can happen, anything goes.

Suddenly you're hot, suddenly you're cold, suddenly you're burning and fevered and sweat-soaked in your hospital bed. Your bladder and bowels quickly freeze up. Suddenly, nothing is regular anymore.

Everything is different, and everything is completely new. When it's not scary, frustrating, or challenging, it's annoying, irritating, and confusing. It's also permanent.

And so, just like the time it takes to recover from that confused state of slumber we've all experienced, the same is true when rehab begins. It takes time to get your bearings and patience and hard work to return to normal.

Unfortunately, the analogy ends there. In the sleep scenario, waking up doesn't return you to Square One. There's no new learning process and no set of requirements to reach some new normal to continue living.

But for those, like myself, who have faced the world of broken backs, shattered spines, surgeries, hospital stays, sleepless nights, pain-filled days, therapy mats, and recovery rooms—our minds will forever hold vivid memories of how they once had to start over.

I will always know exactly what my Square One looked like.

— — — — —

I knew about the issues of bowel and bladder from the start. It's a big topic of concern for new SCI's during this time of constant questioning. When can I go home? Will I ever walk again? And how do I…ya know…go to the bathroom?"

One issue about my internal system I discovered on my own was temperature control, or lack thereof.

If my body had no clue about up or down, the state of onset shock smacked my system upside the head so hard it rendered it equally clueless as to what was hot and what was cold. It couldn't figure out the difference nor make up its mind.

My Stupid Internal System is stupid. So, it goes back and forth one extreme to the other. Even now, over a decade after those first futile arguments with it, the thing remains wackier than ever. Ask my wife.

— — — —

In rehab you have a schedule—for everything. When I say everything, I mean everything. You have an hourly schedule, a daily schedule, and a weekly schedule.

Day one you are given a schedule for when you see your PT and when you see your OT. Group meetings and shrink sessions are set to a schedule as are breakfast, lunch, dinner and the daily delivery of meds. Vital signs are checked by on-call nurses who keep scheduled rounds day and night. Family and friends come and go according to the visiting hours schedule. To allow blood-flow to skin under my butt and to ward off bed sores, I do pressure reliefs in my chair on scheduled fifteen-minute intervals.

It's all planned out, carefully.

This has a schedule. That has a schedule. Everything has a schedule. I'm sure my parents even attended scheduled meetings about my schedule. I did very few things during my hospital stay that were not on a schedule. Shoot, I even peed according to a schedule!

This last one was done for a specific reason.

In the same way I had to train myself to do everything all over again, I had to train my bladder. Regularity and consistency were key in this aspect of rehab and recovery otherwise I'd be left wet in all the wrong places at all the wrong times.

I first had a catheter that emptied into a rather conspicuous leg bag. Once that was removed, I learned the tedious process of intermittent cathing with one-time-use catheters inserted and discarded each pee.

However, this included a whole song-and-dance that I particularly loathed. It wasn't simply the single packed catheters I use now.

It was a damn survival pack for paraplegic peeing featuring gauze, iodine for sterilization, medical gloves for added sterilization, a small packet of lube that got everywhere, a catheter, two yo-yos, a deck of cards, and three protein bars for sustenance since this took forever.

I had to deconstruct this entire kit and unwrap everything inside regularly, day and night. Over time the regularity of it trained my bladder to go only when the pee kit was needed, but it was hardly a guarantee.

If I beat my bladder, I chalked it up as a success. Success, however, was measured in hourly intervals. More accurately, beating my bladder was a stay of unknown execution.

I won this time and remained dry…but would I be so lucky the next?

The answer—both yes and no.

My bladder was certainly a significant part of all the fallout plaguing me during recovery, but as far as bodily functions go, it certainly was not the worst. In this department, peeing—in a rather ironic way—was, and always will be, number two behind, well, number two. It thus marked the return of something I'd abandoned in life a long, long, long time ago.

Diapers.

When I said that paralysis mercilessly throws you back to Square One, where you have to relearn everything, I wasn't kidding.

I literally had to go about my day, through rigorous rehab, after a morning routine that included putting on a pair of Depends.

The Depends were used by every new member to the SCI community. They were simply a precautionary measure at first. Until, that is, they served their purpose.

I was working with Gregg mid-morning when it happened—when my baby-like body did what babies do best and the thing under my shorts was no longer precautionary.

Gregg realized it before I did.

After telling me to lean forward in my chair a bit, Gregg tugged on the diaper with an index finger to investigate.

I was a man of 21-years-old donning a mohawk on my head. I had tattoos. A few more muscles than most. I was a retired two-sport collegiate athlete with plans to become an officer in the Marine Corps. Having an adult check my diaper was something I assumed I had out-grown two-decades ago.

Gregg's investigation led him to cut our session short and send me back to my room, where a nurse met me.

Not my finest hour.

— — — — —

Imagine a cherished vase on the mantle of your living room. A beautiful, prized personal possession passed down over generations. One day it falls to the floor. In some cases, the pieces are large enough and the damage minimal to where you can begin gluing it back together just as it was.

But what if only shards remain?

"Do you try to put the vase back together as it was, using glue and sticky tape? Do you collect the shards and drop them in the garbage, as the vase is a total loss? Or do you pick up the beautiful colored pieces and use them to make something new—such as a colorful mosaic?"[20]

This is Dr. Joseph's theory of the shattered vase.

It was sad confronting the reality that much of who I was and what I did on two sturdy legs had been smashed for good.

Despite new routines, an internal system still going haywire, and embarrassing back-to-square-one moments, I was able to move forward quickly with my adversity. I accepted that I'd never be able to put my vase together again like it was before.

I credit many things, but after I fell, forward motion came with the deliberate decision to control the few things still within my power...

Attitude, effort, finding silver linings, smiling and working hard.

And as time went on, I became empowered by the notion that I could still create something beautiful out of so much breakage.

Chapter 21

THE LIST

Fall, 2002. The Potomac School. College Counseling Office. McLean, VA.

It was a single bottle of aftershave. An inside joke that had never died. A gift. Opening it, the man with more salt in his hair than pepper proudly held it high. The room rolled with laughter. Dad leaned in and whispered to me. Apparently, the man had a reputation for drinking, of all things, aftershave. The laughter continued, morphing into applause.

What stood out most from the evening's dinner—after I, an eleven-year-old, was made to stand up on a chair and loudly introduce myself to the room— was meeting Dad's fraternity brothers and hearing stories relived and retold like they'd happened yesterday.

I saw what my father had with his Sigma Phi Epsilon brothers. I understood it and I promptly wanted it.

We were on a father-son adventure.

Besides hitting up a reptile park, we took a day trip to Florida Southern College where Dad excelled in playing basketball and joined a fraternity. And this week, coincidentally, was their Chapter's reunion dinner.

When junior year arrived in 2002 and it came time to take the SATs and start thinking about college, it was the single bottle of aftershave—and everything it represented—that steered the search.

Besides playing sports, both football and baseball, a fraternity and a strong Greek life, were the two things I knew for sure I wanted in a college. Beyond that I was lost, except for, of course, the List.

— — — —

Potomac's resident college counselor waved me into his office.

On his desk was a sheet of paper with a column of names. A list. The List. The counselor slid it towards me and I skimmed it quietly.

Students became obsessed with their list, comparing with friends, highlighting this school and that, making far-off plans to visit this one, and crossing off that one. The hallways rang with enthusiasm of what could be and what will be.

There was no escaping this intimidating chatter about Harvard, Princeton, Yale, and Brown that left me feeling inferior and out-of-my-element when looking over my own list. Even talk of Duke, UVA, and Stanford within my circle of friends was enough to make me bite my tongue in embarrassment. These were top-notch schools…none of which were on my List.

It was a list—a short one—that did not excite me.

I'd concealed my disappointment behind forced interest as the college counselor went through it and gave a thirty-second "pub answer" about each, pointing out which he thought would fit best.

I bobbed my head and said minimal things like "Okaayy…" and "Mhmm…" and "Oh, nice" while his words went in one ear and out the other. All I could think about was how I was going to hide this from my friends who would surely ask about it later.

Still, it was a place to start. So, whether I liked it or not, I brought it home and showed my parents the List.

Chapter 22

ON THE DIAMOND

Fall, 2002. The Potomac School. Junior Year. McLean, VA.

At the start of junior year, a girl caught my eye.

The girl with the rosy red cheeks and dirty blonde hair that fell long and straight was lean, athletic, and really tall. She walked more confidently than a 9th grader like her should and less awkwardly than most of her classmates. In fact, it was this that kept me looking. And looking was easy.

Erin had a natural beauty about her. When she laughed her eyes squinted and she had a beaming smile that was contagious and cute as a button.

One day after an assembly, as the entire student body migrated back from the auditorium, I muscled up the courage to strike a conversation.

After that I went out of my way to find reasons to talk to Erin and ensure our paths coincidentally crossed. Eventually I scored myself a date.

If I had trouble balancing all things athletic, academics, family, friends, and college—the added distraction of all things Erin didn't help. Not that I minded.

That my new girlfriend was quite the golfer with a mean tennis game was a major bragging point, too. I was vocally proud of her athleticism and sporting background, which fit so nicely with my own that I hardly thought twice when a golf outing would become a convenient means of delaying homework.

Erin's father had been a standout baseball pitcher in his youth, so it was never a surprise to see Erin (and her father) in the stands cheering wildly during home baseball games—especially when it was my day on the mound as starting pitcher.

Baseball was a huge part of my life growing up and I was blessed with enough ability and God-given talent to excel in it from Tee-ball on. In 10th grade I experienced the greatest of this success under Coach Adamec.

"Coach A" was an influential mentor and coach who has become a long-time friend of our family, after coaching Frank in Babe Ruth when he was thirteen and then again after being hired to run Potomac Varsity. Years later, once my turn at high school ball finally arrived, it was Coach A who selected me to be the lone-freshman-on-varsity.

My snowballing success with Coach A was a trend that continued, on the up-tick, in the ensuing seasons.

I set myself apart on the diamond and was lucky to have enough success that the other league coaches took notice, leading to the first of three All-MAC (Mid-Atlantic Conference) honors in baseball, a handful of All-State nods, two All-Metropolitan Honorable Mentions for pitching—my greatest baseball honor—and one Washington Post Player of the Week. Courtesy of one wickedly sick curve that fooled would-be hitters into thinking I had aimed at their head, leaving them ducking, whiffing, or hopping back to safety before the pitch—as planned—dropped clean across the strike-zone.

It was after that sophomore season, however, that I earned an invitation from Coach Adamec to try out for his elite summer showcase team. The Arlington Hillcats.

On a late-spring Saturday 2002, some of the area's best convened at McLean High School to battle for spots on a team whose sole purpose was to travel to different universities over the summer and play before collegiate (sometimes professional) scouts every weekend. The talent that converged on one field that day was staggering.

Days later, despite a tryout that started rocky but ended strong, it was settled. I was a Hillcat.

My next two summers, as a result, were officially jam-packed with back-to-back road trips and tournaments.

Naturally, being my biggest fan, Dad accompanied me on most of our regular weekend trips to the many university campuses where showcase baseball leagues tend to compete, which allowed us to down two birds with one stone: showcases and college tours.

Chapter 23

GOING WITH MY GUT

Fall, 2002. Randolph-Macon College visit. Ashland, VA.

In 5th grade, 1996, big brother Frank taught me an important lesson. I was cramming for a science test on bones in the body. I'd bombed the first one so bad my teacher graciously allowed me to retake it. Out of nowhere, while figuring out how exactly one "crams" for a test, Frank unexpectedly did the older brother thing.

Despite my station as the annoying little brother and Frank the cool, junior, he sat down beside me at the living room table and helped me study all night until the names and locations of every last bone was seared into my brain.

It was then, after I had second-guessed myself incorrectly too many times, that Frank dropped a pearl of wisdom.

"Dude. Trust your gut," he said. "Always trust your first initial instinct. It's usually right. So just go with your gut."

My second-guesses had been wrong. My first, gut-instinct guesses right.

The next day during the re-take, I remembered his advice. When I wavered on a name, I trusted my gut. And I aced it! A perfect 100.

— — — — —

"Let's at least give it a look, Son." Dad wisely urged.

What harm could it do? We would leave after breakfast and return for dinner. So, I caved and agreed to visit Randolph-Macon College.

Ashland, I discovered, is a petri dish of our American past. She's old, quaint, and her history is rich and fertile.

As the hometown to one of our greatest politicians, Henry Clay—who served numerous roles at the dawning of America, including Secretary of State from 1825-1829—Ashland is more than a Southern small-town.

So small that when visitors pull off at exit 92 from I-95 looking for food or a fill-up, they are greeted by the town's uniquely sarcastic sign. *Welcome to the Center of the Universe*!

I would eventually come to love and appreciate this saying, the town, and the history surrounding Ashland, but for now I was here solely to see Randolph-Macon.

As it happened, it was this equally quaint and historic institute—one of the oldest Methodist-run colleges, founded in 1830—that would come to play an integral role in facilitating my renaissance in the aftermath of the most traumatic and significant episodes in my life.

Pulling onto campus, a pleasing chord struck. The college was strikingly beautiful with an unexpected cozy feel about it, just like I wanted.

The buildings, the towering trees, the pristine lawns and gardens. The scattered dorms, the athletic facilities, the busy quads with busy sidewalks. All of it came seamlessly together.

It wasn't long after our arrival that two facts struck another pleasing chord.

First. Despite an enrollment of barely 1300 undergrads, Macon had an extensive Greek system. *Perfect.* And second. Its description as a "jock school" with a strong ratio of student-athletes across the board who strongly compete in the Old Dominion Athletic Conference (ODAC) at the NCAA Division III level. *Excellent.*

After hearing about their Greek Life and sports programs—featuring a nationally ranked men's basketball program—followed by an ideal teacher-to-student ratio, the only things left once the tour wrapped up were a few discussions with head coaches.

Things got better after meeting the football and baseball coaches.

We'd been in contact before this, so it wasn't out of the blue. I was a casual recruit. My accolades as a local pitcher and running back—despite coming from a comparatively miniscule school by Metro DC standards—caught a few eyes. So, after deciding to go D-III for both football and baseball, we kept the discussion going.

After hearing their State of the Program rundowns and team philosophies, I came away giddy. Ashland had captured my attention and Randolph-Macon had sealed the deal. I felt like I belonged.

A week after the official visit and campus tour, Dad and I were back in Ashland for a different kind of visit.

This time we were sitting on bleachers up high overlooking a packed house of thousands surrounding a field radiant with energy and noise. Not a single seat was left. I looked around, smiling at what I saw.

The visiting side's grandstands as big as ours, packed just as tight. Behind each endzone fans stood two and three-deep. The atmosphere was electric. The animosity between the opposing sides was so thick you could reach out and snag a piece.

Randolph-Macon and Hampden-Sydney. Yellow-Jackets and Tigers. The "oldest small school rivalry in the South." More than a hundred-and-ten years in the making, The Game was the season's capstone matchup.

Having grown up going to Redskins games at RFK Stadium, I was taught that all things Dallas Cowboys was fundamentally wrong. I was Burgundy and Gold through and through and knew the importance of tradition. Gridiron rivalries spoke to me.

Surrounded by a century old rivalry with long-standing traditions, I knew I was in my element.

With kick-off looming, I found myself entranced watching the home guys below. Seventy-something men in black with lemon trim. They were huge. They jumped around amped up and pounded pads.

I was locked onto all of it. I recognized every pad-pounding chest bump, every yell, every adrenaline-fueled beast-like step up and down the sidelines—because I did the same thing moments before go-time.

Then a couple guys removed their helmets, and I saw something rather un-recognizable.

I nudged Dad with an elbow. "Look. Down there." I pointed. "Wonder what that's all about."

It was a lineup of unflattering haircuts. One a checkerboard. One an inverse mohawk. One a full-blown Friar Tuck. Some had been cut more carefully, like the dude with polka-dot swirls. Others crude, random with blotchy patterns and odd designs. All, however, had young faces.

"Freshmen," I said.

Down at the 50, as the walk-throughs wrapped up, a fight broke out. The sidelines cleared. Tigers and Jackets stormed the field, jawing back and forth. At the center, as best I could see, shoves turned violent. Face masks were grabbed and yanked about, and fists flew in the air. The fight became a brawl.

Officials and coaches finally got control. Each team retreated to their bench more fired up than ever. Every man seemed to be chomping at the bit for a piece of the action. The crowds, on their feet now, wanted some, too. Me included.

I turned to Dad and grinned. "Oh, yeah!" I said over the crowd. "This is incredible. This is exactly what I want. I'm definitely going here."

I remembered the advice my brother gave me and felt it. *Go with your gut. Trust your instinct.*

Now, as I walked the manicured grounds after The Game, there in the Center of the Universe, in Ashland—my gut was talking to me again. It was telling me things, good things, about love and home, tradition, and rivalry…and haircuts.

So, I listened. And I trusted it.

Chapter 24

PACKETS

March, 2004. Senior Spring at The Potomac School. McLean, VA.

It arrived in the mail without warning in early spring.

As weeks ticked by, with graduation looming larger, the great inevitability cast its tentacles and Senioritis spread. I watched friends and classmates get accepted into one or more of their top choices from their personalized List.

I was still holding out for my one seed and eyeing the mailbox.

When it arrived, I wasn't home to open it. I was out with friends. It was a Saturday night and I got a call from Dad seconds before walking into the McLean Family Restaurant for a feast. I answered quickly.

"Hey, I'm heading into MFR with the guys," I said. "What's up?"

We'd been on the lookout for the package for some time now, but it hadn't crossed my mind once that night—until now.

"It's here."

Chapter 25

PACKETS II: VANISHING PLAGUE

March, 2004. McLean Family Restaurant parking lot. McLean, VA.

I stopped dead in my tracks in the middle of the parking lot, my heart pounding as I processed the meaning of those two words: *It's. Here.*

"Can we open it?!"

"O-Okay" I said. "Yeah… Open it."

My final campaign through Potomac began rather well. Fall 2003 was an exciting time for me and my friends. Our football team was looking promising, we didn't have to worry about SATs anymore, and being seniors didn't exactly suck.

Life settled into a steady routine. Football from 3:30-5:30 being the highlight and lowlight, but I did spend more and more time with Erin in general. And in class, things had even taken a turn for the satisfactory.

The rancid taste that academics left on my tongue changed slowly at first thanks to a few choice electives. What was rancid would then become a sweet and savory addiction during the next phase of my tale—in a time of my life where I became someone entirely unrecognizable from my teenage self.

I was also doing things the right way, staying accountable to the advice and guidance of Mr. Thomas. Sweating the small stuff. Seeing teachers. Keeping my calendar. Getting help with math.

It was paying off. Tactics turned to habits and over time my juggling improved.

One new habit was an odd one and had set in the year before. Now it was full-blown ritual: the 9:00 o'clock bedtime. At night, I had too many distractions.

Not least of which was the tiny TV in my room that hadn't budged since its arrival freshman year when I was laid up in bed with that cracked femur.

The TV was the main culprit, but things like parents and siblings and dogs and AOL all added to the din that hampered my homework. Thus, I made a conscious decision to turn in early and set the alarm for about 4-4:30 in the morning when the world slept and there was no further room for procrastination.

I can't tell you how many mornings I sat at the family computer, pounding my head on the keyboard, hoping that when I looked up I'd find a miraculous compilation of words and sentences sanely brought together to finally finish that ever-loving paper thanks to the power of something higher: my forehead.

But, alas, it was never so, leaving me to rely on what little brain power I had while watching the clock.

No matter how the chips fell, somehow the work was always completed at dawn. It worked, so I stuck with it.

— — — —

Through the phone I heard a faint rustling and then a swift tear. Waiting impatiently in the dark, I felt my feet start to shuffle and then caught myself mindlessly gnawing an already-too-short fingernail.

Lingering back, I held up a chewed finger to signal the guys I'd be another minute then resumed biting while the crew went ahead. More rustling. *What's taking so long?*

The silence grew… Seconds felt like forever. The positive feelings I'd had faded until it was all but gone.

"YOU GOT IN! *YOOOUU GOT IIIIINNNN!!!*"

Boom. Instant. Relief. "WOOOOO!! Hell yeah!!!" I shouted back, raising my arms victoriously. I called ahead to my friends to share the news. They'd just reached the entrance of MFR. "Yo, guys… GUYS! I got in! I got into Macon!!"

— — — —

Making it to graduation and to have overcome years of uncertainty—battling countless setbacks and slip-ups amidst a litany of storms all needing separate weathering—was a colossal relief.

For fourteen years I was plagued by academic adversity. When I crossed the stage at graduation and accepted my diploma beneath that old, iconic shade-giving Swing Tree, the plague vanished.

Soon, in time, memories of past days feeling not smart enough fueled my fire and became motivation for every hard-earned "A" ending with a Masters degree in American Military History from George Mason University.

That summer I watched my tenure at The Potomac School become part of my past; a departure that was sweet with a pinch of bitter.

So, between all the celebrations, high school-decompression, hangouts with Fathead, Fischer, Amann, Brady and the rest, and grueling college football prep—life was good.

Life was good, yes, but with the good sometimes comes the bad.

I was the reason Erin put an end to our roughly two-year relationship before I shipped off to Ashland.

She still had two more years at Potomac.

PHOTO GALLERY #1

Me, Frank, and Meredith dressed to impress for Melanie's wedding.

Turning clay pigeons into dust on the farm. I was in 6ᵗʰ grade when Dad showed up, pulled me from school for the day, and took me to a shooting range where, for my 12ᵗʰ birthday, he bought me a 20-gauge shotgun!

Heading out for 18-holes with Poppy, Duane, and Dad. Even though a golf day at the beach meant missing hours of surf and sand, it was always worth it. North Myrtle Beach, SC.

Left to right: Frank, Meredith, me, Dad, Melanie, and Mom.

Left to right: Evelyn, Frank, Duane, Rachael, Meredith, me, Leah.

In one of the countless mud pits found (or forged) scattered in fields and forests, Duane and I put the Honda Rancher 350 to the test. Summerleas Farm, circa 2000.

With Duane after a morning hunting deer in tree stands. One of the things I have always loved about our farm in the Old Dominion is the ever-changing beauty of the Blue Ridge Mountains in the distance. Summerleas Farm, circa 2004-2005.

Meredith and I after Mom's Christmas morning surprise. 2002.

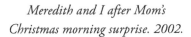

Odds are I'm spinning the ball in my fingertips, settling into the seams for the pitch I know, you, the batter can't hit. Curveball. And I'm aiming straight at your head, confidently. Potomac Baseball, 2004.

Left to right: Me, Amann, Fischer, Locey, Fathead. 80's Day during senior year Homecoming Week at Potomac. Fall, 2003.

Getting my cuts in during our team's senior Spring Break trip with Potomac Baseball. Sarasota, FL. 2004.

Left to right: Fischer, Fathead, Locey, me, and Steve Shashy (who was one of the nicest guys off the field yet one of the fiercest Defensive Lineman in the entire area at the time). Pumped up because more than likely we had just finished dismantling the latest opponent to step on our field. Potomac Football, senior year. Fall, 2003.

Left to Right: Fathead, Fischer, me, Brady, Amann. Senior year, Fall, 2003.

With my high school advisor, Mr. Thomas, at my graduation party. The mentorship and advice I got from Mr. Thomas was invaluable. He kept me in line when I drifted too often. June, 2004.

One of my favorite pastimes at the beach: playing catch with my brother and diving for balls in the surf or hard-packed sand. Days later I would report for preseason football with the Randolph-Macon squad. North Myrtle Beach, 2004 or 2005.

Chapter 26

FLEXIBLE

"It is by remaining flexible that we are most likely to find ways of coping that allow us not only to overcome our problems but also to deal with difficult emotions and to re-author our life stories."[21]
—Dr. Joseph, *What Doesn't Kill Us*

May, 2007. MCV/VCU Medical Hospital. Richmond, VA.

When you sit in a chair all day you get tight. Stretching is a must. To keep my lower half loose, I was regularly stretched by a PT named Barry.

Aside from being a massive, towering human being who could darken a doorway, Barry was famous for playing a mean harmonica, which he toted around in his pocket should the mood strike. This was one of the initial things I learned about him when we first met days into rehab. After telling him about my passion for guitar, Barry and I naturally bonded over our shared love of music.

"We'll have to get together and jam one of these days," he said, looking down at me, cutting off his silent 20-count.

My left leg was pointed straight at the ceiling, resting on his shoulder, firmly in his grasps. His bear paws held my knee in place as he worked my hamstring.

"Yeah! Definitely!" I said. "Just say when."

I was on my back atop the blue-padded table, hands clasped casually behind my head. I watched as Barry mouthed the final counts with his eyes closed before carefully placing the leg down in exchange for the other.

Next, he pushed my knee towards my chest to stretch hip flexors before bringing it down and placing his forearm against the sole of my foot as leverage to steadily drive my toes toward my shin to work the calf. The other side received identical treatments, as always.

The whole thing reminded me of football practices when we did partner stretching in warm-ups. Only this time there was none of that wincing pain attached to tight muscles being loosened that is simultaneously loved and hated.

He counted silently, eyes closed, lips mouthing the pace. I'd looked at him curiously the first time I witnessed his technique. He must have been hearing some music I couldn't, I remember thinking. With each count his body rocked and swayed as if his harmonica had come to life in his pocket and he couldn't help but move to the beat.

Not surprisingly, I came to look forward to these stretch sessions built into my schedule. It kept my lower half loose and made it easier to perform transfers and put clothes on at the unbeatable price of free, never-dull conversations with Barry.

Not only that, it was also a 30-minute window in the mornings when I could lay back, relax, and not do a thing.

— — — — —

The ability to accept situations that cannot be changed, as to be flexible, is crucial for adapting to traumatic life events—and it sure can't hurt for those little daily hiccups we all have.

In *What Doesn't Kill Us,* Dr. Joseph sides with the wealth of research studies used to bolster his book arguing that "compared to people who have an avoidance coping style, individuals who use active task-focused and emotion-focused coping strategies generally do better. These are the people who are most likely to report posttraumatic growth."[22]

Combine the physical and mental strategies, "acceptance coping," as it's called, can appear in many ways:

"Positively reinterpreting a situation, distracting ourselves, venting our emotions, seeking practical support, actively dealing with the problem, denial, religion, emotional support, planning what to do, blaming ourselves, accepting the situation, exercise."[23]

When you're in the grips of change expect to encounter additional practical and emotional problems on top of those that have already rocked your world as you begin plotting your new life course.

But it's never black or white with so many methods at your disposal. If you remain rigid and stubborn in this, your storms are less likely to subside.

Allowing yourself to roll with the punches, to be flexible, and to shift your attitude and effort will be your most effective card to play.

In terms of trauma recovery, "flexibility refers to a person's ability to use different coping strategies in response to changing situations." Knowing when to act on emotions and when to let them go is crucial.

Dr. Joseph provides a compelling example for why:

"If we have supportive friends who are willing to listen to us, emotional expression might do us a lot of good. But," he suggests, "if the people we are trying to talk to are judgmental or distressed themselves or simply not interested, we may come out of the conversation feeling guilt, blame, or embarrassment."[24]

Fortunately, coping and coping flexibility is a universal strategy that only requires a bit of patience and practice.

"Like riding a bicycle, which involves knowing when to shift your weight, when to bear down on the pedals, and when to hit the brake, coping is a skill that can be learned."[25]

Chapter 27

DUDE FROM DURHAM

August, 2004. Randolph-Macon College. Ashland, VA.

I first spoke to Kyle over the phone summer before preseason. Our conversation was quick.

Beyond his name, hometown—Durham, North Carolina—his position on defense and that he was bringing the fridge and me the TV and microwave—that's all I really got. From the sound of his voice, though, I gathered him to be very out-going and enthusiastic—and perhaps over-caffeinated.

Football was the first to arrive in Ashland before soccer, field hockey, and the rest of the student body.

That Saturday morning, car packed and ready, I was up early. Deep in thought. There were endless unknowns ahead to be discovered, experiences to be had, people to meet, and plenty of mysteries I could only guess at as I left Mclean.

How hard would preseason football be at the NCAA level? How many wind-sprints and suicides would I face? What would my new football and baseball coaches be like?

This was a big one, as I was stepping into a new era for Randolph-Macon sports. Both coaches were new, with new systems, playbooks, and coaching philosophies. We were all rookies in Ashland that year.

According to Dad, who kept a closer eye on the situation than me, both Pedro Arruza and Ray Hedrick were brilliant minds in their respective sports of football and baseball, and both were tasked with "turning their programs around." Neither recruited me, however, but I wasn't fazed.

Based on local articles that Dad forwarded to me, Arruza and Hedrick came to Ashland with impressive resumes worthy of the optimism sweeping the Macon community. They were selected, athletically speaking, to bring home ODAC Championships and compete at national levels, which they eventually did.

More importantly, at the top of their philosophies was high academic standards and a strict set of moral codes to ensure their student-athletes grew into well-rounded men.

I was lucky and fortunate to be coached by both.

Nearly two hours after we left, Dad and I turned off Exit 92 and pulled into Ashland, Mom driving her packed Dodge Durango behind us. Our first stop the Brock Center for athlete registration.

Set between Day Field and the iconic train tracks running North-South through town, the Brock is the celebrated activities hub that lures-in prospective students during tours. It's one of the largest complexes on campus.

Thanks to the generosity of famed former alumnus, Macon F. Brock, founder of the Dollar Tree chain, whose philanthropic works often funneled into RMC—she's fully equipped with a gym, racquetball courts, swimming pool, locker rooms with spas and saunas, and three side-by-side basketball courts.

Coaches loved it, too. They found the small, second-floor oval track above the perimeter of the courts ideal for extra conditioning on rainy days. Though tiny with only three lanes (ten laps equal a mile) it served well enough in the absence of an outdoor track.

The Brock Center was quiet and mostly empty now save a team of administrative staffers who welcomed us cheerfully from long tables in the lobby.

I offered my name and information and was directed through the registration assembly-line, making official my arrival. I signed forms, got room keys and my housing assignment, signed more papers, and met teammates along the way before hopping back in the car to confirm my dorm assignment and head to the next stop: Smith Hall. Room 16.

My new home was conveniently situated smack in the middle of what is called the Freshman Village—a cluster of seven single-story dorms at the northeast corner of campus. Some for the men, some the women, a few co-ed. Smith was dudes only.

Smith 16 was the first dorm inside on the left, twenty-feet from prime parking along Henry Street. Having arrived early we had our pick of spots, making move-in exponentially more pleasant.

First, as Dad likes to say, "We got the lay of the land."

Room 16 was rare. She was one of four corner rooms with the luxury of not one, but two windows with two different views. One of Henry Street and the practice fields beyond, the other the grassy courtyard between Smith and Bennett Hall, the last building in the Freshman Village on the far outskirts of campus.

Room 16 also seemed smaller than imagined. Except for two wooden bunks, two wooden desks, and two wooden dressers, also matching, it was bare bones. All this cinder blocked little space needed to become home was a mother's touch.

In her element with hands on hips, Mom thought aloud and turned slowly, verbally painting a picture that made this cinder block space anything but sad. Excitement swelled in her voice as she did her thing.

For anyone who knows me and knows Kyle, and knows us together, they know our bond was instantaneous.

And if you're of those who know us well, you know our relationship is oddly endearing and genuine and neither of us, for the most part, is ashamed to show it.

I can read Kyle like a book. Inside, Kyle is giddy. I hug back with gusto, stroke his back sarcastically so he knows I care. This usually ends the embrace. Feigning disgust, he pushes away. Leaving, I slap him hard on the backside, he slaps my back and we part as friends until next time.

This is my relationship with Kyle. We're silly and stupid but like a flick of a switch it becomes serious and stern if it needs to then back again when business is settled. Back and forth. Because Kyle and I have been through a lot since our paths crossed in 2004.

We've experienced collegiate football together, joined a fraternity as pledge brothers, then drowned in a scandal that rocked the fraternity months before an accident left one of us paralyzed. Our relationship is anything but shallow.

Kyle's abrupt arrival was almost startling, like a bolt of unleashed enthusiasm up two espressos too many.

So, too, the broad-shouldered figure in the doorway filling the frame, cutting a striking presence six-feet-plus. Nothing like the picture I'd drawn up over the phone. He wore khaki shorts, flip flops, with a faded salmon button-down hugging an athletic physique that D-I coaches drool over.

Kyle entered ahead of two women, his tiny mother and girlfriend Emily with blonde tumbling hair. When he flashed a huge smile, it was obvious: my roommate was a very good-looking human being.

Chapter 28

THE TOP BUNK

August, 2004. Freshmen Village. Smith Hall Dormitory. Room 16. Ashland, VA.

When it came time to hit the sack, I made my first, awkwardly unsure climb to the top bunk. It took time before this was seamless, meaning every climb until then was clumsy. There was at least one foot-slip or missed step and it almost always ended in a face plant into the covers.

Night one was total trial and error. Kyle and I bounced ideas off each other on how best to get up.

What happened next is not up for debate.

Because the top bunk is no safe sleeping space, each bunk comes with a removable rail-like board spanning most of the bed's length at the middle, keeping you from rolling off.

When I climbed up, this board was not in place. It was out of the way for the move, leaned against the corner on end. Not wanting to make the treacherous descent back down, I turned to Kyle, still up and about... I asked. He obliged.

But when he did, Kyle did something that I now know—looking back—defined much of who Kyle is as a person, as a son, brother, husband, friend, and to me, a best friend. It was a little thing. Insignificant enough to go unnoticed. But I noticed.

Kyle didn't just grab the board and slide it into place. No. After that, he flattened both hands and shoved them into the crevice between mattress and board...tucking my covers down around me as I lay on my side watching.

He went above and beyond, never batting an eye. Kyle tucked me in. Because that's Kyle: selfless, altruistic to his core, a man to mimic and admire who goes above and beyond what's required.

Like that night at the fountain after that party in 2008, as seniors, four years after we met.

— — — — —

It was a group of us that night. We were walking back home. It was late. Hot. We were all past tipsy and the fountain started calling.

After watching them frolic in the water from the sidelines, it slowly dawned on me that I was sidelined and stuck to my chair. Emotions quickly got the better of me because of what I could not do and my broken body brought me to tears.

I'd hung back after as the group carried on, dripping and drunk. That's when I felt the lump rising in my throat. Then, up ahead, Kyle stopped and looked around.

"Yo, Dude!" He shouted joyfully, wheeling round to see what was up. He was nearly skipping.

When that happened, I couldn't hold it in any longer. The flood gates opened. I dropped my head and continued pushing down the sidewalk, Kyle still skipping to me. Tears rolled over my cheeks.

Kyle realized what was happening and was caught off guard. "Yo! What's u—oh. Ooh…" He stopped mid-skip. His care-free tone severed at the sight of my condition.

And then Kyle did what Kyle does. He listened, wrapped an arm around my shoulder as we walked, and made me smile and laugh.

I never had to ask, and yet, when faced with a situation that my new "legless" reality prevented me from experiencing, Kyle was there—helping me.

Chapter 29

TWO-A-DAYS

August, 2004. Preseason Football on campus. Ashland, VA.

"**D**AG GUM!" He looked at his watch.

"Each and every one of you is LATE!" He reprimanded. "You know that?" A few guys managed to mumble a response that did little. "—Where've you been?!"

We'd been enjoying our last bit of free time during a midday hiatus. Thinking we'd be early, we strolled up campus and reached the front of the science center with five minutes to spare.

It was only when the head man himself threw open the doors, glaring and barking, that I stole a glance around and saw no one. The team was already inside. Waiting.

"Sorry. Sir!" We snapped in chorus. I felt like a whipped dog and smartly shut my mouth.

Another tried quelling his wrath with an excuse to avoid punishment. "We're really sorry, Sir. We thought—"

Coach Arruza cut him off with a hand and said, "Did you already forget the Fifteen Minute Rule?" We stared back blankly, silently. "Fifteen minutes early is 'on-time.' Five minutes early is 'late.' And on-time is the only thing ever acceptable. GOT IT?"

We answered with hurried "Yes, Sirs" and "Sorry, Sirs" and "Never again, Sirs," still hoping to evade the consequences.

Coach Arruza paused, contemplating what to do with us. At length he said, "Good. Don't let it happen again. Now get your butts inside!"

We obeyed and rushed past him, eyes cast down.

With system rules like the Fifteen Minute one, Coach Pedro Arruza—a two-time All-American running back and three-time Academic All-American from Wheaton College—ran a tight camp. He pushed us hard, and often.

— — — —

The days melted together.

Each started with two alarms: first my clock radio, kicking off the day with the always-cackling host from D.C.'s *Elliot In the Morning* show, followed by Kyle's alarm below.

His was all business: a security alarm dressed as a clock. *Neht-Neht-Neht-Neht-Neht.* Then louder. *Neht-NEht-NEHT-NEHT-N—THWACK!* Silence. He knew exactly where to hit it. Time to move.

I swung my legs over the side, checked my landing zone, and slipped off, hitting the throw-rug dead center on sore feet. I wiggled into my flip flops and trudged down the hall to the bathroom.

The fluorescent lights inside the bathroom were always too blinding this early. The noise not much better. You could hear it down the hall, that irritating electric buzz that never stopped.

Mornings were beyond quiet without the other freshmen. It amplified the buzzing, making it exponentially more nagging. I swear it got worse with each sleepy bathroom visit at dawn. I can still hear it now. It took just days before I resented it.

Outside, Kyle and I joined the other rookies on the sidewalk heading up campus to Estes Dining Hall for team breakfast. Across the street, another fresh dew covered our practice fields and low-lying fog was burning off.

Team announcements, as always, followed every meal. After breakfast, Coach ran through the day's itinerary, harping on timeliness and expectations for the next event before dismissing us. From there we hit the locker room—an aging maze of lockers, showers, stalls, and equipment closets that had been neatly cleaned when camp opened.

Once we graduated from helmets-only practices to shells (helmets and shoulder pads), and then full pads, that familiar football odor of sweaty pads and men permeated the lockers for the next three months. You get used to it and even forget about it whenever the whole team is inside gearing up and bantering so loud you can hardly hear the guys next to you.

Then, it was a sprint to the practice fields.

"I better not see you jogging!" Coach Arruza would shout as he darted past everyone, lightning quick to set the tone. "And you better not be the last one out here!" That always got the stragglers moving,

One sweltering day blended with the next, one alarm clock to another, practices, meetings, meals, until days became indistinguishable.

I did my best to do things right and be a good teammate, whether I was working with the running backs and the other fullbacks, trying to earn playing time on special teams, or following coach's orders off the field between more meetings.

After morning practice, if the heat was heavy that day, we would cool off in the pool in the Brock then indulge in Estes remembering, always, "to salt our foods," like Coach told us during his post-practice talks.

After lunch we had about an hour or two to ourselves before suiting up again for second practice.

Showers and dinner came next, then free time followed by a team meeting and full squad film session in Copley 101. An hour later we left Copley to reconvene next door in Fox Hall for individual film with our position coaches.

If we got out before 8:30 we were thrilled. That gave us time to hang out at Lambda. If we got out before 9:00 we were content. Still enough time for Lambda.

If—when—we got out at 10:00, we were pissed. That was the worst. The only thing to look forward to was the pillow.

But hitting the pillow meant deep sleep. But deep sleep meant the alarm going off way too soon and getting to do the whole thing over again starting with the bathroom and those torturous buzzing lights.

Chapter 30

UP ON COLLEGE AVE

August, 2004. The Football Fraternity. Preseason after-hours. Ashland, VA.

Because of these brutal two-a-days, the Lambda Chi Alpha house became our late-night escape. It was our refuge where we could let off steam, gripe about football, and joke around during FIFA tournaments.

It was here, at the house, during these times, that I solidified friendships and earned my first off-field "in" with the brothers.

It was also where I went through a pre-orientation orientation and learned about the culture and character of our team, the campus overall, and the reputation of campus fraternities and sororities at the time in the early- and mid-2000s.

During my time at Randolph-Macon, Greek life was what you did. Roughly half of the student population were Greek, and, from my experience, if you weren't Greek or on a sports team, people didn't know you. And it was in Greek life that reputations and rumors flourished.

At Lambda I learned who threw the best parties, who hardly partied at all, who the more popular girls were and the details of their social goings-on. I even learned which houses certain athletes gravitated towards come Rush Week.

Although the "football frat," of the entire Greek system at R-MC, the Lambda Chi Alpha chapter had the highest cumulative GPA on campus—and they didn't let people forget. Lambdas were talented, intellectual, proficient in the weight room. My kind of people.

Speaking of…

It was during football hours and these Lambda late-nights up on "College Ave" that, again, friendships with my teammates and future brothers budded into something special.

Something that—when the time came and the bad news spread, souring that Sunday morning in April 2007—would one day spur them into action and answer the call when one of their own was in trouble.

Luke—one of the other fullbacks sleeping beside me during film with Coach McConnell—was one of my closest friends.

Luke hailed from the back roads of Charlottesville, Virginia, a country boy whose love for country living and hunting matched, of all things, his surprising passion for rap. His ear for music and rap lyrics likely explains his knack for writing poetry and songs, which were surprisingly good.

Over the years, with my guitar skills having drastically improved, Luke even composed songs that we half-heartedly spent time putting to music senior year. Along with our shared love of the emo band AFI, Luke also did his best to get me hooked on whatever rap he was into at the time. It was because of Luke that I ever even had a "Lil Wayne phase."

It was also because of Luke that I've spent zero dollars on haircuts since 2004.

Two weeks into preseason football my hair entered its pre-fro phase that I despised, which always led me to Kwon, my haircut lady back home. But with Kwon 90 miles away, it was Luke's casual offer to buzz my head that kicked off my new shaved-head look. It has since stuck.

Tyler and Madgar were two more teammates who found their way into the circle Kyle and I shared.

Tyler was a bit like Locey from high school: a tall, statuesque, ball-slinging quarterback, lean with a chiseled jawline. Unlike Locey, Tyler hailed from the small town of Honaker in the south west corner of Virginia, home to Pittsburgh tight end Heath Miller. It was here that Tyler earned the nickname Honaker and received his deep, southern drawl. Tyler is as goofy as they come and laughs at everything.

Madgar was somewhat the opposite. Though blessed with a similar set of muscles as Tyler, Madgar played on defense as a linebacker, which was fitting. You see, as much as we loved him, Madgar had a bit of a temper; great for punishing ball carriers, bad for the golf course.

Still, Madgar and I became close friends, especially later, after we both retired from football and he happened to luck into a room in Lambda in only his second year. We spent afternoons playing Tiger Woods golf between our routine workouts down at the Brock.

While those guys became quick friends, Kevin was...different.

A seriously smart lab rat who studied chemistry and biology, Kevin Kvasnicka was a stout defensive lineman—the type who coaches love at that spot because of a certain physicality. He was (and is) strong in the legs and stocky up top, worked hard, and did his best to mix things up, but it took time for us to warm to him, a fact that now seems absurd given how close all of us have remained.

Our first doses of Kvasnicka, however, who lived directly across the hall from me and Kyle, were hilariously rash. He was loud, possessed a witty vulgarity that knew few boundaries, and spoke his mind to a refreshing degree, telling it like it was to whomever about whatever. And he laughed in a hearty yet high pitched, unmistakable guffaw that came out more *huh-huh-huh* than *ha-ha-ha-ha* and has since become a Kevin trademark.

Nick Jones—who we referred to using both first and last name—was a year older and had a menacing presence of his own. It was entirely football-related, showing up whenever he took his place as middle linebacker.

Nick Jones came to Ashland from the small town of Poquoson near Newport News, Virginia. He loves to fish and drive his boat, is built like an ox, parties as hard as anyone on campus, and speaks with a noticeable southern drawl.

When Nick returned for his senior year of football, the man left absolutely everything he had on the field, every practice, every game, every play. As a star middle linebacker for the team, Nick was a force to be reckoned with. And opposing teams knew it.

Nick Jones could lay the wood and knock running backs and receivers flat on their backsides with the best of them.

Chapter 31

GROUP DEPRESSIONS

"People who are more open are more likely to reconsider their belief system."[26]
—Richard Tedeschi, "Growth After Trauma"

May, 2007. MCV/VCU Hospital. Richmond, VA.

I scanned the room from my place in the circle, like I did my first day in SCI Ed 101. I studied eyes and faces and tried to fill in the gaps of stories I hadn't yet heard. *How did she wreck her car? Who shot him? Why was he stabbed? What caused the stroke? Why did I fall?*

From one to the next we were different; different wheelchairs, different diagnoses, different hearts, different paths, different futures. But it was a stark similarity hanging silently over the room like a dark cloud that connected us: our new forevers.

When someone suffers a SCI, hospitals are as concerned with your mental state as they are physical.

For many, depression and an inability to cope is a very real possibility. I'm one of the lucky ones. Plenty of people, as I've both witnessed and heard, don't accept their injuries quite like I have. To combat this, group sessions are integral to the in-patient curriculum.

Like SCI Education, group sessions met in the same room with everyone in a circle and an instructor to facilitate conversation and provide whatever assistance was required—be it the answer to a question or a motivational pep talk. And like SCI Ed, I entered my first session unsure what to expect.

But it was an open forum. That I did know…so surely we would be talking about our problems.

The opening introductions revealed little more than everyone's names, where they were from, and what type of tragedy landed them here in the first place. It was, by far, the most surreal round of "Hi my name is" I've ever experienced.

Nevertheless, I gleaned quite a bit from these short, reserved answers from a group of strangers who hadn't yet warmed up to each other.

Some spoke softly, others more assertive. Some looked physically dejected, others emotionally so, while some appeared both next to others trying to mask rainy-day feelings. But our circle was not all doom and gloom. I saw a few flash smiles while a solemn face or two cracked, betraying a hint of happiness.

I took mental notes of my fellow residents, chalking them up as this or that as we finished the last of the introductions. I kept a straight face and casually glanced back at those who smiled or were close to smiling.

They should make it here, I hope.

I scanned the circle further and sized up those wearing tight-lipped scowls. Looks alone told me their time here would not go smoothly if it wasn't already.

Hopefully they at least have some family or friends close by, I thought. *They'll need it.*

As the new guy in my first meeting, I was still in my "sponge state," as the doctors say, taking everything in with open ears, eyes, and mind. Besides the occasional sympathetic nod or a word or two of encouragement or advice, I mostly sat and listened as one problem after the next was addressed and superficially diagnosed by the group.

Hearing the litany of tribulations being dealt with had such a profound effect on me that two things occurred to me before the session closed for lunch. Rolling back to my room, it consumed my thoughts. When I reached my room, I had the revelation processed.

One: Emotionally, compared to most, I was in a much different place.

Two: The group session, despite its good intentions, was depressing at best.

As far as I knew and heard, for whatever reasons, "acceptance" had yet to find the others sitting around that circle. Not all, but most.

To me, the circle was one big pity party with an endless parade of "why mes." It did nothing but bring me down. During a time when my sole responsibility was to heal, these little talks simply did not help.

Three meetings later, I was done, and without telling anyone I decided simply not to go.

So, at a time when my faith had been renewed—or, rather, ignited—over the last year and then solidified during my fall, I chose instead to spend this hour in my room alone doing something I never thought I would do on my own free time.

I read the Bible.

— — — — —

Because "traumatic events happen to the best of us," as she aptly puts just six paragraphs into *Bouncing Forward*, Dr. Haas hits us with an important reminder about life's uncontrollable forces when fate intervenes:

"Whether it's an everyday crisis…or a 'capital *T*' trauma…it is crucial," she says, "to know that the trauma is not the end of our story. We cannot control what happens to us, but we can master what matters most: our response to it—our mind."[27]

Attitude and Effort.

While the emotions of those in the group weren't what was best for me, it's important to acknowledge that there's no set time frame for recovery and growth and that those range of emotions in the circle are all part of the healing.

According to Tedeschi and Moore, "In the days, weeks, months, even years after the event…some people experience sadness and grief…others struggle with intense anxiety." Adding that, "depending on the type of trauma, anger and rage may be the biggest emotional hurdles to clear…and then there is guilt or blaming yourself for what has happened."[28]

Sadness, grief, anxiety, anger, rage, guilt—all of it can affect one person to the next in countless ways for however long that persons' personality foundation will or won't allow.

And while these are normal, understandable reactions to abnormal events, they still exist as "negative emotions" and can be very real impediments for growth.[29]

When it comes to coping and growing, negative emotions towards that which you cannot change is a waste of time. Those who can accept their new reality "will do better."[30]

Maybe my range of emotions didn't sync with the group. Maybe they mastered their mind's response to paralysis soon after leaving in-patient. Maybe not. I can only hope that they've found acceptance after all these years and are out there living happy lives.

I hope, yes, but truthfully, I'd go so far as to throw money on the table and bet they *have*, and that they *are* because of one fun little fact:

That despite its baggage, bull, and ever-present hiccups—most people with spinal cord injuries are living life happily. It's true. Science says so.

In 2016, a team of researchers published a study on resilience and happiness after SCIs to identify factors associated with resilience among us spinal folk.

After mailing surveys to 1,800 participants, which included an open-ended final question about the ability to bounce back when faced with a challenge, data from nearly five hundred participants revealed that happiness was not only common, but a partial result of "cognitive perspectives."

Furthermore, they reported that a "positive, optimistic approach to life" was important for levels of happiness, and that "the role and importance of 'attitude'...as a factor impacting quality of life and adjustment."[31]

Studies like these bode well for the future of those in the group whose attitude and mindset weren't quite there yet. And yet the mere fact that they sat around and openly shared the good, bad, and ugly stuff inside their heads and hearts was undoubtedly a positive step.

They could've sat back, crossed their arms, and shut down—but they didn't. They embodied two critical traits that Drs. Tedeschi and Calhoun identified as likely predictors of PTG.

They plucked their heads from the sand, opened up, and committed brave acts of extraversion that I'm sure have led to far more smiles than what I once witnessed.

It may seem like abandoning my depressing group sessions was a cold copout to skip class, but my recipe was my recipe, buoyed by an attitude and effort based on positivity.

It fell in line with an important caveat by Dr. Haas in *Bouncing Forward:* That at times "it can be necessary to distance ourselves from people who are depleting our energy or who burden us with unhelpful advice."[32]

This was simply me being flexible and finding that community support elsewhere when I didn't have family and friends around, didn't have patience for negativity, or when I wasn't hanging out and getting to know some of the other residents after-hours like I often did.

Chapter 32

SNATCHED UP

Late-August, 2004. Preseason Football. Ashland, VA.

Near the end of week two, classes still four days away, some guys and I were invited to an off-campus party by some older Lambdas. Seeing us as potential pledges, they wanted to take us out, show us around, and get us properly introduced to college.

The party was a few blocks from campus, in a townhouse rented by two seniors.

We arrived at a typical townhouse bash: music blaring, people crowding a small living room and even smaller kitchen, overflowing into the backyard where beer pong was played on a grimy ping-pong table. The older football guys welcomed and embraced us like royalty. They armed us with drinks, plied us with shooters, and introduced us around whenever new groups of sorority girls appeared.

Later, while waiting my turn on the beer pong table out back, something made my ears perk up and my heart pound.

"So," a guy at the table began, lightly holding the ball in three fingers lining up the shot. "Who's this Murphy kid I've been hearing about?"

As if mishearing, I threw him a look as he shot. The ball careened off the rim of a red Solo cup. His opponent fetched. "Damn." He turned to me. "Yeah man, this guy Murphy. Kept hearing one of the Thetas talking about him inside. Asking who he was n' stuff. Sounded pretty interested."

My stomach turned with excitement. "Uhh…" I said, in disbelief. "I'm… Murphy."

"You are?" He snatched a ricochet with a quick hand, dunked the ball in the water cup for a cleaning. "Well, not sure what you did, but seems like Veronica's got an eye for you." He sunk a high arcing shot, leaving one more for the win. His second sealed it and brought me to the table— But my mind was elsewhere.

Eventually I was introduced to Veronica.

Over the next weeks and months, Veronica and I hung out more and more. It didn't matter that I was two years younger, either. I felt on top of the world— even with my grueling practice schedule and eye-opening course load.

Hindsight really is 20/20. As much as I complained about it at the time, Potomac prepared me. It made me aware of the fact that, as a student, I could not kick back and breeze through just by showing up. Grades never came easy and they weren't about to now.

I therefore developed a reputation for always being in the library and, as my friends would say, "trying waaaay too hard."

Sure, I messed around, partied and goofed off, but for the most part I did my best to stick to a regular routine after practice. I knew what it was like to fall into a hole and get behind early on, so I consciously created good college habits. Potomac tested me, trained me, and put me through intellectual trauma that spurred me to learn (about myself) and grow.

After practice and Estes, I would return to Smith for a shower and quick hang-out with Kyle. Then I'd pack my things and head to the library for a few hours.

And I had yet to discover the wonders of coffee, so weeknights in McGraw-Page Library, and how well of a study-sesh they turned out to be, was always a matter of how well I could stave off exhaustion and keep my eyelids from slamming shut. Some nights were better than others, depending on the day, the assignment, and which textbook I had my nose stuffed into.

But I was there regardless, putting in the work. Committed to furthering the person I knew I could become, I was finally doing things the right way and settling into a routine of good study habits. The positive note I'd left Potomac on nurtured this new self-imposed library discipline to be better.

Of course, I was also equally motivated to knock out my studies because of a girl.

Veronica and I had been talking more and more and evening hangouts at her place or mine slowly become a regular thing. The sooner I finished my schoolwork, the sooner I could pack up my books and go see "V."

And like that, I found myself walking around campus and going about my days on cloud nine.

While I was just another new freshman on the football team, I felt different. Walked a little taller. After all, I was hanging out with an upperclassman, in Theta, who also happened to be a standout athlete on the Volleyball team!

It wasn't long before Veronica and I started dating, officially, scoring me invites to events like the Theta Fall Formal, an exclusive Christmas party, and, that spring, the fan favorite Fox Fields day trip, where bus-loads of students from local colleges dress up and pretend to watch horse races while day-drinking in a huge field.

My friends got invites as well, after a sister here and a sister there took a keen interest in guys like Luke or felt an event would be lacking without an "as friends" invite to guys like Kyle, despite being "wifed" up before coming to Ashland.

It's safe to say then, that when I arrived in The Center of the Universe, I was snatched up faster than a starving snake on prey.

Chapter 33

LOCKED IN

December, 2004. McGraw-Page Library. Ashland, VA.

First semester of college went by in a whirlwind. The rigorous schedule and expectations implemented by Coach Arruza—from practices to meetings, workouts, and study halls—kept me constantly busy while I learned how to be a freshman and manage my time. Even at the D-III level, football felt like a full-time job. But Coach constantly drilled the policy into us that we were students first and athletes second.

Before I knew it, weeks and months rolled by and suddenly it was finals week in early December.

— — — — —

Maps fascinate me. I love looking at them. Love to know why it looks the way it does and how it's changed. Studying History answered these questions.

Before I settled on a Major, I had no clue what I wanted to do or study. Most of my friends took the Business/Econ path. I could easily have taken that road too, which might have set me up for a career, but that didn't interest me at all. And thanks to a little piece of advice that convinced me otherwise, I avoided that path like the plague.

Before college, numerous people bestowed upon me a gem of wisdom I've since taken to heart. "Do what you love." I was told. "And study your passion."

Senior year at Potomac I'd taken Mrs. Cook's AP *Art History* class, hearing it was an easy A. But that's not why I excelled. I excelled because it immediately grabbed me.

Learning about the ancient Egyptian, Greek, and Roman civilizations and their worldly contributions to art and architecture, sucked me in. This was the first academic experience where my ability to master material and succeed wasn't motivated by a passing grade, rather, a desire to learn about the world and honestly understand its past.

History wasn't something I always loved, though. It took an AP class to lay the foundation…and then one unexpected all-nighter—my first at Macon—to see it differently. It was early December. Finals week.

The hour was late.

Our study room upstairs had become home for what seemed like an eternity. Books and papers were everywhere. Coffee cups had long gone cold next to crumpled food wrappers. And, having secluded ourselves in our tiny space no larger than eight-foot-by-eight, undoubtedly a funk had settled in as well.

We'd become so enmeshed in our studies we didn't realize how quiet the library had become… Hours slipped by unnoticed. Only when the lights abruptly cut off did we pluck our noses from the books to investigate the now darkened stacks and corridors.

"Uhh, where is everybody?" I asked slowly.

"Beats me." Said Eric, a new, non-football friend I'd made over our first semester.

We tip-toed around upstairs like two intruders, looking down the aisles between the book stacks. Deep shadows and still silence lent the library an ominous feel. It was eerie, and utterly unfamiliar.

"Dude," I whispered. "I think they forgot about us."

The night before the final of our World History survey course, in one of the coveted private rooms in the library, Eric and I poured over the twenty-five short answer questions and essay options we'd soon regurgitate come sunrise.

Long lectures, memorized over a distinguished career, were what awaited Professor Reinhardt's students. He'd stand against his podium spouting history in narrative form, stopping only to scribble a name or event on the chalkboard.

Seasoned Reinhardt veterans knew that the list on the board at the end of each class was an outline for the three tests and one final.

Before that final, he'd read you a list of short-answers—you'd pick twenty to answer at test-time—and three long essays that covered the semester. The brilliance of his teaching philosophy was that if you got an A on the final, you should be rewarded with an A in the class, regardless of your current grade.

Armed with the test, there was no excuse for not preparing like crazy—even if creating a comprehensive study guide and committing the answers to memory verbatim took long days and late nights to master. Eric and I prepped separately, with a plan to join heads, compare notes, and fill holes.

The day before our final exam, I found him in the lunch line as I was leaving Estes. "I'll try and go snag one of those study rooms for us up in the library." I said, shouldering my backpack.

"Sweet. I'll meet you there. Catch you in a bit."

We headed downstairs, venturing further into the dark. I was beginning to believe myself. Maybe they had forgotten us.

"I... I think you're right. Ha!" Eric chuckled, amused.

Faint safety lights cast low, spotty glows, but otherwise the ground floor was equally dark and shut down. Not a soul in sight. I tested the front doors. The first opened. At the second I saw a thin sliver of a bolt connecting the glass doors. I gave it a test-nudge anyway. Nothing.

I laughed maniacally and called to Eric, busy elsewhere doing his own investigating. "Yo! Dude!"

His voice was far off in the stacks. "What's up?"

"Looks like we're pulling an all-nighter. Place's locked up! Tight!"

Jittery from coffee, we were now hopped up on the novelty of being locked in the library alone at 2:30 in the morning six hours before the final. We had a solid understanding of the material by this point, so we took some time away from the books to enjoy this rare moment and explore parts unknown in McGraw-Page.

After a while we relocated our things downstairs. We revisited the material then caught some shut-eye on the sofas before dawn.

I awoke around 7:00 to the cleaning crew unlocking doors. The women seemed surprised when they saw me, but not overly shocked. They returned my wave and went about their business ignoring us.

I sat up, yawned, stretched, and found Eric busy at a computer behind the A/V desk, looking like he worked there. "Yo!" He hadn't heard the cleaning crew. "Yooo! We're free. Let's hit it."

Three hours after it began, with material burned into our brains after our peculiar evening, I exhaustively put my pen down—for the first time—when Professor Reinhardt announced, "Time's up!"

Three hours. I wrote nonstop for three hours, taking the full time allotted to purge myself of all knowledge I'd soaked up. My hand was cramped, curled like some hideous claw. I'd filled up nearly two full Blue Books in one-hundred-eighty minutes.

What's more was I hadn't just learned everything to regurgitate it in the exam…I absorbed it.

I consumed it to the point of complete understanding and true appreciation. I didn't just memorize a litany of dates, facts, and short answers—I knew causes and effects, why this happened, that happened, how one thing led to a second which caused a third. History stuck with me and resonated in a way I'd never experienced.

As I packed for winter break, I found myself still thinking about the exam material. Something I'd never done. I thought about my still-lingering mystery, what to Major in. Then it hit me—what direction my studies would take at Randolph-Macon College.

Do what you love. Study your passion.

After being locked in the library, I did. History now made sense. And I liked it.

Chapter 34

EMBRACING THE SUCK

January, 2005. "J-Term." Ashland, VA.

My decision to play two sports in college came from my love of athletics, my passion for football and baseball, and a blissful ignorance due to simply not having been in college. This ignorance was both a blessing and a curse.

The curse came when my obligations transferred to sport two once J-Term (January Term) started and the stink of the football locker room had long aired out.

It was January 2005. I was now the newest pitcher for the Jackets and the only one pulling double-duty as a two-sport student-athlete. What excitement I had towards finally joining the team would vanish in a hurry as pre-season got under way led by new skipper, Ray Hedrick.

J-Term is supposed to be a breeze, I'd heard. It's an entire semester condensed into one month. Students typically take one class that meets daily for a few hours, leaving students time to enjoy the so-called "Play Term."

January of 2005, as it happened, was the single worst month of my college career.

— — — — —

At center court, Coach Ray Hedrick circled us up and formally welcomed me to the team.

I'd been absent all fall but he assured the Yellow-Jacket baseball squad that my time with Arruza was no vacation and that I was joining now far from a soft couch-potato. I knew some of the guys already; the others closest in the huddle welcomed me with nods and back pats. Then we went to work.

We fanned out into a wide circle and launched into push-ups and abs.

The Crenshaw Gym was old, now used for mostly non-sports stuff beyond casual shoot-arounds. Its coolest feature was a raised track circling overhead too rickety for use.

I was just beneath it now, on my back, sweating through my shirt minutes into the workout. I stared up at it, wondering what it was like in youth and who ran around it as I scissor-kicked inches off the ground. Anything to distract me from my burning thighs and lower belly.

Coach Hedrick barked, and we obeyed, switching to the next exercise, waiting for the next order. Bark, obey. Bark, obey. Flutter kicks, leg raises, sit ups, wide grip push-ups, close grip push-ups— I swore it would never end.

Just when I thought it was over, the longer pauses I mistook for the end felt more like a gut-punch than the breathers Coach intended them to be.

I eventually threw hope to the wind after deciding assuredly that there would never be a light at the end of the tunnel and that my workout-welcome would carry on into the wee hours of the morning then on through the afternoon. That's not to say that I gave up half-way or half-assed it.

If anything, I worked harder, embracing the suck start to finish as I felt like I had something to prove.

So, I worked. Miserably. Bark, obey. Bark, obey.

After what seemed like hours, Coach Hedrick ended our hell. We gathered, took a knee, and sucked wind through teeth while he went over scheduling for the coming days. The echo in Crenshaw bounced our collective huffs and puffs around the gym, forcing Coach to speak up.

When we broke and dispersed, I walked back to the Freshmen Village with a few guys.

"It's never been this bad," one said, breaking a short silence.

A second teammate agreed. "Yeah, Hedrick was probably trying to show off and intimidate you. Trial by fire, ya know?"

I nodded.

I went to bed that night assuaged knowing my first day was likely the high-water mark, and that I could expect things to lighten up from there on out.

Things, I quickly learned, did not lighten up from there on out.

Like August to football, January was baseball's preseason. Except August was academic free. January was not.

Yes, I had one class. But a full course condensed to a month led by a nice but demanding professor, is tough. An hour-long class becomes three in January and two or three meetings a week become five. And when preseason baseball is anything but two to three hours a day (a nice fantasy) and it's all you can do to squeeze in time between meals, meetings, class, and practice to study at the library—free time is nonexistent.

I enjoyed baseball and I enjoyed Dr. Terrono's Art History course, *The American Renaissance*. But I did not enjoy them together. And I certainly couldn't enjoy Play Term with my endless routine of class and baseball, baseball and class.

Class was three hours of projection slides and lectures that were equal parts fascinating and boring. Practices were long and cold. Mandatory team study halls unproductive. Evening workouts exhausting. And library time became a battle, me versus a set of eyelids that fought valiantly to fall shut and sleep. There was little productivity as they grew heavier each night while my nose was in the books. I'm still not sure how I managed to keep up with material and assignments as I half-studied, half-slept.

J-Term break was dark and snowy. Lonesome. Baseball had its ups and downs, yes, but the best moments came off the field bonding, away from coaches.

Alone on campus we had free-range of the place. Nights were ours to do as we pleased.

Chapter 35

INTO THE FRAY

Early-February, 2005. Spring Semester. Ashland, VA.

Now, after years of waiting, years of living with the aftershave story, spring 2005 had arrived. My chance at a lifetime of friendship and brotherhood was at hand.

Come Rush Week, the choice was obvious. I was a football guy and Lambda was the football fraternity. Simple as that.

While plenty of other freshmen sampled the assortment of fraternities and sororities on College Avenue, Kyle, Luke, Tyler, Kevin, Madgar, and I plus some others made one house visit only. Rush was nothing but a formality. The odds of getting bids were heavily in our favor but we still had to jump through all the hoops.

We sat around the living room and listened to the Execs babble on about life as a Lambda and all the benevolent work the Chapter did. Then we went around the circle introducing ourselves to a house we already knew, minus the handful of unfamiliar brothers and Rushees not affiliated with sports.

Like this one guy, he was tall and wiry thin, and he spoke with striking levels of confidence for someone who'd probably never seen a football field through the facemask bars of a Riddell helmet. When he introduced himself, the moxie in his unmistakable Southern drawl grabbed the attention of the Lambdas that night like no other non-football playing freshman.

126

He had a first name that started with a J or something, but he insisted otherwise. In wrapping up, to the room of Lambda Chis he said, "But you can call me Fitz."

A few days later the verdicts were in. The houses had spoken. You either had a bid invitation letter in your mailbox, or you didn't. Regardless, Macon had its latest crop of pledges.

《〉》

Our pledge class was a band of ten athletic misfits who at the push of a button could go from upstanding gentlemen to raging weekend-weirdos before walking into a classroom and acing a test they didn't study for.

And most of us played football, except one.

Lambdas' lean toward the football type helped create the reputation that it had. Only rarely did someone walk in during the meet-and-greets of Rush Week, leave an impression, and earn an invitation having zero prior ties to football.

The stick-thin Southerner with confidence left that impression.

Fitz can be your best friend or your worst nightmare. About five-foot-ten and a buck-fifty soaking wet, he was raised in the country, possessing book and street smarts to a great degree and comes across like the most innocent, sweetest guy you could meet. This is all true.

However, Fitz has—and I cannot help but grin writing this—a most unassuming side that doesn't take crap and will gladly dish it back if you annoy him, press him, piss him off or test him. His shoulder angel is always there and vocal, his halo constantly on display, but his horns are always at the ready.

Fitz is not one to stand down from a fight and provided countless entertaining rants and stories in college because of it.

Most notably though is that Fitz is a loyal-to-the-core friend, and a damn good one at that. If you have someone like Fitz in your corner, you're good to go. Guys like that are never far when you need them.

In fact, it was Fitz above all else who quarterbacked a certain gift which was given to me on my sixth night in the hospital. A reminder that the undying support of an entire house of brothers was there for me when tragedy reared its ugly head.

Being a pledge was nothing like I imagined growing up.

Television and movies had left me with a certain expectation, but as I discovered, pledging Lambda was different.

According to *Animal House* and *Road Trip*, I found myself wondering just how bad Hell Week would be.

Luckily, within the house and brotherhood of Lambda, a moral code pervaded and pledges were never forced to do "that which a true gentleman himself would not do."

«»

As far as my duties to Lambda were concerned, I was at least lucky to be in a fraternity that prided themselves on gentleman-like qualities.

We had a lot on our plate in spring of '05 with tons of events and responsibilities to balance as a pledge class including menial, tedious tasks like cleaning the house, food runs, playing chauffer to brothers—all part of the interview-entrance process masquerading as "pledging."

That was the more annoying stuff that made you roll your eyes. Lucky for me I had baseball obligations that became my handy-dandy Get Out of Jail Free card with no If's, Ands or Buts about it. And the brothers knew this.

Very rarely did my phone ring or my AIM messenger flash with one on the other end needing an MTO from Sheetz or chicken tenders and fries from Macon Coffee.

As athletes themselves the brothers knew how things worked in season. When I had spring sport obligations, the brothers knew not to mess with me.

Thus, I was far down on their line of options whenever boredom set them to scheming or a case of munchies demanded a food run. And who better to deliver entertainment and food than a pledge?

Despite enjoying my Get Out of Jail Free card, baseball did cut into some of the more memorable parts of pledging, like random weeknight mixers with sororities or any form of daytime fun at the house on Saturdays because of home games, if I was even on campus at all.

Away games were another matter entirely. This was never really an issue though, except once when the annual Big Brother Reveal night rolled around on the same Sunday we were set to play two games at Lynchburg College. It was a key night I'd heard about for months, one I technically could miss but had zero desire to.

Heading into the weekend with a team bus trip down south, I faced a serious dilemma.

With no way out of the baseball obligations I gladly signed up for, I had no idea how to make both the Lynchburg trip and return for Lambda's most anticipated night of the year: when new guys got big brothers. This was one of the reasons fraternity life caught my eye years ago in Florida at Dad's Sig Ep reunion.

‹‹›»

My predicament was policy related.

When word got to me that Coach was on record against players joining fraternities, the die had already been cast with Bid Night. I had no choice but to keep my pledge status even more hush-hush.

My secret had remained safe to that point. Not a single coach on the baseball staff knew about the double life I'd been leading up on College Ave until our senior catcher—one of the team's goofball jokesters—got hold of a microphone synced to the loudspeakers during a sound check. Even the coaches laughed as Goofball sang and danced about.

My mind had switched to thoughts of dinner when his booming voice stopped me dead.

The question or comment didn't register at first, but the second I heard the words "Lambda," "pledging," and "Murphy," I knew what it meant.

Going into that double-header weekend I was nervous over having to ask Coach to grant the special request that would solve my dilemma and allow me to meet my Lambda family on Big Brother Reveal.

I determined that driving home with Dad—who made all the road trips he could—would be the only way to make it to Reveal in time without missing the games. The bus would be too slow.

As the game commenced that Sunday, I grew more nervous of my post-game request than I did the outcome or getting the signal to come in as late relief.

But as luck, and good coaching, would have it, we snatched victory from defeat in the final innings, sending the Hornet swarm sulking back to their hive.

Riding the victory high, Coach Hedrick came around, albeit reluctantly, after I explained the importance of Big Brother Reveal and how it was not just another frat party. With a "Have fun," he shooed me away.

Shortly after, the team loaded onto the bus while I happily took my leave and settled into shotgun beside Dad. A few hours later our car turned down College Ave and pulled into the parking lot next to the house.

Reveal night was just getting going.

Chapter 36
DR. ANDREWS' CLASS

"As you struggle and wrestle…an increased sense of importance of spiritual matters or an understanding of how to live life well may be a result."[33]
—Tedeschi and Moore, *The PTG Workbook*

May, 2007. MCV/VCU Hospital. Richmond, VA.

I blindly turned to Psalms and began to read.

"Psalms is the perfect Book to just open and start reading," she told me. "It has wonderful messages. I promise, you can find some meaning and inspiration in whatever it is you come across."

It took no more than two or three lines for me to instantly draw parallels to what I was now facing in the hospital. It was like a booster shot of inspiration and motivation and like goose bumps I felt the chill of it surge from deep within to cover my body head to toe.

Whether I felt it or not, above or below the spinal damage at the 9th thoracic vertebrae, I still felt it. I still felt the hand of God touching my life, working in His mysterious ways to shape my future and fix my path ahead—the one I thought was broken, astray, and blocked forever.

— — — — —

I grew up in a semi-religious home going to church and sitting through Sunday Schools, but I was never religious. Frank, Meredith, and I mainly went to church because, well, we had to.

That was all Mom's doing. She took after Mommom and Poppy and always maintained a strong relationship with the Lord. While I was raised a Baptist Christian, I never felt like I had a strong, meaningful bond with God like Mom and my grandmother.

Sophomore year at Randolph-Macon that changed.

To meet one of the two Religious Studies requirements, I coordinated with a bunch of friends the previous semester and together we signed up for one of Dr. Andrews' most popular class. According to campus chatter, this was a veritable cakewalk, a must-have for anyone who's not majoring in Religious Studies and simply needs the credits.

But after hearing more, it seemed the reason his course, *The New Testament*, filled up so fast was because of the man teaching it.

Dr. Andrews was loved by students and faculty alike, including me, and was a regular at the Brock Center gym, where on any given afternoon you could find him sweating it out and mixing it up with students. Dr. Andrews was a Randolph-Macon institution.

After his passing, the college honored his legacy and contribution by putting his name on one of the newest buildings. Andrews Hall is now a senior housing top-choice offering prime views in the northern end zone of the renovated Day Field.

It's because of Dr. Andrews and this 2006 New Testament course that my relationship with the Lord and my faith in God budded the way it did.

To connect a few distant dots, this eventually led to my ensuing a faith-based mindset in the hospital and later to a tattoo running down my left tricep, which itself stems from my staunch belief in the presence of Angels who carried me in freefall that one starry night.

— — — — —

"Really? You really mean that?"

Relief and joy and disbelief came clear over the phone. I knew from the sound of Mom's voice that she had been waiting for this moment, when religion and God finally meant something to me.

"Yes, really," I assured her. I repeated the news of my recent revelation to her once more to be sure. "I really and truly have found God, I think. This class has really made a difference. I've learned so much these past weeks!"

Silence.

A moment later I heard what sounded like a happy sigh of relief coming from the other end, 90 miles north. Her youngest son had finally found the relationship with God she had always wanted him to have.

"Ooohh, I am so happy. I am so happy to hear that. Doesn't it feel wonderful?" She asked.

"Yes, actually…" Hearing the words surprised me as much it did her. "It does. It really does."

What really drew me in was how Dr. Andrews tied in the history of it all, of how the New Testament came to be, of the people who made it happen and the broader, influential and historical events from that time, like Pontius Pilate and the vast Roman Empire he served.

I was fascinated by both the class and the subject matter—even if it did meet three times a week *including* 10:30 AM on Fridays, after the typical weekend-launch party that is a college Thursday night.

— — — — —

In addition to literature from the ancient Greeks to today, along with modern novels, television shows, movies and the like—the main ideas of PTG have long been present in the human condition and thus also in humanity's need to express and recreate its experience with that condition.

It also happens to be an essential aspect of the religions of the world, promoting the idea that, broadly speaking, suffering can lead to wisdom.

Christianity takes tragedy and turns it into non-tragedies. In fact, the central teaching of the New Testament surrounds the story of Jesus' crucifixion and resurrection, along with countless anecdotes of human suffering—the story of Job, for instance.

Islam "suggests that suffering is something to be welcomed because it is seen as instrumental in the purposes of God." While Buddhism, with its Four Noble Truths guiding the practice, "directs people to approach suffering and learn from it rather than avoid pain."[34]

As a twenty-year-old kid I was fascinated by what I learned in Dr. Andrews' class about the New Testament. I was also surprised by how moved and captivated I'd become at times when we reached Jesus' crucifixion and the concepts of suffering…

Yet I had no way of knowing just how instrumental a person's suffering could be—let alone the clarity of meaning and purpose its wisdom could bring.

When I did the timing would be terrible, and tears would fall.

Chapter 37

SHADOWS AT THE GATE

February, 2005. Spring Semester. Bid Night at Lambda Chi Alpha. Ashland, VA.

It all began Bid Night, before Big Brother reveal, and before the exposure of my secret status as a pledge.

Outside, in the lamplit night, my escort was busy spilling secrets about the Lambda selection process that year.

He'd been a friendly fullback with me and was now embracing freedom post-football. He was a good teammate and a fun senior to have around thanks to his reliance on sarcasm.

Out of nowhere, he abruptly stopped, froze. A look of alarm washed over him. His eyes went wide, starring.

Before I could speak, the fourth-year escort placed a hand against my back, shoved, and barked an order. "Run!"

I snapped back around, confused. *Did he just tell me to—*

"RUN!" He shoved again. "Whatchya lookin' at me for? RUUUN! Get to the house, Pledge! Fast!"

As he said it there was a hint of a smirk. Something was up. I wagered it had to do with Bid Night and smartly took off sprinting.

The lawns of the historic Old Campus were scattered with figures silhouetted beneath lamp posts. The farthest were running after something. The nearest mostly still—except for the unmistakable message betrayed by body language of even the most shadowy figures.

I recognized that bobbing crouch anywhere. I did it too in the infield when a pitcher entered his wind-up. An athletic ready position.

The shadows were waiting for something.

Once I realized that something was me, I noticed that each silhouette clutched…a massive object. I couldn't pinpoint it. Not one was alike and the bulging shapes gave no further hint to what was going on.

With too many questions and unknowns flooding my head, I fell back on my orders. *Run!* So, I ran. *Get to the house. Fast!* So, I focused on that, the house across the lawn beyond the street.

Any other time this short seventy-five-yard jaunt would be cake. However, the shadowy figures bouncing on toes like short stops, armed with who-knows-what, convinced me otherwise as I broke into my sprint.

The figures came to life.

They leapt forward. I felt the swarm of red dot lasers lock on to me as they moved to intercept me. I shot a glance ahead just as the Lambda front door slammed shut and saw the last line of shadows turn back on a dime. They too started running, the house at their backs, the next target in sight.

I'm the next target, I determined.

That's when I caught my first look at the nearest man. He dashed forth from the shadows into the light and stared wildly at me with bulging eyes and a hungry smile, all teeth. I recognized him.

The distance closed between us; others fast on his heels. I altered course, juked left, dodged right. He raised his weapon poised to strike— But I zig-zagged past out of reach. The object sliced the gap with *woosh*. Then it hit me. I smirked.

Pillows.

They were decent sized pillows; I'll give them that. Fluffed up nice and good, too, with hearty down filling for optimal pummeling.

They're defending the house!

I barreled through with forearm shivers and well-timed stiff-arms knocking them off balance, buying me time to make a break for the next patch of open ground across the courtyard.

It worked well enough. I faltered once but found my feet in time to recoup, dodge a guy, and size up the last defenders on the street.

They awaited my charge in ready positions, unleashing a battle cry as I plowed forward determinedly, doing my best to appear the intimidating fullback out for a fight. They grinned madly and pounded their weapons, ensuring a perfectly puffed pillow to stop me from reaching the doorstep.

I squared them up like linebackers in the hole, me the fullback.

The first attacked with a chest bump, the pillow held against a barreled gut. I deflected with a left forearm. He staggered and the man beside him was on me, doling out a flurry of blows. I stepped close, shoved hard, and moved on, crossing College Ave.

The final three fanned out, ready to absorb me, Lambda's lawn at their heels. Running, I made a last-second gamble to focus on the middle shadow and to ignore the others. It worked, other than the flanking swats that landed like flies, more nuisance than nightmare.

Then there was one. I received his first hit like a champ and ran on thinking it over. But the middle dude was tough and unrelenting. He attacked rapid fire, hitting like a video game boss in his final death throws. But my forearm was ready, deflecting a dozen blows from his feathery weapon with ease.

I let out a cheer, part scream part laughter, and darted up the steps to slap the doorknob. It opened… A host of brothers ushered me inside breathless and led me to the couch where I joined the other gauntlet-runners.

In a bizarre turn of events brothers of Lambda Chi started to wait on us hand and foot with drinks and back-pat congratulations. This was Bid Night.

As a sign of respect and loyalty to our new house and brothers, come sunrise, we upheld the tradition that had the new guys scrub the house, top to bottom, post-party antics—paying full, necessary attention, of course, to all the nitty-gritty details, no matter how small.

I'm talking toothbrush-in-the-toilet level of cleaning.

Chapter 38

DARK SIDE OF THE MOUND

February, 2005. Day Field with Yellow-Jacket Baseball. Ashland, VA.

After impressing coaches and teammates with my first pull-pen workouts, Coach Hedrick pulled me into his office one afternoon a week before the season's opening games.

Ten minutes later, walking back to Smith with a skip in my step, I eagerly waited for Dad to pick up and hear the news. Two rings later he answered and I blindsided him with said news, detailing our meeting.

"…And then he brought up my bullpens," I said to Dad, "and then he sort of, I dunno, gave me a review of my pitching and what I've shown in practices lately. I wasn't sure where he was going with it, but eventually he stopped, mentioned our opening double-header coming up and shot me a grin…"

Dad quietly, patiently waited for the hook. Giddily, I gave it to him. On the other end of the line came the sound of a proud, beaming father who'd been Fan #1 of mine from the first moment I could kick a ball and swing a bat.

Coach had selected me to start the second leg of the season opening double-header. As a freshman. Amidst a deep, solid Yellow-Jacket pitching staff.

Time with the team, especially off the field, had been unforgettable up to now. But this was one of my best moments. Then, when I took the mound as a collegiate NCAA starting pitcher for the first time, the moment became real.

The knot in my stomach grew ever tighter going through the pre-pitch routine that Saturday. As always, I felt it during warm-ups and as always it intensified on the mound seconds before first pitch. Unlike high school, the weight of the situation was now harder to dismiss, adding extra butterflies.

I veiled my angst and took the mound confidently, chest up, chin up. With my right cleat, I adjusted the foot hole in front of the rubber, spreading dirt about, tamping down lumps with foot taps. Satisfied, I turned, took the rubber, and squared myself to home plate.

I inhaled deep and let out a measured breath, steadying myself. I grabbed the bill of my hat, adjusted it on my forehead, tucked glove to chest, and spun the ball loosely at my side in my fingers. The familiar feel of seams was calming.

High atop my hill, I stood ready. I straightened my back and puffed my chest dominantly as the batter stepped in and the catcher crouched to deliver his signal. Squatting directly behind him, the umpire pointed a symbolic finger at me to start game two.

As dominant as I felt, my first outing as a collegiate pitcher didn't pan out so well. My nerves got the best of me and I found myself distracted by the magnitude of it all; the moment, the venue, my surroundings, all of it. And my accuracy suffered.

I had trouble locating my fastball. Even more trouble with my change-up, which had never been anything more than average at best. And my curveball failed to fall off the table, like it had in high school. Lack of focus and nerves took their frustrating toll against my first college batters.

I walked one. Walked another. And when I finally found my accuracy, I delivered a meaty fastball to the opposing team's imposing catcher. He put an easy swing on it, caught it with the fat of his bat. *Crack!*

The only reason I turned to look was to see how far over the fence it would land. Whether it was a homer or not was never in question.

I was pacing around the mound gathering myself when I heard Coach Hedrick shout.

"Hey Murph!" I glanced over, frustration boiling inside. I found him squatting on a bucket of balls at the end of the dugout closest to home. "Go ahead and let out a fart!" He shouted calmly, for all to hear. "Relaaaax!"

As much as Coach's comment irritated me, I'll admit, it worked. Remembering advice from the past, I maintained a short memory, forgot about the home run and concentrated on the next batter and the first out.

From then on, I was once again my old self—the same pitcher who was once the Washington Post Player of the Week as a high school junior. The same pitcher whose wicked curveball earned him All-Metropolitan Honorable Mention honors two years in a row at Potomac.

One strikeout became two and the tide shifted to our side. Our home fans were back in it as well.

I fed off their energy. I threw another strike and tossed a second to put me well ahead of the next batter. 0-2. The time was ripe to serve up my famous curve. So, I did. The seams bit off my fingertips perfectly. I watched it careen towards the hitter's skull, leaving him wide-eyed and frantic as he bailed from the box, staggering backward to save his cheek bone.

But the precise one-to-seven o'clock spin had done its job. It broke at the last second, nose-diving down and out across the plate, into the awaiting glove. Perfection.

The umpire punched the batter out enthusiastically, ringing up strike three. The crowd erupted. Our bench went wild. Coach popped off the bucket, pumping a fist and clapping at me as I sprinted off the field.

After a shaky first showing I had "retired the side" with three straight strikeouts.

It was an ideal reminder that it is not how you start, but how you finish, and that, when adversity strikes, the most important thing is how you respond and how you bounce back.

Because as long as you have a breath left to give, you are still in the game.

— — — — —

For nearly two decades baseball was life, year-round.

Fall ball growing up, indoor winter workouts and pitching clinics, spring ball, summer showcase teams. I was fortunate to have had success during this, so deciding to continue at the collegiate level was easy. I loved playing, I loved being on teams, I loved competition. Even now, I despise losing more than I love winning.

But something happened during my single season playing for Randolph-Macon.

I would be lying if I said that that passion didn't come down I-95 with me because it did. But it wouldn't entirely be the truth, either.

My experience pitching as a Jacket was complicated. I have fond memories of that season and zero regrets, but factors coalesced leading to a tough yet necessary decision to hang up my cleats and retire the Kelly glove that had become a veritable extension of my arm.

Chapter 39

WHAT YOU WANT. WHAT YOU REALLY REALLY WANT.

April, 2005. Fountain Plaza with the Pledges. Ashland, VA.

From the moment it was announced, the Brothers of Lambda Chi made their expectations crystal clear.

"You guys better win this. You seriously better win this!"

The annual Lip Sync Contest at the Fountain Plaza.

We nodded, stifling laughter at the seriousness of their tone and futile attempt to intimidate. We weren't buying their tough guy act. But their message hadn't fallen on deaf ears either.

Our pledge class was made up of highly competitive individuals. The fact that it was a lip sync contest made no difference—we wanted to win. Period.

We got right into it and wasted little time game-planning even if our outfits and choreography were last-minute. After getting ideas and info from the house about previous performances, we learned what scored best with judges, best with the crowd, and what made a winning routine. From there the matter was settled.

We needed hilarity. Humiliation. We needed to be unquestionably memorable. We'd have to go all-out. We'd have to go…drag.

And for that, only the best song from the best group would do. *Wannabe.*

If that wasn't enough, then a rousing rendition of the Baywatch theme surely would sway the judges.

In mid-spring, Lip Sync Saturday rolled around to one of those cloudless, comfortably warm weekend days you hope for. The excitement I had when we first planned everything was now largely replaced by a serious case of nerves. My gut twisted in knots, refusing to settle.

Neither final outfit prep nor last-minute choreography tweaks could distract me from the thought of taking the stage in a few hours. Beer helped, for a little, but the butterflies only got worse as the contest neared.

Backstage—the basement of Mary Branch dorm—I felt like throwing up as the last two pledge classes before us half-bombed before the crowd.

The crowd cheered. I gave my outfit a once-over and palmed my B-cups, making sure they were adjusted and still in place. I looked around and saw others doing the same.

I was Posh. I proudly rummaged the Goodwill racks for a sleek black dress for my best Victoria Beckham impersonation. I decided to opt out of the high heels.

With a seriousness that surprised even me, I carefully trimmed the dress into a mini-skirt, cut the sleeves into spaghetti-straps, and deepened the neckline to ensure cleavage and show skin. I stepped into it top down then threw on the itchy black wig, adjusting the rug before turning for approval.

Approve, they did, with laughs and cat-calls. I had no defense. I mean, how exactly was I supposed to respond to their probing eyes tracing my every curve? I had pulled off Victoria Beckham nicely.

From backstage we heard the emcee announce us and a great cheer ensued.

Kyle threw open the door and led the charge onto stage, his comically huge frizzy black wig waving atop his head. The crowd roared louder, howling at the sight of us. We indulged them with waves and smiles and promptly took our designated spots on stage then paused, waiting for the music.

That pause felt like forever. Frozen beside Luke, I scanned the crowd and felt the stare of a thousand eyes. The crowd grew softer with anticipation.

I felt exposed and awkward and gave one last look down to fill the void. My boobs had gone askew and so I gave the girls an adjustment. That was all it took to trigger a loud whistle from somewhere in the crowd, followed by catcalls. Tweaking may have started it all, but it was our collective appearance that opened the floodgates.

The beat dropped.

And then, after a steamy, not-quite-choreographed performance with little actual lip syncing, the Spice Girls vanished. One by one dresses and wigs and boobs were stripped off and flung aside revealing ten bare chests and ten red bathing suits.

The Baywatch lifeguards, in a turn of events, had arrived.

As we launched into a slow-mo jog towards the crowd, a loud shout echoed over the plaza. The crowd parted for the lifeguards, moving ever-so-slowly on a mission: a former Spice Girl-turned-victim flailing in the fountain.

The crowd went nuts, cheering on the rescue team to the Baywatch anthem. Scantily clad, the Baywatch lifeguards rushed the fountain, splashed about, and saved the drowning-damsel—still in slow motion.

I can't seem to recall what our score was or what place we came in, but I know one thing: the group that followed us had some big heels to fill and fake boobs to live up to.

The Brothers of Lambda Chi Alpha, in the end, approved.

Chapter 40

ENTRANCE EARNED

May, 2005. On College Ave. Ashland, VA.

"**M**urphy! Murphy! Wake up, wake up!"
I shot up zombie-like, confused and out of it, no idea why these guys were in the room and why they were yelling. Then it hit me. *My alarm!*

When the guys burst into the room that Sunday morning, setting this particularly memorable end-of-spring snafu of mine in motion—they say the look on my face was as if "someone had just shot my dog." Their words. Not mine.

"Dude you're late for practice!" One said.

"Hurry up, hurry up" nagged another. I scrambled for my things. It was chaos.

Calmly, a third added, "Nah, just kidding."

I froze.

— — — — —

Once baseball was over, I returned to the property of Coach Arruza.

I'd watched the football team practice from afar, discreetly, between pitching workouts, after-bullpen running, while feeding ground balls to infielders with the Fungo during on-field batting practice.

The squad had been learning new schemes and wrinkles in the playbook, plays and formations designed to fill gaps and holes learned during Coach's inaugural season. When I came onboard, I was behind and had forgotten almost everything. Thankfully, Coach was understanding and patient as I caught up.

Making things tougher was the fact that my old position—fullback—no longer existed in his scheme. After one year and one year only, Coach scrapped it. By the time he'd return to having a big, blocking running back on hand, I'd already be retired. Until then, I found myself on the line as a (mostly blocking) tight end for my second season, when Arruza decided to put my soft hands and unique catching ability to use.

Spring practice was relatively easy and took up less time than I thought. However, it was the attendance policies that landed me in hot water, sidelined in khakis for the following season's home opener because I couldn't resist—and then because I couldn't wake up.

Far too young and immature to say no to such an epic Saturday night like this one—the culminating celebratory party representing our transition into sworn-in-Brother status—I thus got myself in trouble.

It began the week before, at the start of our last phase of pledging: Initiation Week, or what society has dubbed it, Hell Week. That meant that finally, after a semester of servitude, only four or five nights of ritual ceremonies and gentlemanly tasks stood between the ten of us and the final Initiation proceedings when we'd finally earn entrance into the brotherhood. This last, excruciatingly long evening would culminate, as we all knew, with that much anticipated Saturday night.

Once the last rituals were conducted, and after years of wanting exactly this—camaraderie and life-long bonds the likes Dad has enjoyed all his life—it was finally mine to grasp. Brotherhood. Even just minutes old, the feeling of respect, inclusion, and belonging was indescribable.

And so we celebrated. Music blared. The dance floor hopped. The beer flowed like wine…and the women instinctively flocked to the front steps of Lambda.

By night's end the guys were debating whether to go to sleep or just stay up. Arruza had scheduled an early practice the following morning to cap off our spring workouts. Our celebration stretched into the early Sunday hours, past 2:00 AM, well past 3:00 and when 4:00 AM became 5:00 most decided there was no point in sleeping with practice an hour out. They were the wise ones. I was not.

Rather than heading back to Smith with Kyle, I stammered down the street to Veronica's sorority house where within seconds I was out like a light. I did manage to smartly set my alarm, though. For forty-five minutes later…

— — — — —

Relief hit me like a thunderclap and I looked up to see if I really wasn't late after all, searching their faces.

A fourth, wearing a devious smile, chimed in. "Yeah, practice is over."

Pause. Silence. His words were icy. A ghostly death knell methodically delivered with a sick pleasure that made the men in the room giddy. Then the final blow.

"You missed it." He said. The guys laughed. I shuttered.

I stopped what I was doing to process it. That's when—after his words played over in my head to the point of understanding—my face contorted into the "someone-shot-my-dog" look. Complete and utter despair. I knew I was screwed.

I wasn't simply late for practice; I'd missed the whole thing. Start to finish.

Chapter 41

THE BRIDGE

—Dr. Joseph, *What Doesn't Kill Us*

May, 2007. MCV/VCU Hospital. Richmond, VA.

It's not often that one thanks our Lord for the internet. But looking back on those first few days and weeks, I had to.

"Our Lord has been beside me this whole time," I proclaimed, spilling my heart and soul to the community of followers in journal form. "My guardian angels dropped me square on my back in just the right spot—no broken legs, no broken arms and more importantly no broken neck and no head injuries...My accident could have been a lot worse."

After I fell, Meredith set up a page for me on a site called CaringBridge to update those awaiting word of my condition and on-going progress. This was a unique place that promoted healing, support, and prayer during a community's time of need with message boards, photo albums, and journal options to remind all involved that "Going it alone" should never be an option.

Back then, social media had just been born. Facebook had just opened to the public. Instagram was still a twinkle in its creators' eye. And parents like mine who were still coming to terms with "texting" probably hadn't even heard about "tweeting" yet.

It was from these early, hallowed inter-webs, where connection came in places like CaringBridge, that I drew much of my strength and inspiration to keep going. Because it really could have been worse—a lot worse.

I could have been alone.

Each day, however, the CaringBridge page featuring able-bodied me riding horseback reinforced this realization and reminded me that I would never travel this new road alone.

Loneliness was a non-factor as I read new messages. I was utterly grateful for each message online, as well as in the mail and over the phone. Even now, words still cannot express my gratitude because it fueled my fire and enabled me to persevere.

Without CaringBridge and the community connections it gave me, my recovery would have been far more difficult and painful.

Between the time of my accident and my return to R-MC at the end of summer, I kept my followers satiated with near-weekly updates detailing my days. These became widely anticipated; I heard sometime later that people from all over eagerly awaited entries during that long spring in 2007 and into the even longer summer that followed.

Like the book you are holding, crafting my entries became a labor of love.

My newfound faith played such a role in my recovery I couldn't help but honor it. My faith was plain for all to read and it grew as I continued to devour the book of Psalms and digest the messages within.

— — — — —

"Every person is different, and we all have to find our own recipes." But when it comes to the recipe for overcoming trauma, Dr. Hass points out in *Bouncing Forward* that "the ingredients turn out to be surprisingly similar."

"The number one thing is to acknowledge the trauma and to connect with others instead of isolating ourselves. Nobody can do it alone."[36]

Connecting with others with similar situations is one of the best things we can do. Accepting help and projecting help is a clinically proven path towards betterment and growth.[37]

"Whether it comes from family, friends, or professionals," agrees Dr. Joseph. "The help it provides can be practical as well as emotional…Talking through experiences with supportive others allows us to convert upsetting traumatic experiences into posttraumatic growth."[38]

I'll be the first to acknowledge that I was close to home and even closer to college and therefore benefited from such easy access to everyone and everything in my corner, but hospitals can be restricting. Meaning an in-patient residency like mine comes with at least some degree of isolation.

When the halls went quiet and the visitors were gone, it was during these blips of seclusion—where a mind can wander to the shadowy places it shouldn't—that CaringBridge existed as a constant conduit to my community, a virtual link to love and compassion.

Each time I logged on I healed a little bit more.

Chapter 42

THOSE FAMILIAR BUTTERFLIES

August, 2005. Moreland Hall Dormitory. Ashland, VA.

Moreland Hall became home two weeks before campus life got going in fall 2005. There was no question Kyle and I would live together for year two.

We both knew we wanted to live around the center of campus near the fountain, between Lambda and Estes, so we snagged a first-floor room in Moreland, a building similar in size to Smith but with three stories and on the west side of campus behind Fountain Plaza. A cozy little spot in the heart of Macon.

Like Smith 16, it had bunk beds. I took top. We were short one less set of windows, however, which was mostly covered by our stacked refrigerator and microwave, but enough remained to enjoy our view of Macon's Historic Campus—site of my mad dash on Bid Night through this small open quad between Moreland and Lambda with historic brick buildings on three sides, railroad tracks on the fourth, a center flag pole and tall oaks and elms scattered about.

Almost every building—from Old Chapel to the History Department hub in Washington-Franklin Hall over by Lambda—had some form of old peculiar marking on it adding to the mystery and lore of this corner of campus I loved and now called home.

Time spent in this new home eventually dwindled however, once preseason gave way to the start of classes and a full campus after summer. Veronica, I

148

already knew, would be living down campus in the senior apartments once she arrived in Ashland. Our relationship held strong over the break and it was only a matter of time before half my nights were spent with her.

Waiting on her that last half of August was excruciating. Preseason dragged more than ever, and nights—save Kyle in the bunk below—were often lonely and surprisingly cold without her even in the late summer heat.

For now, though, Moreland was mostly empty—serving dutifully as a quiet retreat to recharge as preseason unfolded.

I was excited to return to Ashland now that I was solely focused on football, but I still had those familiar butterflies that came at the start of every preseason. I now had some idea of what the next two weeks would bring.

However, knowing was almost as bad as not knowing.

I knew morning alarms would come too soon. I knew practices would be long and brutal. I knew my head would pound each practice until I got used to my helmet. I knew wind-sprints would be awful and that if I didn't make my position's time in the 5x60-yard sprint test that Coach's punishment of 100-yard rolls would also be a nightmare. I knew there'd be a million meetings and a million film sessions—and I knew I'd be fighting my eyelids.

But I also knew I wouldn't be alone.

There would be about ninety other guys who'd have to endure all this. Most of those ninety or so I hadn't seen since the spring, so it made the return more enjoyable.

Not to mention that I was now a fully initiated brother of Lambda Chi Alpha. I had full range of the house with all rights and privileges afforded to me, Kyle, Luke, Tyler, Kevin, Fitz and the rest of our pledge class. I no longer felt like an awkward guest—albeit a warmly welcomed one—during evening hangouts playing FIFA and gripping about coaches and two-a-days.

I felt accepted. I felt exactly how I always wanted to. This made being back more special, even if it made football no less easy.

All the things I knew came to fruition. Nights were short. Practices dragged. I was sore in the mornings, exhausted by the afternoon. My helmet hurt. My feet ached. And meetings did in fact peak at the million-mark with meetings that preceded other meetings that followed film sessions and more meetings about meetings.

Chapter 43
ACADEMIA DAWNING

Fall, 2005. Randolph-Macon College. Ashland, VA.

By the start of sophomore year my passion for school, academia, and History had blossomed into full-blown obsession. I had found something non-sport related that truly interested me. Like many aspects of my life at this juncture, I was slowly coming out of my shell.

I had officially decided to declare History my Major. Later, my advisor and I realized that tacking on a few Minors wouldn't be a stretch. A double-Minor in Classical Studies and Art History was feasible.

Mid-fall I unexpectedly found myself at a crossroad, pitting old passions with new ones.

What had been my primary love in life—sports—now entered the twilight of its reign over my attention and motivation. Whereas the dawn of academia, looming on the nearing horizon, was catching my eye. Athletics fulfilled my old life and now academics my new. It was a slow transition, it seems, yet looking back it happened rather quickly.

I had already retired from baseball. I knew I couldn't keep up the pace of school, two sports, and a social life, so something had to give. While I enjoyed football, there was still much about it that I did not like in year two.

Amidst our team's daily and weekly routines, contempt festered and eventually, after much conversation on the sidelines, in Estes, and over Lambda FIFA matches, a few of us ultimately decided that this would be our last year. Some would call this quitting. I prefer retiring.

Like most of the guys, I hated practice with a passion, and having my fullback position removed from the offensive scheme didn't help.

As a result, Coach moved Luke and me to tight end.

I had some of the better hands on the team, outside the receivers, so it made sense, I guess. I just wasn't all that big. My blocking wasn't entirely effective. Next to guys with bodies suited for the position, I wasn't even second string. Most of my playing time came on special teams, which I enjoyed, however my service to the team was far less glamorous—even embarrassing.

Attached to Arruza's hip on the sidelines, I was the designated play caller when the offense went to work. Well, in a way. Using signals that corresponded to different formations, personnel packages, and play wrinkles—he dictated, I translated.

After declaring it the responsibility of the tight ends, the six of us would rotate at practice. When Coach realized I was the only one who could deliver the plays to his speed and standards, he promoted me to full-time signal caller.

My first year-and-a-half at Macon followed a strict regimen week in week out, one head coach to the next. Free time was regulated by study halls, mandatory workouts, practices and games in season and off. There was always someone to report to, always someone watching over my shoulder, and it wore on me.

I knew plenty of people who didn't play sports at all, so I saw what freedom was like for them—and I wanted it. There was another factor still that helped me navigate this crossroad, something quite new to me: good grades.

Actually, great ones.

Statistics was a class I tolerated at first before I found a genuine interest in material that the old me would have bristled at. I found myself putting in time and effort to not only learn and get through the subject, but to understand and appreciate it.

When our professor handed back to me quizzes, tests, and homework with mostly As, I was filled with tremendous pride. It bolstered my new love of academics and further convinced me that I *was* capable…that I *was* intelligent… that the Michael Murphy from Potomac was not the real Michael Murphy.

The "As" only made me want more, and when they came, it wasn't just in *Statistics*.

In *The History of Royal France* I found the nuances of how France came to be in the Middle Ages fascinating beyond belief. Putting in the work was not a burden at all.

For all this fascination, it was a course on *Ancient Athletics* that really struck a chord, taught by the legendary Dr. Camp.

"If you're here to learn about sports in ancient Greece…you're in the wrong place." Dr. Camp told our class day one, which ironically consisted of almost all Macon athletes.

I always found that statement odd because ancient sports is what the course was basically about. Particularly those of the original Olympic Games.

It was a class that combined my love of athletics and my passion for Ancient History. I ate it up.

For Dr. Camp's part, he brought this class to life in a way that captivated me to the point where I was always one of the first to arrive in our upstairs room in Fox Hall. I sat right up close, front and center, working my four-color pen, filling my notebook with facts, figures and sketches of athletic tools and equipment and arenas.

I particularly enjoyed Dr. Camp's dry humor which he strategically deployed at just the right times to keep us engaged.

It was also in Dr. Camp's class that I discovered a knack that once made me hate the subject in the first place: dates. Don't ask me how I did it or why it came to be—likely because I enjoyed it—but I learned how to memorize a plethora of dates and the facts tied to them and to keep them sorted in my head until test time.

Heading into finals my grades were looking good. Tests, quizzes, papers and projects came back not with Cs or Bs, but As and by that last week of class in December I could see a finish line that had been a mirage all my life, a dream fantasy that was real for everyone around me growing up, except me.

I crushed my *France* final, filling up my blue book over the course of three hours to earn an A. Dr. Camp's final went according to plan as well, after I committed every colorful fact and figure in my notebook to memory. It was a simple matter of regurgitating all I knew to solidify my second A.

Intro to Short Novels was considerably more troublesome, but I suffered, survived, and came out with a final grade good enough for an A-.

The last test to complete the foursome was largely a formality. *Statistics.* I'd kept up with my assignments and maintained a firm grasp on the math. The only nervousness had to do with a fear of ruining my clean sweep. A B+ or below wouldn't ring in the apocalypse, but it would certainly be a blight upon so much hard work.

As I worked out the final problem and turned it in, half the class still had heads down. Usually being done early meant I had no clue what I was doing, but not this time.

Handing in my *Statistics* final, I knew: Never have I left a test with such a spring in my step and smirk on my face.

Days later the grades came in on the school's website. And there it was…

The mirage of my academic youth was tangible. That fantasy of As a fantasy no longer. After all my academic ostracism, real or manufactured, I'd finally achieved what had always been an elusive impossibility in my life across fourteen years at Potomac:

Straight As.

Chapter 44

LAMBDA LUAU

"J-Term" and Spring, 2006. Randolph-Macon College. Ashland, VA.

In early 2006 I returned to campus.

It was odd at first not having a coach to check in with, a team meeting or mandatory study hall to go to or someone else's schedule to worry about.

I took to this freedom shaky and hesitant, generally unsure, feeling I always had to be doing something, but old habits die hard. And things ingrained in you don't easily vanish. I may have cursed all those workouts under Hedrick and Arruza, but it never spoiled my taste for lifting and exercise.

Once, while still playing, I thought all the hellish workouts and endless wind sprints would sour my relationship with the gym and make me never want to see a bench or barbell or painted basketball court line again. I thought that once I was on my own time, I could avoid the Brock Center however much I wanted.

Freedom gave me an entirely new perspective on my time each day.

Sometime either during J-Term or early spring semester, I started pulling self-inflicted two-a-days for no other reason than to shed the pounds I'd put on to become a tight end and to trim up for beach season.

It was easier to find lifting buddies in the afternoon, so I dedicated mornings to cardio. I would set my alarm early, throw on whichever t-shirt and shorts were next in the workout rotation, bundle-up in sweats and a hoodie and make the short walk from Moreland to a Brock Center that was relatively quiet at those 7:00 AM hours, save the few student and faculty early birds.

Now that I was solely a student and not a student-athlete, life as a Lambda Chi brother was drastically different.

For one, having pledges was utterly unlike being pledges. Sure, we had a few pledges during the fall, but since Rush is only open to sophomores and above we were lucky if ours exceeded four or five in all.

Remember, Macon's enrollment hardly exceeded 1,200 students.

After a small pledge class that fall, my first foray into the world of Brotherhood rituals and secrets when I wasn't in class, in books or in football pads came as a nice change of pace. I relished my new sense of freedom and all the perks that came with it. Primarily, the type of fraternity life I'd imagined.

After Rush Week and the handing out of Bids, Lambda ended up with a nice crop of about a dozen pledges all hailing from the football team. In many ways the group reminded me much of my pledge class. They were close and out-going and had our same blend of jock-athleticism and intellect.

It served well in adding to the reputation we prided ourselves on: Having the highest cumulative GPA among any Greek house.

The rituals of our fraternity—like that of Bid Night plus the added pomp and circumstance —whether you're subjected to them as a pledge or dole them out as an initiated Brother were all carried out with equal parts seriousness and reverence, sarcasm and hilarity.

We respected the traditions and upheld them to the best of our ability knowing that everything we did was part of something bigger.

No other time was this more apparent than during Initiation in the final week, where nightly rituals took place by candlelight in a darkened house filled with Brothers in hooded robes, and where snickering and stifled laughter were as ever-present as the fraternity's symbolic objects and images taking center stage.

"Another airplane bottle! Mark it down!" Someone would invariably call out from the dark as they monitored the passed-down script word for word, ensuring the penalty for that infraction wasn't forgotten the final night, once Initiation was complete and the ceremonious tallying-of-errors began.

One of the highlights that spring was the hotly anticipated Lambda Luau of 2006.

It was an annual springtime tradition for our house and a quintessential Saturday celebration as summer drew near.

The big draw was the massive, homemade tiki bar and elevated stage for the band, fashioned entirely out of locally-harvested bamboo from nearby woods that was then cleaned, cut, and assembled by the brothers of Lambda Chi.

Each year the bar and stage got bigger and more elaborate. From the pre-planning stages to the party itself, Luau preparations were taken so seriously blueprints were drawn up albeit vague. Stations and jobs were assigned by the oldest brothers to keep things moving and there was a foreman elected to oversee construction.

We had teams with pickup trucks that ventured into the forest wielding machetes. They came back hootin' and hollerin' with huge piles of bamboo, foliage and branches dragging on the pavement. Another team helped unload the Luau lumber and piled it to the side while the truck peeled out of the driveway to get more.

Meanwhile, a horde of brothers descended on the first payload to begin an assembly line to sort, strip, and stack each bamboo tree. Leaves and branches were set aside in another pile to be used later for roofing and decoration while the clean trunks awaited their fate beneath the siren scream of the circular saw.

Everything unfolded like clockwork in the days and weeks leading up to Luau. Weekends and afternoons were dedicated to construction since most of us were free, except for the football guys who had spring practice. But even during the week you could always find at least one brother out back doing something before or after class and sometimes during.

It was never out of the ordinary to see some of the upperclassmen skipping classes to help keep construction on schedule. More so if they were seniors on cruise control making the most of their final few weeks.

With only a handful of weeks before exams, Luau Saturday finally arrived, blue-skied and bright.

The house was packed. Last-minute preparations and beer runs were underway as alumni made triumphant returns. Family members showed up, too.

Out back, on the bamboo stage, the band conducted a sound check. Then the crowds came dressed in their best Hawaiian attire. After being verified on the guest list every entrant kicked off the party the same way: by immediately descending on the massive bamboo bar.

That's where I was stationed, proudly.

I played bartender side-by-side with nearly a dozen other Lambdas. The early rush was frantic and fast-paced with drink orders being shouted at us by the dozens. A beer here, a bourbon and coke there. It was a madhouse.

I'd be lying if I said I didn't savor the behind-the-bar power of being one of the few in charge.

As the sun dropped, Luau transitioned inside, and the evening's registered party got underway. It was a sloppy occasion to say the least.

Suffice it to say, though, that when Sunday's sunrise came and the Lambda Chi brothers finally rallied for food, the Estes sesh that morning was unrivaled in its time.

We must have sat there for two hours. Everyone had a story; everyone had some sinister, juicy gossip tucked up their sleeve. And not just at our two tables.

Judging from that morning's breakfast, I swear the whole campus was hungover or still drunk with the latest Lambda Luau the talk of the town.

Come Monday it was back to reality: classes, homework, the looming spring finals. Like so many others, I spent the week leading up to the exams—and exam week itself—holed up in a private corner of the library or the Copley computer lab, cramming.

I read, wrote, memorized and if it came down to the wire I fueled up and pulled all-nighters.

In the end, the suck paid off and I came away with another strong academic semester. I fell just short of the straight set of As I'd been eyeing, but I was satisfied nonetheless—mainly because I was ready for summer and sleep.

Chapter 45

STRENGTH RENEWED

"Posttraumatic growth requires us to face the struggle and tend to the wounds. The pain is the catalyst for growth..."[39]
—Dr. Haas, *Bouncing Forward*

May, 2007. MCV/VCU Hospital. Richmond, VA.

I grabbed the next envelope from the stack of cards scattered across my lap. I studied the front, checking handwriting and return address. The last hadn't rung a bell, a friend of a friend of a friend the note had said. This one I recognized.

Before peeling it open, I grabbed the bed remote and hit the up-arrow to sit taller. I'd been at the stack for a while. Comfortable again, I slid the card out.

Religious. Faith-based, judging from the front. I read slowly, opened it. On the inside left page, across from a cursive inscription, there was a Bible verse.

One card in every three had at least a Bible verse. The popular ones often repeated, so it was always the sender's penned inscription that I looked forward to, but this one was new.

Halfway through reading the verse something about the words struck me and I felt a tickle under my nose. I read again.

Strength... Soar... Walk.

The words were powerful.

Strength... Reading them I felt powerful.

Soar… I felt the tickle again.

Walk… A knot at my throat.

What verse is this?

Below the final stanza read *Isaiah.* Chapter *40.* Verse *31.* I read the verse once more from the top.

"Those who hope in the Lord," it began, "will renew their strength… They will soar on wings of eagles… Run and not grow weary… WALK…and not grow faint."

My eyes misted over. The tickle. The knot. And like that, the tears streaked down. Tears full of hope and resilience and determination. It was unlike anything I'd experienced, a true religious awakeni—

Knock knock!

I snapped to, lost in the moment. The knocking stopped. From the entrance a voice called out, upbeat and familiar.

"Mi-ster Murphaaayy!" The man hollered strolling in. *Marcus.* I'd quickly learned that knocking was never a request for entry. It was an announcement. "What up, my man! How you feelin?"

Marcus was one of the regulars on the hall, and one of my favorite nurse-orderlies. In the short time we'd known each other, Marcus and I had developed a friendly rapport based on sarcastic banter, similar attitudes, and a love of sports. I always liked it when he stopped by.

Except for now.

Silently, I cursed the bad timing as I hurried to dry my eyes and cheeks. Marcus had only ever seen me at my best, smiling, laughing, strong in all the right places and lobbing his smack-talk right back.

Now I was vulnerable with emotional bloodshot eyes…and Marcus had stumbled in, catching me with shields and armor down.

I lowered my head to pretend like I was organizing get-well cards until I gathered myself. Marcus was mid-banter, already running through his checklist starting in the bathroom. Then he was at the foot of my bed. Then he was beside me, swapping medical supplies and pressing buttons on machines…

But *Isaiah 40:31* was still with me—and out poured a second round of tears that I couldn't hold back.

"Yo. Dude. You good, man?" He said, cutting himself off when he saw what was happening.

"Y-Ya, man. I'm goo—I'm good." I said, choking up.

Head still down I held up the card. I could barely speak.

"It's just—The verse. In this card. It's ju—It's just really powerful. Hit me hard. Outta nowhere." I took a deep breath, wiped my face, and found composure. "Ugh. Sorry 'bout that, dude."

He swatted the air and shrugged. "Nah, man, 'sall good! You good, though?"

"Y-ya… Ya I am." I smiled. A resolute calm washed over. I really was good.

After this *Isaiah 40:31* would follow me.

Like a bad penny, it began appearing at random until it worked its way into my head and heart where it stirred my soul and fueled me.

Coming from a Book I knew little-to-nothing about, and had read even less of, the verse that popped up in get-well cards, infomercials, books, and Sunday sermons resonated with such astonishing accuracy, it ultimately changed and defined my time in the hospital and my recovery. Even my beliefs above.

— — — — —

As you work towards fitting the narrative of your trauma and its reality into the beliefs you held leading up to the "event"—an increased sense of spiritual matters or new understandings of how to live life well can be very real with impactful results.[40]

It's a process that takes time, flexibility, and openness, and a willing desire to actively author your new story as you stare down at the vase shattered on the floor. Because reconciling new realities with old principles is hard.

It involves (and requires) the adoption of new perspectives, about religious beliefs, spirituality, or simply your life's philosophy, and something as heavy as this is no picnic.

But there's always hope and help, and Tedeschi and Moore reminds us so.

"Many people find guidance in scriptures while others seek it in more secular teachings and ideas. Many people find their own truths not in the words from others but in a very personal way that seems to come from within."[41]

Throughout *The Workbook*, statements from survivors, acquired over the course of their fifty combined years of research, who've experienced all or some forms of PTG are used to highlight different points pertaining to growth and adjustment.

When it comes to understandings of life's purpose and meaning, and changes in spirituality, the statements themselves may be helpful in pinpointing this aspect of growth.

I have a greater clarity about life's meaning.

I have a greater sense that I am part of the fabric of life.

I feel better able to face questions about life and death.
I have a deeper sense of connection with the world.
I have a better grasp of what life is all about.[42]

Dr. Joseph also highlights religion in *What Doesn't Kill Us* as it relates to the "emotion-focused strategy" of coping that goes hand-in-hand with its more practical, physical sidekick—that "task-focused strategy" we touched on earlier.

In addition to providing someone with a sense of meaning, religion can "help people elicit social support" through, for instance, a prayer chain or simple, good old fashioned compassion and companionship from the congregation itself.[43]

But you don't necessarily have to be "religious" to feel or benefit from spiritual or philosophical revelations. So, let's call it Ecstasy.

An overpowering emotion or exaltation. A state of sudden, intense feeling. Rapturous delight.[44]

This was my unstoppable reaction to one tear-jerker of a greeting card: a state of sudden, intense feeling, overpowering emotion, and rapturous delight.

There was something else about this moment too. Because "acceptance" was nearly instantaneous, you could say I'd already begun the process of "tending" to my "wounds" before PT ever even started.

Heck! You could even say I was patching myself up mentally with sutures and staples before I went into surgery.

But that quiet afternoon was different.

Going through get-well cards and being so completely caught off guard by the *Isaiah* verse was a catalyst moment that helped me see and face my struggle in a new light. Knowing that my strength could be renewed in unfathomable ways fed me from within.

It gave me fresh morsels of motivation to attack each new day, each new therapy session, and each new abrupt roadblock that sprung up to fight me with the tenacity of a fierce linebacker poised for a goal-line stand on 4th and 1.

And I did so while staying happy—with an almost permanent smile thanks to a revitalized joy upon having glimpsed the meaning my second life could have and the future strength I could develop to not merely live life, but live life well.

Strength... Soar... Walk...

When I opened that card and discovered *Isaiah* book *40* verse *31*, ecstasy wrapped me in its arms, filling my head, heart, and soul so quickly with spiritual fervor that—*Bam!*—like that—a flip was switched and I saw life through a new lens, with new perspectives and new beliefs.

The timing had been perfect and terrible, the tears that fell powerful and true.

With Marcus by my side I was one step closer to total growth—to being completely and utterly AWAKE.

Chapter 46

THE LAST SUMMER

Spring/Summer, 2006. McLean, VA, to Ashland, VA, and back again.

Veronica and I had a good run full of great memories.

She came to football games and I watched her volleyball matches. Over breaks and holidays, she came to McLean for visits and I traveled to Baltimore. I met her parents and she mine. I introduced her to my hometown friends and she to hers.

But it was our differences—age for one—that brought our time to the end of its course.

Veronica's looming graduation was a major wrench: her college days were ending, mine at the midway mark resulting in opposing views of what came next. On the cusp of entering the real world, one of us envisioned a more permanent future…the other did not.

Eventually, inevitably, we split.

— — — — —

I looked forward to the Summer of 2006 for many reasons—other than the fact that it was summer.

Enter Hanover Project.

I was going through the normal routine of deleting junk email early on into the recent spring semester when one email caught my eye. From the History

Department. Something about an internship, it said, with an organization called "The Hanover Project."

I read it over. I perked up at the mention of three History credits tied to an internship. I removed my cursor from atop the trash icon and decided to investigate.

A few days later I went to the meeting mentioned in the announcement. I was one of three. They were happy to see us.

We learned about the project and heard more about a special history book being written about the County of Hanover in Virginia. Interns, they told us, would be assisting the head historian over the summer by investigating an aspect of Hanover of their choosing before producing a lengthy, three-credit-worthy paper containing original research for the book.

I jumped at the opportunity, adding a new wrinkle to the upcoming summer that now found me back on a quiet campus.

Almost weekly I stayed in Ashland for two nights and mapped out two, sometimes three, days of time to do research for my paper. Not only was I studying a topic I loved, it was a good excuse to return to a place I loved more: Macon.

My trips here, considering what I now know awaited me twelve months later, reside permanently, and vividly, in my mind.

At Macon I enjoyed the quiet lull that had descended upon campus and often took time to walk the sidewalks through the Historic Campus and the grassy courtyard facing Copley. I strolled around the Freshman Village and the athletic fields thinking about my project between fond reminiscence.

I even worked in a few lifts at the Brock, took advantage of cheap meals in Estes, and dipped my feet in the Fountain Plaza.

Nostalgic by nature, I enjoyed driving around, too. Wherever I went, I remembered things, stories and moments associated with each corner, crosswalk or crevice I passed. And I wondered, with two full years ahead what memories awaited me at whatever I drove, slowly, slowly by.

But mostly I was holed up in the library, hard at work on the Project, which got bigger by the week as my constant research stole time away from actually writing, leaving me a slim chance to finish the thirty-pager by the end of August.

Those three history credits I so foolishly saw as simple snatch-and-grabs became anything but the certainties I'd chalked them up to be.

Surely there was wiggle room for an extension. So, I sent some emails to test the waters of my wiggle-room theory, which turned out to be accurate.

No longer pressed by time for my research paper, I spent another week or so going about the summer routine I'd settled into.

I enjoyed plenty of nothing when I wasn't doing more nothing with the guys. After morning workouts at the gym, if we weren't playing golf somewhere, this "nothing" typically involved plenty of pool time or playing video games with Fathead, Fischer, Amann and Brady.

After long hours in the sun, and if there wasn't a big house party to attend, the afternoons and evenings followed a predictable pattern: a 7-11 run for Slurpees and snacks, a dark basement, a large television, and marathon video game sessions into the dead of night.

The other half of my routine, reserved for the Project, was quite contrary, and switching wasn't so simple. Some days took longer to boot up between the ears.

In the end, the fall semester was half over by the time I finished the paper. A full course load slowed me down considerably, but eventually I did it. My name was listed in the front of the official hardback history in Martha W. McCartney's *Nature's Bounty, Nation's Glory: The Heritage and History of Hanover County, Virginia* (2009).

For a history of one of Virginia's most influential regions, the impact of World War II on Hanover between 1945 and 1965—my chosen contribution to the book—was received only brief attention compared to, say, Revolutionary and Civil War issues. Still, though, my stuff is covered.

Then it was over, summer 2006.

From that spring into summer, I look back feeling lucky and fortunate to have had so many experiences that remain in my memory vivid and fresh. Memories of things. Things that bring out a smile the way they did in the moment, then again at August's end, and again now.

Only now the smile is different.

Because until God says otherwise—or science intervenes—the Summer of 2006 would be my last on two good feet. Should that change, cool. Should it not, cool, it was a damn fine one to go out on because I assure you…

The one that followed in 2007 was a living nightmare of unimaginable proportions.

Chapter 47

MURPHFEST!

September, 2006. Lambda Chi Alpha. Ashland, VA.

"**S**houldn't you be hitting the road soon?"

"It's getting pretty late. You don't want to be too tired on the drive back, do you?"

"I thought you were leaving…"

Initially I thought nothing of it. When the first few asked me about when I was leaving, I chalked it up to curiosity.

Then, when the same questions were asked yet again, I started to wonder. I knew my family was looking out for me, knowing that I was heading back to Ashland that night, but it seemed odd.

It was September 30, 2006. Not long before this bombardment, my Aunt Paige happily married Steve at Summerleas under the white colonnade façade of our mid-19th century main house. It was a perfect day on the farm.

While our families celebrated to a live band, I began to question the questions concerning my departure.

I found them so odd I had to ask about it. Mom assured me everyone was just looking out for me. The logic seemed sound enough. I then made my way through all the good-byes and before long I was in my Jeep headed down the long gravel driveway then dark country roads back to Macon.

I pulled into the parking lot next to Lambda. I was busy at the trunk when I heard a greeting from behind.

"Yo, dude!"

I turned. A shirtless Kyle walked over through the dim glow of street lamps. The night was comfortable. He wore a cheerful smile and seemed happier than usual in his short shorts and red Croc sandals.

Our talk had turned to the weekend when we hit the porch. I asked Kyle what we should do tonight, hoping for some fun. He shrugged, and I punched in the pass code above the doorknob. The lock retracted inside, and I gave Lambda's weathered green door the extra little shove required to un-budge the hinges and open it.

I stepped in.

Junior year marked the beginning of a new lifestyle at college: my new home. Same roommate, but a new home.

In fact, it was largely because of Kyle and his role in the fraternity that made moving in for the new school year so exciting. No more dorm life. Instead, a frat, like I'd wanted.

On the middle floor our room was the first in a cluster of four on the right wing of the house. Prime location; layout basic. It had a window onto our small backyard, the brick wall hiding our dumpsters, and the college's Physical Plant buildings across the fence. The flat roof of the closest of these had been a graveyard for tossed bottles since who-knows-when.

Our living room was square and simple with two tall dressers, space for a futon, a love-seat and a table, and maybe a bar of sorts, which was a must. What made the rooms uniquely badass were the cave-like sleeping holes.

They sat one atop the other like bunk beds on a big shelf that ran the width of the room. A thin wood wall sealed it off creating the cave. Just the sort of nook I love.

Sticking with tradition I snagged the top; my ladder a futon armrest and mini fridge. Inside, the mattress took up the back third of the cave with less than an inch to spare. I outfitted the rest with a small dresser, a minier mini-fridge for myself and a tiny desk fashioned from A-frames and a wide piece of wood, with a step stool chair.

Besides the love seat I brought from home and the new futon, the highlight of the room was Kyle's bar. With help from his mom—meaning, he provided measurements and she made it—it had been crafted specifically for Lambda, because, well, bars are a must.

During parties, each room on floor two becomes its own little party—and a party needs a bar. For months it was all Kyle could talk about.

Expertly made, the bar was solid wood with shelves in the back, sturdy, tan, and perfect for hosting. And! It was built to the precise height so Kyle could rest his elbow on it comfortably while leaning all casual like against it, giving his best "Oh, hey there ladies, what can I getcha?" face.

That bar served its purpose and then some for our final two years. It gave us so much until its fiery demise graduation eve. Surrounded by a crowd celebrating their final night of college, that thing went out in an epic blaze of glory.

But that was still two years out.

The single semester I spent living in Lambda was some of my best three months in college.

There was always something going on: brothers hanging out, people playing video games, friends day-drinking, front porch hangouts on stained and musty sofas and chairs, registered parties Saturday night, "late night Lambda" after another frat's party, desperate "door knockers" going room to room hoping for a hook-up, pledges cleaning post-party mess, and random people showing up searching for that lost item; clothing, a wallet, a phone.

It was the parties that truly made the experience. Campus favorites like Save a Horse, Ride a Fratboy and 80's Night.

The most memorable, however, came early. Though just one month into the new fall semester, there was no question that MurphFest was the party of the year.

"SURPRIIIIISSSEEEE!!!!"

The stentorian shout that hit me half a step through the doorway caught me entirely off guard, nearly knocking me over. A mob of dudes crowded round close, filling the front hallway. It was all I could see and hear. I was floored. Speechless. Eyes agape, jaw dropped.

There is an awesome picture taken of this exact moment that perfectly captures the mood of that eruption, my look of complete shock and the shape of the night that followed. It's one of my favorite candid photos. Ever.

It is also one of the pictures that would be used later for a certain poster created by my brotherhood to honor one of their own. To carry him in a time of great need.

Until I walked in the front door that Friday night, two days after my official 21st birthday, MurphFest was a tightly kept secret.

In the weeks leading up to my big 2-1, Mom and Dad again and again kept asking if I wanted something special, and I kept saying thank you, but no. They eventually relented. Or so I thought. Little did I know that they were busy conspiring with Kyle.

With a veritable blank check in hand from my far-too-kind parents, Kyle took the reins. Soon, something small became something entirely opposite. Assuring my parents that he'd take care of it, Kyle went all-out.

He had a massive ice luge brought in for the third-floor attic. Food that was catered. Kegs for each floor. And enough liquor and beer to drown a Munich Oktoberfest.

But what really made MurphFest "MurphFest" were the shirts. White with different colored sleeves from blue to red to green each had "MurphFest" emblazoned on the chest.

Kyle clapped me on the back and then stepped around me. He took his place before the still-cheering mob unmasking himself as the brains behind the operation.

"Surprised?" He said rhetorically. He grinned a toothy grin and met my shock with pure pride and smugness as he wallowed in the satisfaction of the mission's success.

Still stunned, I said nothing.

"Well," Kyle said officially, "Happy birthday, bro!"

Lambda Chi Alpha erupted. Wild shouts exploded up the stairs and filled the house. Then they led me to the Delta room cheering and MurphFest was a go.

The Delta room makes up a third of the fraternity's ground floor with windows on two walls, a plexiglass memorabilia case on the third, and a bar across the back next to an exit in a corner. No couches. No chairs. Occasional wooden riser for bands. Low ceiling. Tile floor.

It's the perfect dance floor. Great for bands, DJs, and mischief.

Tonight, the Delta room was not bare. It was filled with great cheer, the wafting aroma of dinner, and the perceptible hint of the evening's coming debauchery where the only ritual was that of brothers celebrating a milestone where fake IDs go useless.

Here, the crowd eagerly presented me with two tables of hot, catered food. They honored me with a plastic gold crown, pinned the blue Birthday Boy ribbon on my chest, and slapped a footlong Sandano's steak and cheese in my hand bursting with the works. The foot-long was still warm.

Due to popular demand I tore into it as the house launched into a testosterone laced rendition of Happy Birthday more shout than song.

It was deafening.

From there the night unfolded magically. It was as good as it gets.

When the guys told me that every sorority on campus was on their way, I knew it would be epic. What seemed like the rest of the student body arrived in droves. Soon the house was crawling as a steady flow of coeds flocked to Lambda stuffing it to the brim.

The first floor was packed, the Delta room a dance hall. The second floor swarmed with eight parties that spilled into one up and down the hall. And in the attic, beer pong tournaments and side-by-side tracks in the ice luge made floor three the MurphFest hotspot.

PHOTO GALLERY #2

The day Kyle and I met inside our new Smith 16 home. Hours later Kyle would go above and beyond. August, 2004.

With Mom and Dad after a home game at Randolph-Macon. They have always been my greatest fans and never missed a game. Ashland, VA. 2004.

With Nick Jones, riding dirt bikes and ATVs during a summer weekend between sophomore and junior year. Summerleas Farm. June, 2006.

Left to right: Madgar, me, Brian, Fitz, Tyler, Kevin, Luke, Kyle. Our pledge class during one of the Lambda Luaus.

Left to right: Fitz, Brian, Kyle, me, Luke. The Spice Girls stealing the show at the annual Greek Life Lip Sync Contest at the Fountain Plaza. Spring, 2005.

Lambda Chi Alpha kicking off MurphFest. The t-shirts really were a nice touch, I must say. September, 2006.

In-patient rehab wing with two preeetty great parents. Yup. That's the mohawk. And that's the Shell I lived with for 3 months. Richmond, VA, 2007.

Whether its hunting, messing around on the farm, or jamming out—I have always had a special relationship with my Uncle Paul. Duck, NC. Summer, 2008 or 2009.

With my wickedly talented Aunt Paige at one of her art shows. We have always had a special relationship, too, but once I became the second family member to bust up their spine, the bond I had with Aunt Paige grew.

US Para-Alpine Nationals. Full of nerves and adrenaline halfway into my first ever Super-G ski race a year after joining the NSCD Competition Team. Mammoth Mountain, CA. March, 2018.

Geared up and ready to race moments before the U.S. Cycling Time Trial National Championship. Soon after I would (smartly) transition to skiing. Chattanooga, TN. May, 2014.

In recent years, the whole "Never give up" mantra has become so pervasive (thanks in part to social media) that the message has become watered down, almost to the point of cliché. But in 2007, when I received this gift from that SEAL, it wasn't. I still draw strength from this.

With my amazing wife, Casey, and a young Gunner at one of our favorite places. The Finger Lakes, New York. Fourth of July, 2016.

Chapter 48

THE SLANT BLADE

January, 2007. Home. McLean, VA.

After Christmas and New Year, I was again packing to return to Ashland, a week away from a trip to Rome, Paris, and Amsterdam to study the history of art and architecture in ancient worlds.

Because of my double Minor, I jumped at the chance to sign up for a *Baroque Art History* course taught by Dr. Eve Terrono, my J-Term professor from freshman year when life was nothing but books and baseball. A description highlighting an extensive Euro-travel itinerary caught my eye, but it was the word "Rome" that sucked me in.

After a week in the classroom studying and analyzing slideshows of paintings, architecture, and sculptures, plus a surprising amount of homework, our class of fifteen set off to crisscross Europe for three weeks studying art in an impressive list of locations.

Before we left, I was contacted by the website/media offices of Macon and asked if I'd be interested in keeping a travel journal for the school's website. I was knee-deep into my newfound love of writing, history and academia at this point, so I jumped at the chance to document this experience for myself and others.

Soon after landing home in Virginia, J-Term break ended. I felt the excitement of the spring semester. The high I carried with me after so much globe-trotting put a bounce in my step and I hopped about my room the night before returning to Ashland. I was giddy with a plastered-on smile, riding my high…until it all came crashing down.

It began with soft, fatherly footfalls on stairs.

Oddly cadenced, the measured pace was different, new, forcing me to pause and look towards the door. When curiosity turned to concern an entire chapter of my recent college life came flooding to the fore.

Scandal and controversy burst forth from its shadowy cell of forget, deep in the recesses of my mind, where semester's end and a trip to Europe had cast it not two months early, veiling it with better things.

J-Term had been the perfect distraction, but now I remembered the thing waiting for me that could permanently change my college experience.

I waited, breath baited, mouth sealed, for Dad to reach the landing. My mind raced. In a matter of heartbeats, I weighed a dozen different what-ifs, contemplated an unknown future fraternity-free, and basked in the beautiful memories of the very brotherhood I'd been waiting for.

Thanks to a few infractions over the years, and popular and widely attended parties, Lambda Chi Alpha was under the scrutiny of Greek Life.

Admittedly, mistakes were made that led to minor infractions. This created a reputation that didn't match the character of the guys in the group and ended up putting a target on our back.

Without going into details, I'll reiterate shared sentiments from many Lambda brothers and even some faculty: the way Lambda was viewed, judged, and treated for more than a few years was unfair and unjust.

To some, I'll venture, we were just jocks.

But that was our reputation. No matter how much we tried (and succeeded) to improve our image and change perception, our endeavors ultimately failed. Even with stand-out students and athletes, there was no way to prevent the camel's back from breaking when one last straw was thrown into the equation.

When it did in 2007, at the end of junior fall semester, it came crumbling down.

What had been my first semester in the house, was my last.

By the time I was packing for spring, the future of my chapter was decided.

The footfalls stopped at the landing and my father stepped around the corner to fill my door frame. Stone-faced, he met me with unmoving eyes, heavy by some unseen weight. I knew it to be that of the verdict.

"What?" I muttered softly.

"News about Lambda. President Lindgren did everything he could—"

"Just tell me." I interrupted sternly. There was no point in beating around the bush. He cut to the point.

"They're pulling your charter."

Boom.

Deadly, the words dropped, like the slant blade of a guillotine. Swift, with no mercy. It struck me clean and complete, and final, a four-word verdict on the razor's edge of my father's voice, severing parts of me whose roots were born long ago in the spring soil of a Florida trip with Dad and a reunion of brothers.

It happened all too fast. The lever was pulled. The blade fell. Lambda was gone.

Chapter 49

PROGRESS AND THE PEOPLE IN MY CORNER

"Asking for help is one of the most important ingredients..."[45]
—Tedeschi and Moore, *The PTG Workbook*

Mid-May, 2007. MCV/VCU Hospital. Richmond, VA.

In-patient therapy reminded me of summer days at Camp Friendship when I was young.

During the orientation process, I was given two copies of my schedule. One went to me, the other was tapped to the back of my on-loan wheelchair for easy viewing. Just like camp, my days were planned out in blocks of time for different "activities."

It was a tough schedule Monday through Friday. Mornings and early afternoons were typically my busiest times with OT, PT, group sessions, SCI Education and other necessities, like stretching.

The only free time I really had was lunch break at noon for about an hour-and-a-half, two on a good day. After that, the schedule was usually a bit lighter before punching out for the day around 3-3:30 when I was then free to do as I pleased.

Depending on the day, and the number of visitors at a given hour, I'd pass the afternoons on the computer, reading all the heart-warming CaringBridge

179

messages or working on my next entry, which usually took a few days to compose. Some days I even got a few extra workouts in using the equipment in the rehab room under PT supervision—something I looked forward to.

With my legs now on permanent vacation, it was up to the top half of my body to pick up the slack.

Lifting became integral for my physical and emotional rehabilitation. I hit whatever weights and exercises I could to strengthen the above-injury muscles to promote healing and make wheelchair life more manageable. The stronger you are, the easier daily tasks become.

If working out wasn't part of a day's PT, I'd do my best to squeeze it in at the end, usually off the clock. I had a good relationship with the staff so sticking around a few more minutes to supervise me was never a problem. Usually they were straightening up anyway while I put together a make-shift lift.

This was the tricky part. As far as actual gym equipment goes, it was slim pickings. Luckily, there was floor space open for a multi-purpose machine with cables for an all-in-one workout, and an odd-looking contraption beside it that was lever-based.

I had not seen this contraption before but took to it fast after realizing its unique design was for tricep work. Between two bars resting at upward angles with handles to push down on, space had been left open for a parked wheelchair. Holding the inclined bars against the ground behind this was a stack of adjustable counterweights. It was an adaptive dips-machine.

So, some Seated Rows for my back, some chest presses and biceps on the cables followed by tricep pushdowns, and I was good to go.

Lifting weights was something I loved and missed. Once I was old enough, it became a mainstay in life and part of my able-bodied normalcy. During my days in ICU lifting had been a legit unknown, the feasibility of it being something I often wondered about while staring up at the ceiling. Having this back was phenomenal. And important.

There were plenty of days, of course, when I could not wait to crawl back into my bed and watch TV or take a nap after the end of my last afternoon session. It was usually complete and utter exhaustion—mental and physical—that did it.

But on those other days I always felt better after a lift knowing how I was that much closer to reclaiming normalcy. Even if it was something as small as sweat and the feeling of strength from moving heavy things.

《》

After living like this for two weeks I was making meaningful steps to becoming as independent as possible by the time of my release date: May 31st, 2007.

Settling into routines, however, did not equate to smooth sailing from here out. I was helping myself bounce back in every way possible, but I still suffered regular rough patches that nagged my sanity.

One particularly pesky problem came after sundown each day and became such an issue that reaching out for help was the only option left to help myself.

Every couple of hours a new face on rounds interrupted sleep to give me a cup of meds, check blood pressure, turn me to prevent bed sores, or make sure I was still breathing. Sleep was already tough enough to find, being limited to left and right sides and flat on my back (I've always been a stomach sleeper). After so many nights of interruption, I'd had it.

The mounting exhaustion—unrelated to therapy, mind you—took a toll.

"It's annoying as crap!" I vented to Mom one morning, following another restless night. "I mean, can't they all just come at once or something?"

Lucking into a stretch of, say, four straight hours of deep, interruption-free sleep, would've been the miraculous equivalent of my spine suddenly fixing itself on a whim. It didn't happen.

"Is there someone you could maybe talk to? Someone in charge or something? Someone who can actually help? Please. I talk to the nurses but nothing's different!"

Mom heard me loud and clear, and Mom had my back.

That same day she pulled a few choice officials aside and relayed my suggestion.

My gripes did not fall on deaf ears. For the rest of my tenure my sleep schedule was at least somewhat less eventful than before. Oh, don't get me wrong—it still sucked. They still had to interrupt me to turn me and monitor meds and vitals but at least now it sucked a little less.

— — — — —

The list of ingredients that, when actively fostered and cultivated, lead to betterment has been well established since PTG received its name. As you'd expect of course, it's been hotly debated by shrinks and academics alike, but the list, for the most part, has endured, with certain such ingredients repeatedly rising to the top.

Like help. Finding it, asking for it, accepting it: "While self-reliance is important…so is finding and accepting support," argues Tedeschi and Moore in the *Workbook*.[46]

But asking for help isn't always easy, particularly for men, according to research.

Tedeschi and Moore equate this in part to how "we are inundated with messages from television, movies, and newspaper and magazine articles about how we should 'be strong' and 'not rely on other people for our happiness'…But taken to the extreme" this overly independent, go-it-alone mentality can lead to prolonged isolation, for example, and can be detrimental, interfering with recovery and growth.[47]

It is easy to simply say to someone suffering, "Oh, just ask for help" and that's that. But even something small like asking for or accepting assistance in the form of decent food or letting, say, a parent or sibling go to bat for you just so you can sleep better requires being vulnerable.

I'm okay being vulnerable, but I know not everyone is.

"Following trauma, people tend to withdraw from others and refuse to ask for help."

Tedeschi and Moore chalk this up to possible fears of rejection or being embarrassed or ashamed. Perhaps you don't want to feel like a burden, or you feel pressured to kowtow to societal expectations of independence.

Or maybe outdated gender ideals about manliness and masculinity have convinced you to adopt a "go it alone" approach to appear "strong" to others around you, even as it hinders healthy coping.

Thankfully society has been moving away from excuses and reasons like these. We now encourage the expression of feelings and the seeking of help—especially mental help—more than ever before. The "go it alone" approach is a dying breed.

It's because of what professional helpers like Tedeschi and Moore have discovered.

It's because "you need compassion and companionship for both recovery and growth after trauma."[48]

Though small, the help I've highlighted here—the food, the sleep schedule—are examples occurring at the beginning of my own post-trauma journey wherein "help" was a constant presence and necessity in my day-to-day existence.

I needed it in the hospital. And I would need it more once I left the hospital.

Whether it was a close friend taking me for a drive to get out of the house, or a very close friend carrying me in his arms for one last dip at the Fountain Plaza before graduation—help is why I'm here.

It's how I've become me.

Chapter 50

THE 7-11 HOUSE

February, 2007. Off Campus. Spring Semester. Ashland, VA.

Randolph-Macon was abuzz.

Wait. Didn't you hear? They're gone. The Lambda guys... Yup. Kicked off!

Four of us found a provisional home mere blocks from campus past the train tracks: Kyle, the inseparable duo of Collins and Norrett, and I. We rented out a spacious first floor in what became known as the "7-11 House," thanks to the convenient store next door.

Since I'd been in Europe it was the other three who found the house. I was lucky to be Kyle's roommate. I hardly lifted a finger house-hunting. He was on top of it fast and chose well.

The house was larger than imagined. Older with dated fixtures and appliances, but it made no matter. It had a front and back porch, a cozy living room at the front plus a bigger one off the back, a suitable kitchen, two bedrooms, two baths, a small office area, and a labyrinth of halls and doorways connecting it all. Against her unassuming exterior, the interior was far from cookie-cutter.

The place had character and I liked it. And not just because of where I lived within.

Being the fourth addition, I got leftovers and shacked up in the unused dining room. It was great. I was on the complete opposite side of the house, so even though I had nothing but a curtain for a door separating me from the kitchen, I enjoyed considerable privacy.

My dining room digs was luxurious with views of the street and the side yard through two windows and more space than I knew what to do with.

If my kitchen access wasn't sweet enough, door two led to that cozy living room at the front. A favorite little perk after lucking into last choice. With extra furniture and a cable hookup, it became my private hangout. The others preferred the larger one closer to their side, so they had little interest.

And while I missed the excitement of living on College Ave and being in the fraternity house, like my other housemates, I saw through the storm clouds and was grateful to see sun. This new situation of ours, I decided, wasn't too terrible. For what it was.

Though I was only taking four classes, an easy load is not how I would describe this seminal semester. Not after picking up my reading list.

After browsing the bookstore stacks, my basket brimmed with seven or eight books per History class plus a few hefty Norton Anthology English tomes. *The Modern Middle East, The Revolutionary Period, World History II* (the second half of the general history course) and, finally, a *19th Century American Lit* class. Not a cupcake course in the bunch.

I checked out and stepped into the crowded Campus Center atrium. I grasped the handles of the plastic bag and looked down at the ominous heap staring back at me, this imminent three-month undertaking.

I took a breath, gave the bag a jiggle, and silently calculated their collective meaning. It would be a daunting task this bag, but it was a bed I had made.

I was well into my Major and Minors and the hours and hours of reading and writing ahead was my paid-price for pursuing passion—and this would be the first semester I would truly be knee-deep in it. Three History classes and one less-than appealing English obligation I could no longer ignore. A fearsome foursome to say the least.

I shook my head, smiled, then doled out a sarcastic self-reprimand.

"Well," I said to myself, walking outside. "Looks like we got a few all-nighters ahead!"

Nice job, Dingus! At least it's not Business Econ.

I passed the fountain where a thought hit me, making me smile again. The simple fact that I liked what I was studying.

Chapter 51

A MIND TO SERVE

March, 2007. The Brock Center. Ashland, VA.

I left the 7-11 House an hour after the fair started. It lasted a few hours, so no need to rush.

It was a lovely spring day with scant clouds marring an otherwise pristine sky. I wore khaki shorts, a Polo, and Rainbow sandals. I clung to them with my toes so they wouldn't fly off as I hustled out the door, hopped off the porch, and leapt over the lawn to my Jeep.

At the last minute I'd considered dressing up for the occasion but convinced myself otherwise.

Even though this was the annual job fair, I went with my gut and decided to be my own comfortable self in my typical attire; a few steps above mesh shorts and t-shirt and a few below pants, tie, and a jacket.

As I walked into the Brock's back doors, where inside the three basketball courts held recruiting tables, a friendly face gave me a once-over in passing and couldn't help commenting.

"Sandals?" He asked. "Bit underdressed, don't ya think?"

He was right. But he also knew nothing of my intentions.

"Yeah." I conceded. "I'm only here for one booth. I doubt The Marines would turn a recruit away for not wearing a blazer."

About my workouts.

I usually hit the gym with Madgar after last class around 4:30 to get a lift in before dinner. There were lots of regular gym rats in the afternoon and we did joint workouts with a few of them. One of these rats was Mike W.

A former football teammate who had hung up his cleats for a purpose greater than himself, Mike W. was a year older and spent a lot of his time with the Lambda crowd. He was big and in shape. When he hit the Brock, he worked hard.

The Army was turning Mike into a soldier and he had to support the rigors of his ongoing ROTC program that took him down to Richmond a couple of mornings each week.

Now, Mike W. was two semesters out from his ROTC graduation and the commission as a 2nd Lieutenant that would later take him to Ranger School, and then overseas. His gym regimen lately had naturally kicked up a notch. I know because I willingly subjected myself to his routines and allowed Mike to play Drill Instructor via his own program of sit-ups, push-ups, and runs after a full slate of weights.

Mike W. was no joke.

The time I spent at the Brock with Mike brought us close and soon conversations revolved almost entirely around the military, military workouts, his Army training, and even meta-stuff like duty, honor, and serving. The impact was tremendous.

The idea of transforming into a soldier and serving one's country took root and grew.

I'd be lying if I said my trips between McLean and Ashland didn't have an influence on my decision to become a Marine. Passing Quantico and seeing Marine insignias on car stickers and signs up and down the interstate undoubtedly affected my psyche and my early inner connection with this idea.

Until heart-to-hearts with Mike W., though, it lay dormant. This mind to serve then evolved steadily from a thin interest to a want, a need, and finally— before becoming the impossibility it is today—it became an obligation led by obsession.

This growing idea was nourished also by the nature of what I was studying.

History taught me the importance of the past. But it was the military I gravitated towards. Policymakers and generals received the honor (and the infamy) in history books—but it was the soldier who spoke to me, in particular.

As my own worldly understanding and appreciation for this past came together in classrooms, my patriotism for America swelled and I found myself wanting to do my part as well.

"Want" became "need" and in that transition I developed a growing sense of duty, honor, and country.

In no time the notion of service to something greater (and the idea of personally challenging myself) opened my eyes to my future for the first time—one where I would do my part while being a badass as I did it. And to me, Marines were badass.

I knew what I wanted. My sights were set.

I had read through the student-wide email and scanned the vendors for the service branches, though I had eyes only for The Corps. I hoped deeply that they would be there.

I also knew I liked history. I knew I liked school, books, and academics. I knew I liked the military, the outdoors, sports and competition, and I knew that one day soon I would be a Marine. These few certainties gave me a vague road map ahead.

Then I found it.

I stopped at a table draped in blue cloth and flanked by a dapper Navy recruiter on the left and a hulking Army Officer on the right.

The lone officer between was statuesque. He had a predictable crew-cut and a Marine's physique beneath a pristine uniform. The very picture of a Marine's Marine. He stood "at ease" when I approached, hands clasped in back and a barrel chest held out proudly.

At my greeting his hands appeared and his chest relented. He adopted a friendlier demeanor and returned my hello. "Welcome. What can I do for you, Son?"

I abandoned further niceties and cut to the chase. "I'm interested in The Marine Corps...Sir." I made sure to sound as professional as possible. "I want to become an officer after I graduate next year."

"Excellent."

He looked slightly up. When he stopped at my hairline the officer further disrobed his tough-guy exterior. I wondered how many people had stopped by his booth that day. Or hadn't.

"Well, I see you've already got the necessary hair for the job!" He smirked. I chuckled. "We could use a man like you. Let's get you some hand-outs."

For the next ten minutes the officer told me about the Corps and Officer Candidate School. He did his best to convince me that OCS was the route for me. I'd brought up the question often with Mike W.

Go the officer route…or go directly into basic boot camp and start bottom up?

I had been leaning with the former. It was the recruiter who helped solve the debate after he showed me pamphlets and covered the basics of how I too could lead Marines one day and oversee my own platoon of forty-three Leathernecks.

I gathered up the pamphlets and he took down my information.

"Great!" He said. "We'll be in touch. I'll make sure of it."

I left the fair bristling with pride. The thought of serving my country, wearing that uniform, and making a difference as professional badass in The United States Marines put a serious charge in me.

Chapter 52

THROUGH THE WINDOW

"It's okay not to be okay. You don't need to hold it all together all the time. Allow yourself to be fully human, in all its beauty and ugliness."[49]
—Dr. Haas, *Bouncing Forward*

Mid-May, 2007. MCV/VCU Hospital. Richmond, VA.

Tucked high in the corner of the cinder block room, a television that usually delivered welcomed distraction spouted meaningless noise.

After a full day of exhausting rehab, I was sinking into a moment of sadness. Tuning out the TV, I fixated instead on the window and the faint sounds of the world beyond.

It had been a rough day. I was in pain, my mood had soured, and I ached for elsewhere. I had never missed the outdoors more.

There was nothing particularly exciting about what was outside. It wasn't the outdoors I grew up with or wanted, though it wasn't the stuffy white-washed hospital ward either.

Yet the outdoors was freedom. And I missed freedom. I wanted it, couldn't have it, couldn't even fight for it…and I sunk deeper because of it, alone in my room.

I wasn't really alone, broadly speaking, but afternoons like these, when smiling was harder and family had stepped out, solitude became a breeding ground for the kind of "woe-is-me" mindset that made things worse. And today I let it take hold.

The sounds outside teased me. The cinderblock walls nagged me. Gossip that had reached my doorstep from Ashland made college feel as distant as ever while commercials touting The Marine Corps' "Few and Proud" on ESPN hit like a hammer. All of it reminded me of what I'd lost days before, of goals and dreams I'd never catch. Of unmovable legs and undoable realities.

I sunk further and sadness took hold.

For some reason, too, reaching for my Bible never crossed my mind. Permitting myself this low point insulated me from my go-to avenues for attacking adversity and forging ahead.

As if wearing blinders around my eyes and brain, Psalms was now out of sight and mind, sitting there shut on the bedside table.

As my mind wandered further through the window, the outside called to me again, stronger this time. It was a chirping bird.

Tucked up in the corner, the television spouted more noise again. A new commercial this time, hyping the "Few" and the "Proud" and I hated it.

My eyes misted over and I drifted into still-fresh memories from a special place and time on two feet, where my love of outdoors germinated…and where there was always a chirping bird.

Summerleas.

— — — — —

In recent years, psychologists have been pushing to change the preconceived notions surrounding survivors and their trauma. Namely, PTSD.

In *What Doesn't Kill Us,* Dr. Joseph takes issue with the industry of psychological trauma and therapists treating patients with PTSD, claiming its overshadowing PTG.

He argues 1) that with words like "disorder," the trauma industry has adopted the language of medicine, placing responsibility for recovery into the hands of the therapist and not the person themselves; and 2) that it's also created a culture of expectation in which there's a mistaken assumption that PTSD is inevitable and inescapable.[50]

Tedeschi and Moore agree and offer a solution.

They believe that PTSD is a natural bodily reaction to an unnatural traumatic event and that healing and growth can often occur without the help of psychiatric professionals. "We therefore speak of *post-traumatic stress injuries* (PTSI) that produce symptoms and also set in motion natural growth processes."

Tedeschi and Moore even prefer "to use the word 'injuries' to emphasize that the reactions that have been called PTSD have a basis in a natural response to extraordinary circumstances," and how for the survivor it's important to remember that "just as injuries heal naturally and growth occurs naturally, there are circumstances that hinder healing and growth and circumstances that facilitate it."[51]

I realize my brief episode of sadness pales in comparison to what the typical person imagines when thinking about traditional, society-held concepts of PTSD, or in this case PTSI. However, this wasn't my first low point after my fall, and it certainly wouldn't be my last. Dark days would come, I assure you.

I use this though to highlight a bigger point—that it's okay to not be okay. We humans are emotional creatures. It's what separates us from the steely-eyed synthetic cyborgs.

So, as you heal—as you bounce back from your injury in natural ways—embrace the emotional roller coaster. Close the door and have yourself a cry, punch a pillow, or rip a phonebook in two as you scream because it's all part of the process.

Because it's okay to not always be okay.

Chapter 53

BREAKING NINETY

Saturday April 21, 2007. Ashland, VA.

As the only roommate without football obligations, on Saturdays I could do as I pleased. So, I took this freedom to polish my golf game.

I had grown up playing with Dad and Frank and as frustrating as golf is, I loved it. Luke, Kevin and Madgar—others who'd also "retired"—played too, and once nicer weather came to Ashland, we hit the links and driving ranges semi-regularly and soon my game drastically improved.

Until that spring something had been missing in my golf game. I wasn't bad, but my swing had never clicked. And then it did.

I was at the range with Madgar and Luke, testing a new driver when everything came together. Hands, hips, arms and legs moved fluidly in one motion that just felt right.

I crushed ball after ball and my excitement grew, realizing I'd found my swing. Luke and Madgar took notice. There were even kids beside us who wandered over wide-eyed, watching as I'd tee up and hammer another.

Each drive soared so straight and true that they cleared the six-story high net wall some 250 yards out, disappearing in the treetops behind the range.

"Watch this one," I said, teeing up the next. Hands, head, hips… And I held the follow through and watched the ball climb steadily higher and vanish. Each consecutive tee-shot, with added mileage factored to "go yard" over the net, was easily 300 yards.

On Saturday April 21, 2007, it came together again over the course of 18-holes.

❮❯

We loaded up mid-morning and with beers in the cooler and a supply of cigars, a big group of us took to the back roads for one of our go-to courses. Per usual, the smack-talking started early in the car.

It was perfect golf conditions. We were excited to hit the links and then College Ave that night. SAE was registered and it was their annual 80's Night and a band was scheduled to play.

The Hollows Golf Club was twenty-minutes west of campus through the countryside. We got carts, paid greens fees and kicked things off with zero warm-up, heading straight for tee-box one.

Golf often played second fiddle to screwing around.

Hole to hole we joked, laughed, bickered, gave each other crap about X, Y, and Z and raced the carts with a stupidity that only 21-year-olds could muster between brief moments of what one might call golf.

Luke was his regular old Charlottesville country self, his antics one-of-a-kind.

"Heeeeehaawww!!" He'd yell from the fairway after a good shot with a little extra Southern as he struck up a jig, hollering, "Gooooshdang wouldya look at that?!" Then he'd eye me and cock his brow. "Wooooo boooy! Whatchasaaaay der Pinche??"

I shook my head at my friend and laughed, readying my shot.

Luke's demeanor was a far cry from Kevin's. Kevin had been working on his game and it showed. He did his best to stay focused when he wasn't deflecting the typical barrage of guff that we all rained on each other, which only intensified when he teed-off since it was his turn under fire.

Kevin addressed his ball and Luke chanted, "Sweaaatkaaaa… Sweaaatkaaaa…" a nickname Kvasnicka had assumed from past workouts under the oppressive humidity of the football weight room.

Tyler was there too and heckled in a strong Honaker accent. "Hey, wouldya look at that! Sweatka's sweeaaaating! Hey Sweatka! Naaaice pit stains!"

Madgar jumped in too.

"Sweaaatkaaa…" Continued Luke and Madgar, nearly chanting now.

Standing over his ball, Kevin turned his head and let out a sarcastic retort, a noise less than laugh-like. "Huuahuuua!" His high cackle was a Kevin staple. "Shut up, losers." He drew his club and unleashed.

He crushed the ball with the same surprising strength that once garnered praise from Coach Arruza himself in a meeting, after Kevin followed up an impressive showing in a D-line drill with an even more impressive number on the squat rack.

"HA HA HA!" was all the response Kevin needed after stepping up under pressure and crushing his shot straight as a string. It was impressive. There was nothing we could say.

The round continued with much the same. Some played well, others bad, some both. I was among the former, as was Kevin and his pit stains.

Madgar had his moments, but they were few and far between. His angry side, not surprisingly, made an appearance after a slice in the woods, a shot in the sand, or a line-drive across the ground. If it didn't go straight, hit the fairway or land on the green, Madgar got mad.

We could only stand by and watch as he cursed and growled and beat the ground with his clubs, and obviously we laughed. That only pissed him off more.

Luke and Tyler were middle-of-the-road, which was about right for their care-free approach, which I could never do and definitely not now.

This was my first real round of golf following my 300-yard tee-shot display at the driving range from about a week before, so I wanted to show off my new skills as much as I wanted to prove to myself it hadn't been a fluke. So far it was working.

With a few holes left I had a couple nice pars racked up and a few round-saving bogeys. My drives were on point, and, not only did I save critical bogeys and pars with sweet putts and precise wedge work around the green, I posted my first round ever with two Birdies (scores of one shot under par for that hole.)

Despite the saying "drive for show, putt for dough," it was my driver that laid the foundation for my scorecard. "Live in the short grass," Dad would say. And today, the fairway was my home.

After the last hole, I tallied my card, then tallied it again, then a third time to be sure. I didn't want to ruin this moment materializing before me by miscalculation. Assured of the math, I stared at the number on my scorecard, shocked.

I shot...an 89?! I SHOT. AN 89!!!

I couldn't wait to call my Dad and break the good news. *An 89*, I thought, still high on adrenaline. *Wow, what a day! He's never going to believe this.*

◄◄►►

We got back to campus at around one. Starving, we dropped off our bags and B-lined it to a much-needed Estes sesh.

On weekends Estes was typically more subdued after 1:00 PM.

Now, it was 1:30 and Estes was quiet, the lunch rush having died down, we talked about the round before turning to more pressing matters: the night ahead. We all knew 80's Night was one of the best parties of the year.

Springtime. Saturday night. 80's party. Live brand. College. And a round of 89. Sadly, no Lambda, but still, could it get any better? I was so excited I even looked forward to Sunday's Estes brunch come morning.

We had a hunch that things were about to "get weird," as we'd often say.

Chapter 54

ON THE EDGE...IN MY 80'S SUIT

After lunch, I returned home to relax and get ready for the night. In my room, I looked over my outfit from Goodwill.

Rummaging through the racks of Goodwill I had come across a tracksuit with pants to match the zip-up shirt. It was a blue velvety material soft to the touch and had red stripes down the arms and legs. I would be wearing my famous Velcro shoes as well.

By that evening our house had livened up. Music was blaring, the crowds surged, and drinks kept landing in my hand.

A while later, it was time to make moves towards campus.

We joined the sea of students descending on the SAE house, dressed in tracksuits and leg warmers.

Inside, the party raged wall to wall in every room on every floor. The air hung hot and thick. Music pumped, thumped, and the crowds surged to the beat. Eventually, the later it got, events of the party became distant and blurred together. Then, at some point, I left.

I made my way down campus, to the SLAM house.

There, I met some friends outside in the backyard. Nick Jones had just inched the bed of his truck carefully against the rear wall of his own house. A makeshift ladder to climb to the roof.

I spent a lot of time down campus at this so-called SLAM house that spring.

For my good friends and teammates Nick Jones, Steven, Richard, and Ryan, SLAM house was home. For their senior year, the foursome applied to live in one of Macon's special interest houses on the merit of their proposed project to the college: SLAM. Student Leadership and Mentoring. It was a hot spot the entire year.

The house sat on the northwest corner of the Macon Mile across the train tracks beside the old tennis courts. It was small, simple and square. A two-bedroom A-frame cottage with a quaint living room off of a crowded kitchen. The roof reached some twenty feet tall, maybe more.

I gathered myself, stood tall. I tested my footing and judged the slant of the roof in a too-quick calculation before bounding to the top.

I love a good bird's eye view. I looked around and took it all in then climbed down to the perch above the porch. I crouched into gargoyle-mode on the edge and went still. I took in the scene, high and low, and surveyed the campus like an old soul reminiscing. It was beautiful and lit by a thousand lamps and lights that twinkled back to a slate of stars.

Ahead were the football and baseball fields. Beyond that Freshmen Village. I gazed blissfully at it all. I couldn't help but reminisce about my time in this corner of campus and smile fondly.

It was an oddly heavy, moving moment.

A freight arrived, chugging northbound. For a few dozen cards I watched it rumble past then I stood and climbed back to the ridge. Behind me, the steady, rickety chugging continued.

What happened next remains a blur with parts altogether absent.

Chapter 55

DESTINED TO FALL

Sunday, April 22, 2007. The *SLAM House. 2:30 AM. Ashland, VA.*

The crowd around me dispersed. I heard no sirens, saw no flashing red lights. Help appeared out of the night in the form of more dark figures rallying to my side.

This time the figures wore uniforms and had a professional haste about them. Their words matched their speed, but all meaning was lost on me. I only heard gibberish.

I then felt a body-board being positioned against my right side and realized they were trying to get me onto the gurney. I succumbed and tried to help by staying silent and still.

Two paramedics crossed my arms over my chest and rolled me gently onto my left side. Two more slid the board in place. The feeling of their hands left a powerful impression I still recall vividly; how they embraced me, cared for me, how I took comfort in it. I relished their healing touch.

As straps and harnesses synched tight about my body—some I felt, some I didn't—a wave of gratefulness and appreciation washed over me. In suit followed an odd tranquility though the feeling was ephemeral.

I heard a three-count and felt myself rise. A team of deft hands took hold and worked in unison to get me out of there. As I jostled about, I became keenly aware of the device I was on and forgot about the tranquil calm that covered me, the way a warm blanket does on snowy mornings.

The body-board taking me from ground to gurney was rigid and uncomfortable. And the gurney itself was a stark contrast from the much softer yet firm ground—the same ground that caught me from the sky, saved me from death, and wrought my body's new form. My landing zone was truly a miraculous patch of ground.

The path where I hit sat mere inches from a stone slab in the walkway beside the house.

My memory goes dark after I was hefted into the air on the body board. The next thing I remember is the bright bay of the ambulance. Whether we were moving or not with horns blaring, I can't say, but amidst this confusion a couple of things stand out in memory: the cursory medical exam to gauge my injuries and being asked for a number to call home.

At 2:36 in the morning, my father answered that call.

I still could not hear the sirens from inside, if there were any, and I could tell I was thoroughly tied down. To say I was constricted shoulders up is an understatement.

Straps secured me in place and I felt a thick neck brace hugging me tight, the feeling borderline claustrophobic. Only my eyes were free to move but even this freedom was hampered.

Everything and everyone stirred about me furious and blurry under fluorescent lights that made seeing nearly impossible. I was forced to squint in the bright bay. The only thing my eyes truly registered was the figures of the paramedics attending to me and asking questions.

I looked down. One of the paramedics was conducting an exam to gauge my level of paralysis, to see how "complete" or "incomplete" the injury was.

"Can you feel this?" The paramedic asked, beginning the exam.

I squinted back down and saw him poking at my bare toes. "No."

He moved to the next toe. "Can you feel this?"

Same thing. "No."

Then the next. "What about now? Can you feel this one?"

I knew I was paralyzed and had no feeling or function, so at these obvious questions, with their obvious answers, I got heated and annoyed, fast.

"No!" I shot back, quicker this time, with more force. If my irritation towards this little superficial exam was obvious, he certainly did not pick up on it.

Whether he moved on to the next toe or the other foot after that, I can't say, but all I heard was the same question as before. "Okay, can you feel this?"

Really?!

I only knew two things: half my body was unresponsive, and the EMT's repetitive questions with the repetitive answers annoyed me to no end.

I fired back aggressively, this time cutting him off. "IF I CAN'T FEEL *THAT* (EXPELTIVE) TOE HOW AM I SUPPOSED TO FEEL ANY *OTHER* (EXPELTIVE) TOE!!"

I was only fifteen miles from where I fell in Ashland, Virginia. It may as well have been 15,000. Never before had I felt so far from somewhere so special.

In 2004, Ashland and Randolph-Macon College was where my life—my intellect, personality, passions, and desires—had fully begun to bloom. It was a place where I became a completely different person.

Ashland is where I discovered my passion and where I realized my potential. Ashland is where I became the person I am today.

Then, on the night of April 22, 2007, more than three years after that renaissance began, Ashland, and the little campus of Randolph-Macon College, once again became the site of my other transformation, another renaissance, a difficult, rather unexpected renaissance, to be sure.

Nevertheless, I maintain the belief that my accident and the experience that followed happened for a reason—all of it.

I've said it before, and I'll say it again: I was destined to fall.

Those bricks were meant to rip free.

Chapter 56

ALIVE AND BREATHING

"The loss or threat of loss forces many people to confront how precious life can be. This confrontation can lead to a radical change of priorities and to a greater understanding of what is truly important."[52]
—Tedeschi and Moore, *The PTG Workbook*

Sunday, April 22, 2007. Intensive Care. MCV/VCU Hospital. Richmond, VA.

The US-36 Bikeway in Colorado hugs much of highway 36 connecting Denver to Boulder.

A half-hour drive from downtown Denver, it's a scenic cruise northwest to Boulder over rolling foothills. Atop a final cresting rise is an overlook with a postcard vantage of the quaint college town below, tucked against the Rockies.

Wending closely alongside this like a Remora to a shark for sixteen miles is the bike path. Bikeway 36 is a different ride; one that rewards just as soon as it challenges.

Long ascents up gradual, grueling rollers test riders of every ilk only to reward them with long descents that make every painful second worth it. Of the sixteen-mile stretch, the greatest challenge and sweetest reward comes on that last rise to the overlook before a sweeping downhill into Boulder.

It was here, while suffering towards this sweet reward, late in July 2016, that a song came on from my playlist that fueled and motivated me unlike anything I've ever experienced.

As I cranked a steady rhythm, fighting the hill in my handcycle, I suddenly discovered new meaning in the song's chorus I'd long known by heart. Goosebumps riddled my flesh. Chills coursed through my veins.

Something in me came alive, something primitive and powerful, a slumbering dragon startled from sleep that took me from my already-tough 9 mph pace to one exceeding 12 miles per hour.

Even I had to do a double-take after seeing this on my Garmin.

Beyond the barrier to my left, morning traffic *whooshed* by rhythmically against the soaring vocals of Sia.

Adrenaline and newfound meaning poured a power I didn't know existed into each turn of the hand cranks. The crest inched closer. Another flash of chills hit and I climbed faster, harder. Sia was hitting her highs, belting out her mantra with astonishing pipes.

Over and over the words "I'm alive…I'm alive" fueled a fire within, hitting me greater than any other wave of song-induced chills. They carried me to the top, over the ridge, and sent me down the arrow-straight descent.

Verse changed to bridge, to chorus, to crescendo, and back to climatic chorus. It was a new favorite, but I knew the song well. Yet, suddenly, the lyrics stirred up different emotions than past listens.

"But I survived…"

This time, as Sia called out "I'm alive…I'm alive," the meaning I found manifested not only as goosebumps and chills.

"But I survived… I'm still breathing…"

This time they surfaced at the corner of my eyes in pools, streaking away in the wind. The tears were warranted. Real. And I knew exactly where they came from, because I lived it.

"But I survived… I'm still breathing… I'm still breathing… I'm alive… I'm alive…"

Inches off the ground, reaping my reward and satiating my adrenaline addiction with speeds nearing fifty miles per hour plus, my tears stood little chance of falling like real tears fall, succumbing instead to the fierce wind buffeting my face.

A cold current flowed wet along my temples, running eye to ear then vanishing.

Flying at these speeds, here in Colorado, was the last place I'd expected to be overcome with emotion, but in my head Sia made sure of it. Strapped in my handcycle, I have a tendency of being mentally transported to places and times according to certain songs.

This time, Sia took me back home to the east coast, nine and a half years ago. To Richmond, Virginia.

I'm Alive.

— — — — —

When I came to in the hospital I was inundated by lights and noisy ICU clatter.

On top of the lifting head fog, I was still drunk and heavily drugged-up; I had trouble making sense of everything and struggled to put pieces together. Even now the memory of those first moments at the hospital are dicey. But I remember the sound—of everything.

Besides constant noise and fluorescent lights, the general sense of concern and a feeling of love and support engulfing me also still stands out.

It took time to remember why I was there and until I did, it was the presence of nurses and doctors coming and going and the sight of familiar faces that kept me largely worry-free.

I awoke early Sunday morning the same way I had hours earlier. More lights, people gathered round, nurses and doctors, the same drawn curtains, head still foggy. But I processed things easier now, which was both good and bad.

One of the first things I wanted to do that morning was call Nick Jones.

Only after hearing the tiredness in his voice did I realize how early it was, but I didn't care. I wanted him to know that I was okay, and that things were fine.

Sunday was largely a blur after that. Very few things I did or conversations I had remain clear amidst memories of that first day and my entire ICU adventure. Except for one.

It was a single moment of clarity.

A Modern Marvels rerun was on at the time, my bed inclined to watch it. Exhausted and properly numbed, I stared blankly at the screen with Mom there next to me.

In that moment the severity of my accident became clear. I was struck by the fragile simplicity of life and how precious it is. And, how fleeting.

Quietly, a smile worked its way across my torn-tired face until there was no holding back the toothy grin that emerged, nor hiding the out-of-place glint in my eye, conspicuous as a shiner fresh off a fist fight.

Mom sensed it. She turned and looked. The happiness plastered across my face caught her off guard.

"W-Why…why are you smiling?" She asked, hesitant and unsure.

Her confusion was not out of line. So why *was* I smiling?

Softly, I said, "I'm…alive."

"I'm here." I said, slightly louder, my voice growing with every syllable. "I'm alive. I'm…*alive!*"

The last word came with conviction. It dripped with added emphasis that made the very word come to life and fill the room.

I tested the very fragility of life itself. I poked the bear. And the bear woke up, angry.

And though I live with the consequences, it's that key word that's largely responsible for establishing the tenor of my outlook in the days, weeks, even years to come: Alive.

I was alive. I'd survived.

— — — — —

The descent leveled out and my speedometer fell from its adrenaline-inducing heights. The chorus faded. And with it my ICU memories of those two little words.

When I was twenty-one, I found myself smiling in a hospital bed, beneath white sterile sheets, where a pair of once-strong now-motionless legs represented my new forever wrought by a shattered vertebrae and severed spine.

I faced a long, hard road after my fall. And still I smiled. I probably should not have. But I did. Because of life. Because I could.

— — — — —

Growth isn't universal. It doesn't make everything suddenly better. And it won't magically eradicate your suffering. Like most psychologists in this academic field, Tedeschi and Moore openly recognize this in their PTG *Workbook*.

But it is commonplace, it can provide meaning, and it can sow the seeds for important positive changes, changes that while varying from person to person show up in common ways:

An Awareness of new opportunities. A Warrior Spirit featuring strength never before seen. New Attachments to people and relationships around you. A Knowledge of Self that makes you appreciate the air in your lungs. And spiritual Ecstasy that can awaken your faith or open your eyes to new meaning and purpose.

In the best examples of PTG, survivors reporting growth in all five areas— for the purpose of this book—can be thought of as living life AWAKE.

When I woke up in the ICU with a toothy grin, it was because I had unknowingly tasted the power of PTG and what psychologists had been unearthing for the first time. I had a newfound appreciation for life, an understanding of its fragility, and a fresh sense of my fortunate place still in it.

It was this Knowledge of Self—the mere fact that I was alive—that made me smile so happily.

This "radical change" would not have occurred "without the shattering experience of loss" that forced me to confront and evaluate my priorities. That morning I knew what was most precious and I awoke to a life-changing understanding of what was truly important.[53]

Tedeschi and Moore highlighted it best, getting to the core of the matter and pinpointing the Knowledge of Self theory:

"Perhaps one of the most common lessons learned from experiencing loss is that life has much to offer…For survivors of trauma, each simple aspect of life may be a wonderful gift."[54]

Chapter 57

CLAD IN COAT OF WHITE

April 22, 2007. Intensive Care. Richmond, VA.

Sunday afternoon my doctor came in. Pushing aside the curtain, he stepped in and greeted me.

Clad in coat of white, he knelt bedside. Something was up.

Doc hemmed and hawed for a minute, shifting from a knee to a crouch as he beat around the bush and recapped the nature of my injury and what had taken place when my spine exploded. Hearing but not listening, I waited quietly for the news.

I was staunchly sure it would be good news too, and that whenever he got to the point it would include a certain departure date, some timeline for me to hop up and walk out of there.

Searching for the right words before continuing, Doc paused, then leveled with me. "Michael, as far as where you are right now and how much function we can expect to return…I'm afraid this is as much as we can expect."

A flurry of thoughts hit me. Any hopes I had of walking out vanished, along with any possibility of making it back to Ashland for the last five weeks of the year.

That alone was as crushing a blow as the sudden permanence of my injury.

Before now, I had been imagining a simple recovery scenario of learning to walk again on those metal parallel bars you see in therapy rooms. Sure, my fall had set me back some, but until this little chat, I had considered nothing else other than regaining my feet on those bars. I had even imagined some cute physical therapist at my side wearing a pretty smile with a steadying hand guiding me.

That too was now no more.

And then I thought ahead. I remembered my summer plans and pictured the acceptance letter from Dr. Camp inviting me to Athens as the newest volunteer archeologist at the renowned Agora Excavations. I scrambled to find a way to still make the two-month trip-of-a-lifetime happen, but that was also now a fantasy.

Everything seemed ruined, shot to pieces.

My dream of joining The Marine Corps gone—but that realization wouldn't hit me until later.

Chapter 58

CRACKED RIBS AND CONVOYS

Monday, April 23, 2007. New Intensive Care room. Richmond, VA.

I was wheeled down the hall to a corner room free of curtains, full of privacy. It had actual walls, a door, and a window. I found out this was the staff's response to the flood of visitors that had descended on the ICU from the time of my arrival.

It began with my immediate family around 3:00 in the morning together with Dean Hull and President Lindgren from Randolph-Macon. From there it was a constant stream of more friends and more family.

The fact that the ICU staff offered to move me to a larger, private room is a testament to the incredible support I so fortunately had in the wake of my fall.

My small, curtained quarters may have served for Sunday, but by Monday— maybe Tuesday—it reached critical mass. Well-wishers from all over spilled beyond the curtains.

Sunday morning news of what happened reached The University of Virginia.

Initially Fathead ignored the call. It was unusual for him to get a call from my sister, even more odd on a Sunday morning. Thinking it a butt-dial, Fathead let it go to voicemail and returned to his pillow.

But when *Meredith Murphy cell* flashed a second time, Fathead picked up.

When he got word, it didn't take long to inform fellow Wahoo Brady and rally the troops. In no time, a carload of childhood friends were on the road and

209

Richmond-bound. Elsewhere on the eastern seaboard other friends like Fischer assembled from places like Duke.

Sometime later, they appeared at my door, an unfortunate but grateful reunion. Besides the hospital setting and a new token wheelchair guy to the group, it was about as normal a hangout as one could have, and I could not have been more thankful.

It meant a lot to have them come to the hospital at the drop of a hat. Their visit only solidified what I had been discovering: that without question I had an army supporting me in this traumatic time.

— — — — —

I clenched my jaw, sucking air through teeth to stop from crying out. I balled my fists tight as wave after wave of piercing, agonizing pain radiated through me.

I focused on the next round of morphine and the time until the next dose. Out of sheer desperation I did my best Jedi mind-trick to telepathically hurry them along.

It didn't work.

After surgery, my broken back needed a cast. It was in my private room that I was fitted and molded for what was officially called a TLSO—Thoracic, Lumbar, Sacrum Orthotic.

The process, I'd come to learn, was not pain-free.

With surgery a day away, a nurse escorted two orthotists to my side. I knew they were coming, but between bouts of sleep and a particularly captivating Modern Marvels episode, I had forgotten all about it.

I welcomed them in with an upbeat smile and made small-talk as they set up tools on a bedside table.

Despite wanting a cast growing up, because of all the attention and popularity it garnered, I never had one, even when I broke my femur. The process of getting a hard cast was thus completely new to me. I watched them with a wary eye.

I was mainly on the lookout for sharp instruments that could have once doubled as medieval torture devices but did my best to not betray my angst.

When I saw nothing more than a bucket of water and a pile of cloth-plaster cut into long strips, I relaxed considerably.

When the team of two was ready they explained how it worked. It seemed straightforward enough. I gave them a thumbs-up to begin. At that, the assistant turned to the pile of cloth strips and started systematically dipping them in the bucket.

One-by-one she carefully laid them out on the table while the man in charge, orthotist number one, examined my bare mid-section, feeling around as if my torso was a piece of produce and he was searching for the right one, testing how ripe I was.

He made a sound and said, "Okay. Shall we?"

Unable to sit up, the orthotists were forced to make the plaster mold of my torso with me lying prone. The stomach was easy. I even bristled as they placed the first few cold strips across the parts of my belly that weren't numb. I had to stop myself from giggling. "Hey, hey!" I said, squirming. "That tickles!"

"Woops!" The man said, flashing a smile. He paused before applying the next piece of plaster and looked to his left. His assistant played along. "Did we forget to use the warm water again?! Ugh. Happens every time!"

"Yeaaah, yeah." I waved at the air smiling, permitting them to proceed.

The fitting was going as planned. It was indeed straightforward; my prediction of it being pain-free looked to be true.

Once my front was coated in sopping wet plaster, the orthotists had to finish the job. The Shell wasn't one-sided, and they needed molds of my obliques and back. The only way to apply the plaster strips then was to have me roll from side-to-side, with a nurse's help.

And so, the torture began.

You'd think it was my shattered spine that would hurt most. Not so. It was lying on my sides with a set of cracked ribs that made it so painful. Sure, the shattered vertebrae inside me didn't help, but the blinding agony I had to endure came from my ribs as they moved me about through the molding process.

I couldn't roll completely on my stomach, so the nurse had to hold me there on my side for minutes at a time while they covered the exposed side and half my back. Then they rolled me over and repeated the molding of the next side.

My discomfort was not lost on them and the orthotists moved quickly with deft, experienced hands. Friendly banter was set aside and the two charged towards the finish, setting the last strips in a hurry before giving the nurse the all-clear nod to roll me back down.

The relief was instant, and a calm washed over me once they laid the last strips and gave that okay. As the team packed up, I closed my eyes and relished the post-torture sensation. It was oddly warm, like looking up at the first warm sun after a long winter.

"Okay, we're all set." Said the first orthotist. "We'll have that brace ready for you in no time. Hope we weren't too rough on you…"

I shooed him off and smirked. "Aahh it was nothin!"

Chapter 59

STILL MICHAEL

Tuesday, April 24, 2007. The eve of surgery. Richmond, VA.

The room was dim. Mom and Dad stood on my left, Uncle Paul to the right, his tall, lanky frame bent over so he could talk close.

He'd brought his girls with him, Rachael, Leah, and Evelyn. They'd made the trip from Summerleas to see me before I went under the knife and had bounded into the room hugging me tight before Uncle Paul stepped up with his own hugs and banter.

"Nooo, no. I promise you. I'll remember this, thisss conversation." I assured Uncle Paul. The pre-surgery drugs were setting in, slurring my speech. Uncle Paul worried I would not remember their visit.

"Okay," Uncle Paul thought aloud. He leaned in and his hair tumbled over his shoulders. "How 'bout this. We'll have a secret phrase, like a password to see if you remember."

"Works for me." My mind was a jumble and the edges of my sight fogged over.

"What about..." Paul looked around the room and saw Leah, whose long blonde hair was her mother's, but tall frame a hundred percent Dad. "How about this: 'Leah goes to the Chesapeake'?" Leah had an upcoming class trip to the Chesapeake Bay. She'd told me about it when I'd surveyed my cousins on the latest news upon their arrival.

"Leah goes to the Chesapeake" I recited. "Done. I promise I won't forget."

I didn't.

The next morning, I was prepped for cutting. An ICU orderly arrived and wheeled me to a curtained prep-room. The trip down the hall was no more than a minute or two but along the way my mind juggled a swirl of thoughts, memories, and emotions for what seemed like hours.

What if something goes wrong? What if they can't fix me? What if I don't wake up?

Staring up at the passing ceiling tiles, the questions rotated endlessly one to the next, like a three-way tennis match: back and forth, femurs to What-ifs, What-ifs to parents, parents to femurs.

Meanwhile, the orderly made small-talk that hardly resonated. I heard him little and answered less thanks to this swirling mental match and the steady hypnotic passing of ceiling tiles.

Back then, my thoughts were solely on these tiles and my inner angst, but as I write this over a decade later, in retrospect I can't help but connect that hallway trip to something that wouldn't enter my life for another 9 months, during the dark dreary, senior year winter at Macon, when I was happy to finally be back at school yet found myself battling low moments I hadn't anticipated.

That something was a book.

An eerily familiar book to be exact; that so deeply resonated and had such a profound impact when I needed it most, that I've never doubted the fateful timing of when I finally cracked it open and read the story of Mark Zupan.

Mark Zupan had his own hallway walk to surgery. He too stared up at the tiles.

Gimp would ultimately come to save me, in more ways than one. I just didn't know it yet.

First, I'd have to go under the knife. Then embark down a treacherous, unfamiliar road to master a new existence before finding, and starting, his book.

— — — —

I last remember the curtained room.

I waited there until a team of surgeons were ready to piece my insides back together. The bones at the center of my spinal column had been obliterated upon impact to the point of no return. In fact, after cleaning out the area around the 9th thoracic vertebrae, reconstruction required another, smaller, incision at the lower right side of my back where doctors then harvested fragments of my hip bone to rebuild my spine.

My final memory before I awoke, and before they cut me open, was of Leah's class trip.

Hours later, I came to in my room in the ICU and found my parents keeping their promise. They hovered over me waiting to serve either Styrofoam cups of ice, ginger ale, or both. I could have as much of each as I wanted, the nurses instructed, but no food, not yet.

Lifting my eyelids required considerable effort. Keeping them there did too, as did actually seeing. My eyes saw but my brain lagged to process it.

I reached out an opened hand at nothing. An inaudible sound escaped my lips and I writhed with discomfort under the sheets.

A cup found my palm and a hand guided it to my mouth. I tilted my head, attacked the cup, and clamped down into the foam leaving a gapped-tooth impression as ice chips and sweet Ginger Ale doused my mouth.

After two rounds of Ginger Ale and almost three cups of ice, I was well on my way to consciousness and understanding. My words were no longer incoherent blabbering and my eyelids had lost their former control. I was awake and gradually distancing myself from the side-effects of being anesthetized.

The pain, however, both throbbing and stabbing, had all but abated.

The morphine coursing through me had only recently been hooked to my IV and hadn't taken effect. All I could do was sit and wait patiently until it did, and do my best to wiggle around in bed, my only means of killing pain.

Nearing normal, the rest of my family came to see me after having stood vigil, waiting out the surgery.

Meredith and Frank came in with cheerful greetings and the usual set of sarcastic sibling jabs. Mommom and Poppy followed, along with Duane, Uncle Paul, Rachael, Leah and Evelyn.

"Remember what we talked about?" Uncle Paul asked, testing me. "The secret phrase from last night?"

The anesthesia had been powerfully effective, but despite my venture into its void and its best efforts to keep me there, I was now more awake, and so too was my mind.

"I do!" I fired back enthusiastically, proud for remembering. "Leah…" I rolled my head to the side to find Leah Bean. Our eyes met and I grinned. "Leah…goes to the Chesapeake! Ha."

— — — — —

Sometime after surgery—whether that day or the next—the same orthotists as before arrived with my new back brace for a fitting.

Instead of a single device, the brace came in two pieces, each a mirror of the other, each tall, shockingly white, and expectantly curved. One had a set of three loops where a stack of three Velcro straps on the other fed through and back over itself to secure the Shell in place around a torso. That was the more obvious difference.

Subtler was the shape of each side's bottom edge; one tapered and curved to fit the lower lumbar, the other straight for an easy fit in front across the lap.

This Shell would become part of my life for the next three months.

Doctor's orders required me to wear it always in my chair and whenever I moved to an inclined position above thirty degrees in bed. There was even a level on the bed, so I could raise my head and sit up at exactly the right height and no further before the Shell was needed.

It was nice being able to sit up—if only partially—because putting on the TLSO was a process.

I learned exactly how much of a process after the orthotists put me through the paces during my final fitting trial. I'll explain how later.

Chapter 60

A TORRENT OF TEARS

Thursday, April 26, 2007. Newer, non-Intensive Care room. Richmond, VA.

N ow that I was stable, ready to mend, and sporting a shiny new back brace to commemorate the occasion—the time had come to leave the ICU. My in-patient rehab wasn't for another four days, however, so the hospital had to transfer me elsewhere to make room.

I had my own bathroom (which I personally never used), space for visitors, and a couple of windows to help assuage the feeling of isolationism and detachment from a long hospital stay.

As if being in the hospital wasn't bad enough.

Thankfully my roomy, sun-lit home for the next few days warded off this cabin fever.

— — — — —

My first true set of tears came after a phone call, on an afternoon that Duane happened to be visiting.

I showed little signs of cracking. I wasn't sad. I wasn't depressed.

Besides, the incredible show of love and support surrounding me made it almost hard to be sad. Tears, as it were, were not really part of this story—even when the doctor knelt beside my bed and told it straight.

Until, that is, the moment Dr. Camp called and the words of this world renowned, History Channel-featured Classics professor caused my immediate reality to set in.

When that happened, I broke, pouring my emotions into the shoulder of my cousin.

— — — — —

It goes back to when I discovered my love for ancient history, but its true origins stem from when I first heard rumors about the archeological excavation in the Athenian Agora in Greece.

Excavations there are on-going and led by Randolph-Macon's own Dr. Camp, who has published numerous books and appears on History Channel programs. Each year the Agora Excavations sorts through world-wide applications for volunteers hoping to take up picks and brushes to dig up artifacts for eight weeks in the summer.

There was no question—how could I *not* apply? I wasted little time gathering information from Dr. Camp about the application process and soon had it in the mail. I had a good feeling, too.

When the letter finally arrived, my hands shook ever-so-slightly as I held the envelope before I tore it open and skipped the niceties looking for that one sign. I scanned the texts furiously for it.

The fate of my upcoming 2007 summer all came down to this.

And then I saw it. That one word. *Congratulations.*

I stopped; that was all I needed to read at that moment. I let out a huge sigh, threw my hands up and unleashed a "Wooooo!!!" that carried significance far greater than simple excitement from becoming an official volunteer for the Agora Excavations.

The letter was tangible testament to my hard-fought classroom battles.

Which brings me back to the reason for this brief biographical tangent down memory lane: the significance behind the summer of 2007. Not the one that was, but the one that was supposed to be.

Six weeks after crying on my cousin's shoulder, those summer sessions kicked off in Athens. Little chisels and tiny tools went to work in the dirt, the volunteers searching for the ancients there in the high shadows of the Acropolis and the Parthenon.

I was 5,000 miles away, starting over.

Chapter 61

THE WOMAN WHO PAINTS

The 90s. McLean, VA.

G rowing up I was lucky to have most of my extended family in short driving distance. Like Uncle Paul and Duane out in Centerville. Even closer was Mom's little sister, Paige. My Aunt.

Coincidentally, Aunt Paige lived across the street from the CIA in the same neighborhood as Potomac.

Naturally, I spent a lot of time at her place. Besides the farm and Uncle Paul's house, hers was the only one in the family with a nearby pool.

Duane and I spent muggy Summer days swimming and playing in her pool. There was no diving board but there was a slide that kept us entertained. It was always fun at Paige's.

Her cockatoos squawked on and on whenever you walked in and her golden retrievers would come scrambling on the hardwood floors to greet you.

I was only a toddler in 1987—when the car she was in ran off the road and she was thrown against the roof, causing her neck to break. I never saw Aunt Paige as a "quadriplegic." I was too young to know any different.

I never really knew what paralysis or spinal cord injuries were in the first place. Aunt Paige was different, that much I knew, but not less, so I've only ever known her as she is now: The Aunt Paige with long golden hair who loves 60's Rock n' Roll and tattoos of flowers and butterflies. The Aunt Paige who has just enough hand function remaining to steer that big power wheelchair of hers.

Whenever I saw her, the first (and most favorite) thing I did was run up to her chair, greet her with a hug and a "smooch," as she calls it, before promptly pressing the button on her armrest control panel to sound the "horn."

Today, it's seeing her latest painting, among other things, that we all get a kick out of. We marvel at her detail, her precise brushstrokes, how life-like her flowers and animals are or how gorgeous her sunset is or the moonlight reflecting on water.

Come to think of it, we marvel at the whole thing. The painting, the person, and the process.

"How does she do it?" we'd often say, baffled. "This must've taken forever." Or, "They just get better and better" and "Those gardens she first did were amazing, but now this! Remarkable!"

Then someone invariably follows with something like, "I don't get it. Most people can't even paint this well with two good hands…she uses her mouth! And gets paid for it!"

That's because, as a professional member of the Mouth & Foot Painting Artists association, Aunt Paige's work is just that: marvelous.

Growing up I enjoyed a close relationship with my Aunt Paige. But twenty years after hers, it would be my own accident that would bring us closer.

Before my now-hometown of Denver and her 1960 Colorado Springs birthplace added another common thread between us, Colorado style, it would be our shared experiences of being dealt New Normals and coping with rerouted lives that ultimately brought a welcomed hope to each of us as a newer bond, stronger than before, was formed.

And, under the circumstances of not one but now two SCIs in the family, a newfound happiness, too, that came quite unexpectedly.

Chapter 62

THEIR BROTHER'S BOAT

Friday, April 27, 2007. MCV/VCU Suite. Richmond, VA.

As I've said, the incredible army of friends, family, and strangers made it easier to cope during my darkest hours. The response from my friends and the touching things they did made me feel loved in a different way.

On Friday night, three days after surgery, some of my closest Macon buddies surprised me with a pizza party.

I can't remember whether I knew they were coming, but if I did, I certainly wasn't aware of how many were coming or that they weren't there to simply have pizza and hang out with me.

I was laid up mindlessly watching the History Channel when they poured in, noisy and cheerful. They crowded round, showered me with hugs and high-fives and head rubs.

Before everyone settled in, Fitz stepped forward to present me with a surprise he'd been orchestrating since my fall. I'd noticed it when they first arrived but paid little mind to the large canvas-poster-like thing rolled up tight.

Unfurling it carefully, Fitz spoke for the group in a tone both ceremonious and poignant.

His exact words escape me, but Fitz talked about the impact my accident had had on our band and how much I meant to them and them to me. They wanted to show their support in a way that would stay with me during this fight, even when they wouldn't be able to visit in person.

Once fully unraveled, Fitz laid it out across my unmoving legs with others holding down the corners.

The poster must have been four-feet long and three-feet tall. In the center was an enlarged image from MurphFest. It was from the series of photos taken moments before the party got underway, when we gathered in the Chapter Room at Lambda wearing our MurphFest shirts for a big group photo.

You could almost hear the rowdy chorus echoing ghost-like in the image. Raised arms hoisted beers. Gaping mouths cheered. And funny faces around me summed up the mood. And there, in the center, me and my crown of plastic gold, humbled and still utterly surprised, managing only a tight-lipped smile as I toasted my massive stein of beer into the air.

The choice photo took up most of the canvas and was flanked by smaller pictures at each side, some from MurphFest, some from other Lambda moments. But between these, and below the central photo (easily ten-times bigger than the rest), there was a quote.

A Hindu proverb, to mark the occasion. It lifted my spirits.

Help your brother's boat across and your own will reach the shore.

My friends wanted me to know that I wasn't alone. That they were with me through this trying time. Not that I didn't know that already, but this gift solidified that commitment.

After that the pizza arrived. We settled in, eating and gossiping between moments of TV watching. I told them how things were going and what the next steps were, but mostly I wanted to hear about Macon.

On cue, they filled me in on the latest news until I was up-to-date.

Their visit, like so many others to come, buoyed my spirits, inspired and motivated me to stay strong, keep smiling, and bounce back like no one else had, could, or would.

Such visits kept me busy that weekend, but it was far from the only thing.

Chapter 63

BEFORE THE STORM

The Weekend of April 28-29, 2007. MCV/VCU Suite. Richmond, VA.

For the next two full days I had absolutely no obligations. To keep busy, build strength, and get acclimated to wheelchairs, one thing I did was go for pushes around the halls.

I'd get help with my Shell from two nurses who then helped sit me up in bed and position me for the transfer to my chair. It was more like a shimmy or a slide than the type I'd eventually come to perfect.

That level of independence was still a long way away. At this point I wasn't even close to sniffing my future hospital graduation, let alone graduating to unassisted transfers—that essential component to an independent New Normal I'd begun hearing about.

For now, I had to get used to the drill of getting in my Shell, out of bed, and in my chair. It involved the precise placement and under-butt-wedging of a transfer board so that it rested safe and secure with equal ends on bed and chair, forming a nice butt-bridge.

Eventually, I'd learn to assist, leaning and lifting where I could, making placement and wedging smoother. The best I could muster for now was a feeble little tilt that freed some weight from half my ass. I wondered how much good I was actually doing since this never really went smoothly.

One out of four tries required a do-over because of hiccups. Shorts catching on the board often mucked things up as did uneven placement with one side lacking. More than twice a nurse or therapist had to jump and catch me mid-shimmy after my butt and body dislodged the board and it slipped from the bed's edge into the chasm.

Were it not for my vigilant helpers, I'm sure I would have plunged into the gap four or fourteen times.

Once in my chair, I spent time getting comfortable on hallway pushes. Even if the benefits were minimal, at this early stage, pushing was as therapeutic as it was practical.

For one, it got me out of bed. And two, chair acclimation.

Aside from twists and turns and pushing methods for optimal and efficient arm strokes, I was also advised to take notes on likes and dislikes about the chair. After a litany of loaners, I was told to be prepared for a barrage of wheelchair-fitting questions when it came time to narrow down the different specifications (specs) and order my own.

I'd have to think about every little detail to ensure a comfortable chair for a comfortable life.

Is the height okay? What about the positioning of my legs? Where do I want my knees and feet to be? How's the width? What about the height of the backrest, the design, the style? What sort of frame do I want? What color? What kind of front wheels (casters)? What kind of rear wheels? Treaded tires or bike tires? What sort of cushion would I prefer? Foam? Air? What about gel? Custom fit? Neutral fit? How susceptible am I to pressure sores and skin breakdown? Which of these models if yes, which of these if no?

These were things I started thinking about when pushing around the halls, bantering with the pretty-eyed, pretty-haired nurses who quickly took a liking to me and my entourage.

Getting out was also a morale-booster. Lying in bed watching TV to pass the time between meals, medication, and vitals checks can sour a mind. You can only watch so much Sportscenter and Modern Marvels reruns before your mind drifts towards the negativity.

Pushes kept me active and forced me into interactions with fellow residents, nurses, and orderlies who went from familiar to friendly because of it. It was a therapeutic time-killer, a breath of fresh air for the mental and physical.

Still, it had nowhere near the powers of healing nor the remedying effects on boredom as *Ashley*.

Though I was aware of her powers during the latter half of high school and then college, I was still a week or two away from realizing the true manner of the medicine that a simple guitar can have when life throws you a curveball.

I was an in-patient resident week two when *Ashley* was brought to me. From that day forward, held in my hands, *Ashley's* wooden, sleek black frame and six strings, tight and tuned, would harmonize to make more than music. What that was is hard to answer.

Perhaps the best answer for what *Ashley* gave me would be a life jacket because *Ashley* never failed to scoop me up and rescue me from one storm after the next. She was there when I needed her, night or day, clouds or clear sailing, my own personal Coast Guard.

Ashley filled a role that hallway pushes had filled first, though hallways didn't have quite the same feel or sound. Still, they served the purpose of spirit-lifting, the way visitors did, or the way a new haircut can buoy a mood. And I do mean that literally.

For whatever reason, I entered the hospital sporting a strip of short, dark fuzz, and the look stuck. I thought it looked cool, but it became apparent that this was more than just a haircut.

It was a conversation piece that had nothing to do with spine injuries. It offered lightheartedness and gave my Mom something to smile about.

So, when my hair started to grow back, I decided that parting with my racing stripe would never be an option as long as my hospital bracelet itched my wrist. The itching lasted five weeks, the mohawk a day longer.

Hospital haircut one was done in my room with the help of Frank. Mom and two nurses watched on after wrapping me in a makeshift barber's cape. Frank was meticulous with the clippers, making sure the stripe ran even.

Afterwards he wiped me down and carefully removed the cape, bundling it up then tossing it flippantly into the trash as he stepped back to examine. Like a stone-faced detective, he eyed every inch, peering in close then stepping off for a wide-view analysis. He cut strays and aligned my sideburns before one last look.

"Looks good, Buddy!"

I tilted my eyes upward and raised a hand to feel around, brushing the stripe front to back blindly assessing. It was a stark contrast to the course, near-hairless landscapes at each side. The mohawk was perfect. A work of art.

Chapter 64

MIDNIGHT ON MORPHINE

Saturday night, April 28, 2007. MCV/VCU Suite. Richmond, VA.

On morphine, anything goes.

I experienced one such episode in the midnight hours.

Forgetting my paralysis, for some reason I woke up convinced I was in the hospital because of some viral infection covering my body and part of the treatment involved the IV cord running from the back of my left hand to the hanging bags and beeping machines bedside.

Half-asleep and heavily medicated, I emerged from a dream state and found myself smack-dab in the middle of what I thought was the instructed, completely sane, far-from-abnormal treatment procedure for healing the superficial virus covering my skin.

Holding the looped IV line in my right hand, I methodically traced it up and down my arms, across my chest, and over my stomach the way a security guard wields a metal-detector at a checkpoint.

I was dead-certain that what I was doing was business as usual.

I fully believed that waving the looped IV line—it had to be looped—over my body—without touching it, of course—would remove the infection, like a vacuum over a dirty carpet.

From there, as confusion set in, plus an unflinching belief that this virus was real, I found myself in a kind of limbo, frantic and worried, baffled.

After scanning the body parts I could reach, in my mind, I was infection-free. The cord treatment worked! Time to go home!

Now what... I thought, unsure what to do next. Now the cord was the one carrying the infection, so the last thing I wanted was to let it touch my skin and infect me all over again. That was out of the question.

Holding the looped cord as far away as possible, I froze, arm outstretched, not a muscle moving, eyes wide and staring. I still had absolutely no clue what to do. I couldn't move or go anywhere and I damn sure didn't want to set the virus-laced cord on anything and spread it.

I held the looped IV out further.

Regardless of how ridiculous it sounds and how hilarious it was in hindsight—I was truly confused and nervous. Lost, I looked around in the darkness for a solution and found nothing.

"What am I supposed to do with this thing?" I asked myself. Then I remembered my call button.

I quickly hit the intercom and the voice of a front desk nurse came through the hospital bed speaker.

"How can I help you, Mr. Murphy?" The voice asked softly.

Unable to process my predicament, I reached blindly for words not there. "I, I don't...I don't know what to do," I muttered, staring at the cord in hand like it was an alien fetus.

"Are you okay? Do you need some assistance?"

I struggled again to relay my concerns to the nurse, which were fast approaching actual fear.

"I...don't know what to do with it..." was all I managed. There was a pause before she responded. My words hung in the air mid-sentence, unfinished and cryptic.

Hardly a rookie, the nurse sensed my confusion. In a comforting tone she said, "I'll be right there," and ended the call.

Just then things started coming together as I emerged further from the morphine-injected dream-state that triggered this mess in the first place. I looked around the still, sterile blackness of my room connecting the pieces.

By the time the nurse peaked past the curtain, the debacle made sense and I realized I had been hallucinating. I couldn't help but laugh at myself. I explained and she too chuckled in relief.

She asked if I needed anything else then clicked off the light and headed back to her post.

I smiled again, shaking my head in amused disbelief. I took a deep breath, exhaled, then sunk into my pillow. Without question, this was one of the more bizarre episodes during my hospital stay.

— — — — —

The morning of my transfer arrived. The time had come to start the long process of bouncing back. It was inevitable, I knew, but parts of me hoped a nurse would come in and say rehab was under rain delay.

I'd grown accustomed to my accommodations with little requirements of me, as the weekend came to an end, and I did not want this to end.

I had other reservations—one involving my morphine drip. What had been a lifeline over the past days would soon be gone. It was officially adios to my sweet euphoria-inducing friend. I also didn't want to leave because, despite the paralysis, life really wasn't that bad.

I had nice nurses; a few of them cute. I could watch as much History Channel and ESPN as I pleased. And school stuff had been shelved. I enjoyed the three History classes and English course I was taking, but the amount of reading and writing this semester was too daunting to try and keep up with while hospital-bound, which the college understood. It was nice having zero academic obligations.

And then, of course, the stream of steady company that kept things interesting while boosting my morale.

My battle had barely begun, though, and trudging ahead was the only way home. This easy weekend was merely a time-out to catch my breath, and I had. It was time to start fighting—as if my life and all I knew depended on it.

Monday morning two orderlies arrived to wheel me away, bed and all.

Flat on my back I watched the ceiling tiles steadily pass while the man behind navigated the gurney down hallways and into elevators.

He hovered over me and we made small talk. My mind raced, stomach knotted. It reminded me of when they took me to surgery-prep with similar chit-chat, steady as the passing ceiling squares.

I had no idea what to expect when our stroll ended so I kept my eyes up. I knew rehab would be hard, but I had no idea I was facing more work than I could have ever imagined—all without morphine.

I also couldn't foresee that I was closing in on the most painful night I would ever know and the worst moments and lowest lows of my existence that would test me and put me on the brink.

I was being wheeled headlong into the fight of my life at the hands of a chipper orderly.

Chapter 65

NO BLOOD

Early-90s. Home. McLean, VA.

I have this memory, it's old and symbolic.

I'm asleep on the couch, still small enough to be held, and its bedtime. Mom comes over, gently scoops me up, puts me on her shoulder, and carries me up the stairs. Halfway up, I stir, crack open my eyes, and look down.

The staircase runs along the wall in our front foyer. Upstairs the small landing outside our rooms is like a balcony overlooking the clean, manicured entryway.

Looking over Mom's shoulder, as a toddler, it looks like it's ten stories down over the railing. I remember feeling dangerously exposed, like I was standing on a cliff-side precipice—but not once did I feel afraid. In Mom's arms (and Dad's), I was untouchable and safe.

When I wasn't, I was taught to be tough—but even then, I felt protected.

Like that time when I hit a divot in the driveway and flew over my bike's handlebars.

Even with the three rocks implanted in my elbow, and the trip to the Immediate Care for stitches that followed, I barely remember crying as I stood in my parent's bathroom. There was something about how Dad knelt before me, calmly assessing my wounds and what he said that made me buck-up.

I watched him say it to Meredith once in a home movie after she'd scraped her knee. I was a new-born at the time. He'd assessed it like he did my elbow,

230

using his prognosis with that same upbeat voice that could either magically dry up tears, or prevent them all together.

"No blood!" Dad said simply.

And that was that. The rocks had sealed the laceration. I was fine.

I've always been fine. Even when things appear to be scary or the roads been rough and rocky, I've always felt safe, comforted, and never alone.

These emotions were pivotal ingredients of my upbringing—it helped mold my mind and my spirit. It set me on a path wherein the safety I experienced and the feelings I had of being protected and not alone played a role in developing the character that allowed me to cope during my darkest times and my most transformative traumas.

Chapter 66

FORTUNATE MISFORTUNE

"In your struggle to survive, to cope, and to prevail, you are given an opportunity to develop a strength you didn't know you had."[55]
—Tedeschi and Moore, *The PTG Workbook*

Sunday, April 29, 2007. MCV/VCU In-patient Rehab. Night one. Richmond, VA.

I didn't notice it during the day because of all the distractions from transferring to the in-patient wing. Pain and discomfort were there, yes, but I generally forgot about it as I met staff and doctors and toured the facilities in my new home. The light of day had me lured into a false sense of security.

But nighttime in hospital is different, quiet and lonely.

Minutes and hours drag. Gone are the busy comings and goings of doctors, patients, and nurses in the hall, and though Tramadol was now my new pain-pill, its relief was nothing like the morphine drip.

As Heisenberg said in *Breaking Bad*, when it came to Tramadol and Morphine drip, it was like "grade school tee-ball versus the New York Yankees."

Pain launched its assault at midnight.

It started as a dull ache that went from mild to bad then worse to excruciating. Sharp, stabbing bolts between every pounding throb coursed through back and ribs, consuming my entire torso, pummeling every inch.

I repeatedly called nurses, pleading for them to do something or give me more meds, but I was on a set pill schedule. Their hands were tied. Nothing could be done now that my IV was gone. All I could do was moan in agony. I tried moving around as best I could to find comfort, but it was no use.

In the quiet morning hours, I was all alone, on the brink of tears with no end in sight.

As I held out for the next dose of Tramadol that I knew would not come soon enough, I found further discomfort elsewhere.

Soft as cement, my bed was a battleground of epic proportions. Something more akin to a Dark Age torture device than the place of solace it would eventually become.

Writhing in place, then, was my only recourse for comfort. Through clenched teeth and balled fists, it was all I could do to fight back against the searing, crippling agony that was racking my body, infecting my mind, and corrupting my soul. It was a futile effort, at best.

As the aching increased, I found myself struggling with reality. I knew this wouldn't last forever, but in those minutes and hours I was beginning to question if that were true.

When it finally became unbearable, I pressed the call button beside my head. Thirty-seconds later a nurse entered.

"Isn't there *anything* you can do?" I pleaded without preamble when she showed.

The agony in my voice was not lost on her, yet she could not help.

Leveling with me she said, "I can give you another dose of Tramadol here shortly but nothing more beyond that. And we can't do any more of your sleeping pills. You're maxed out."

She was sympathetic in wanting to comfort me but dealt honestly. I groaned at the answer. As far as dose-limits go, I understood. Protocol had tied her hands.

I nodded and mustered a faint "Okay" through teeth.

"I'm really sorry, Mike. Is there anything else I can do for you?"

"No. Thank you." Misty-eyed, I turned my head away.

"Okay." She said solemnly. "Remember, we're right around the corner so don't hesitate to call. I'll come back with more pain meds in a little while."

I grimaced as another wave of pain pierced my sides, oblivious to the nurse leaving. And on the battle raged.

To make the pain go away I tried imagining myself in distant lands in Europe and Africa.

I thought of happier times with my family and fun moments with Meredith and Frank. I revisited hilarious episodes from high school and focused hard on the most recent memories with my Macon friends. None of it helped beyond a couple of minutes.

Same too of the latest Tramadol dose from the nurse who promised to return. The interruption was better than nothing, even if the meds were about as effective as a Tic-Tac.

Eventually, since pills were useless and sleep a pipedream and all other mental distractions ill-equipped against the onslaught of pain and his minions, I sought help elsewhere and reached for my phone. It was well-past 2:00 AM and I knew she'd be asleep in her dorm, but I was out of options and hit call regardless.

I looked at the screen. *Calling Kristen…* It began to ring.

— — — — —

Back on campus, when someone asked what you were doing Thursday night, "Break Time" was the common response. Ashland's Break Time Sports Bar seemed to be on everyone's Thursday night schedule to kick-off the weekend.

This smoke-filled dive in a nearby strip mall was nothing special, but it was a favorite pool hall of Ashland locals and Yellow-Jackets alike. It was something different, a change of scenery and only a short walk away.

That and their Thursday night DJ turned Break Time into something we all looked forward to.

It was also a venue for fraternities and sororities needing a cheap alternative for formal, invitation-only parties. It was here, at the Phi Mu Christmas bash, that Kristen entered the picture.

Kristen was a senior, with straight jet-black hair that fell past her shoulders when it wasn't up in an athletic ponytail. Her personality matched her smile and her wits, alluring in every sense, while her preference for humor and a sarcastic retort was fun, contagious, and never dull. It was over drinks and appetizers that we formally met.

Together we laughed and joked alongside a circle of my friends and hers, all of us dressed for the night in red, green or some hideously loud Christmas sweater. It was also here that I learned of her athleticism.

Kristen was a jock, a fact that fittingly added to her personality, which I'd quickly been privy to in only a short span. At the time Kristen was in her final year as a point guard for the women's basketball team. Beautiful. Hilarious. And athletic? Small wonder that my eyes drifted her way more and more as the night wore on.

To my surprise, hers did some drifting as well. I capitalized. Luckily there was some overlapping between her basketball friends and my football buddies, which made hanging out easy, natural, and, best of all, frequent.

As winter break inched closer, our time together increased. I liked Kristen from the start, but as I got to know her, I felt myself being drawn to her more each time I saw her around campus, at her games, in Estes.

When exam week rolled around, we even holed up and studied together in the Copley computer lab.

— — — — —

Kristen was more than a fling but less than a girlfriend in the months before my accident. Things had recently slowed down between us but hadn't yet come to a complete halt. As they often do in trying times, my accident fanned the embers of our relationship and brought it back to life.

During my time in the hospital, Kristen was a huge source of support and comfort when I needed her most and on this night, I needed her the absolute most.

I held the phone close and shut my eyes as the line rang and rang. I felt bad waking her up but there was nowhere else to turn.

Finally, a prayer was answered. A soft, tired voice came through and I swore the pain receded just a bit.

In a jumble of incoherent phrases and moans and groans, I tried to explain everything and tell her about the incredible pain I was in, that the nurses were doing nothing for me, how the throbbing hardware in my back was a living hell, and that I was sorry for waking her. There was little she could do beyond offering kind words and letting me vent to someone besides a nurse.

Again and again I told her she could go back to sleep and again and again she refused. "No, no," she said each time. "It's fine. I don't mind at all. I wish I could be there to help you."

We talked at times and shared the line in silence at others. Fighting the all-out assault was much easier with Kristen there on the pillow in phone form.

In a way Tramadol could only dream of, Kristen's presence, and even just hearing her breathing, gave me a new line of defense against the relentless enemy armed with sledgehammers and biting blades. Who knows how long we stayed on the phone. All I know is that Kristen helped me fight on.

Sometime past 3:00 AM Kristen's responses grew faint and I knew sleep was getting the best of her. I didn't want to keep her up just to listen to me groan all night, so I told her she could go, and again she refused. I managed to convince her I was now fine and as sleep drained the fight from her, she relented.

We said our goodnights and goodbyes, her with sleepy stupor to her voice and me with, well, one much different from trying to conceal suffering like it wasn't there. She wished me well and promised to call me in the morning. When I hung up, I returned to the same solitude and physical despair as before.

Only this time was different.

If nothing else, while still fighting my pain in bed, our phone call lifted my spirits and offered me hope. I found I had new strength in my resolve and a will to endure that wasn't there before. Now, the battle for mind, body, and soul was being fought on my terms.

Soon, the siege began to lift. The waves of Hellish hurt receded and the river of tears that had welled up so heavily ran dry.

Then I saw it. Far ahead a speck in the darkness, a flash of hope signaling a way out, offering salvation from this Night of Nights; the beacon I'd been fighting for.

Dawn. And in the dawn, I discovered gifts…

A new source of strength. Undaunting courage and determination. Perseverance. A fresh set of confidence and a force of will unearthed from deep within, far deeper than mere broken bones. Through suffering and despair I had tapped into a lifetime reserve of personal fortitude that would follow me forever.

They were gifts that, when things got tough, would always be there to remind me with a whisper in my ear, saying, "You got through that night, you can get through this."

— — — — —

It happens to be that personal strength is a key weapon that humans must use to cope successfully with trauma and "trauma may be a testing ground that reveals these strengths in you" because "the struggle can make you stronger."[56]

In other words, says Tedeschi and Moore, "just as necessity is the mother of invention, for many people, trauma may be the mother of strength."[57]

But in their PTG *Workbook*, a second type of personal strength is addressed.

Relying on one's self and the ability to face hardships is a factor that goes directly to the core of developing and discovering that Warrior Spirit that is not just common and synonymous with growth, but pivotal to making growth a reality rather than just a theory.

It's both proof of your independence and proof that you're independent.

As Tedeschi and Moore say to their audience of survivors, some parts of what you're going through must be done alone because no one but you is going to live your life for you. Regardless of your new circumstances in life, it's one that you and you alone have to live.

"The ability to face up to this," they explain, "and to see that you can live this new life using your own personal resources, can be a source of pride and comfort."[58]

That night I was alone, but I didn't necessarily make it to morning alone. It was an individual effort, but a team effort as well. Something from within got me through, but help from others got me through, too—Kristen, the nurses, thoughts of friends and family.

But above all, I knew deep down that it wouldn't last forever, and that even with people and forces pulling together in my corner of the ring, it was still up to me.

This wretched night has a bigger meaning as a metaphor for all I've endured and what I would face in the days, weeks, months, and years to come. Victory over despair came in the form of the next dose of painkillers, a voice on the phone, and the light of a new morning.

To achieve that, and get from one to the next, the price was the endurance of pain.

This has been my life, in a nutshell, since April 2007.

Through searing pain, severe suffering, and one severed spine, I found the gift of relativity and perspective in the form of strength, courage, determination, perseverance, confidence, and a force of will that's allowed me to push myself further and harder than most.

And I found it all waiting for me in the darkest hours of my darkest days, in this Hell-sent blessing I'm grateful for—my most fortunate misfortune.

It's from this that I can now forever whisper to myself that simple, slap-in-the-face reminder as needed:

"Dude. You'll be fine! If you got through that...you can get through this."

Chapter 67

SQUARE ONE

Like it does for all fresh-faced patients, whose broken and battered spines were rebuilt with rods and screws, rehab starts slow. Duration varies person to person, case by case, but it's always a long, arduous journey home.

After their crippling event, whatever it may be, all SCIs go under the knife. When they wake, they find themselves at the starting line of something big: their new life.

No matter who you are, spinal cord injuries are the great equalizers. Everyone is forced to restart. Once the doctors do their thing, and you're healed up enough to go forward, rehab becomes the starting gate.

In a race to recovery, when it comes to Attitude and Effort, my money is always on the military or military-minded. PTs and OTs love these people because they have incredible motivation. My hopes for the Marines dashed, my only option was to be the military-minded type.

But this race is fixed. No matter how fast someone wants to accomplish and master one objective and move on to the next, a team of race officials disguised as doctors, nurses, PTs, and OTs, hover close, watching your every move, governing pace in the interest of safety.

SCIs are also great equalizers because the road to home follows a certain universal route accepted by the field. *The patient needs to do this first before that. To do this, learn that, he/she must demonstrate the other thing before the next thing. You have to crawl before you can Parkour.*

238

The process demands baby steps, especially in weeks one and two, to give you, your body, and your mind the time it needs to come-to and sort things out.

During my five-week residency my primary goal focused on becoming as independent as possible by the time I went home. *By the time I go home.*

This denotes some sort of established time frame, which is true. However, just like one person's rehab to another's, timeframes vary based on what delivered you to the in-patient wing. For SCI's (paras here, not quads) in-patient is typically a few months depending on person and motivation levels.

Well, abnormal personal motivation aside, I established my own time frame, believe it or not.

Since the accident happened in late-April, rehab began approximately five weeks out from graduation. I had friends making final preparations to walk the stage at graduation and I fully intended to be there when they did. When I told the doctors this some were shocked, even skeptical.

They explained again the severity of my injury and how time was an important factor for healing.

"Blah blah blah."

I explained how I had every intention of leaving the hospital graduation morning, whether they, or the insurance companies, liked it or not.

And, so, it was, that nearly ten days after those chimney bricks ripped free in my hand, I started this long process of rehabilitation to reclaim independence and discover my New Normal with sights locked on that first Saturday in June.

The time to reroute my rerouted life had come. Adversity had struck. It was now time to strike back, to attack, tenaciously. To reroute my rerouted life and dream new dreams.

Learning to sit up and put shoes on was only the beginning.

Chapter 68

THE STRENGTH OF A SEAL

Early-May, 2007. MCV/VCU. In-patient Room. Richmond, VA.

Mom doesn't remember being in the hair salon that day. She doesn't remember talking to the Navy SEAL's wife. And she doesn't remember telling this stranger about her youngest son, and why exactly she was in Richmond.

In fact, Mom doesn't remember a lot about my time in the hospital that April and May in 2007.

"It was just such a traumatic event," she tells me. "It's like my mind blocked it out on purpose, like it wanted me to forget…I have zero recollection of talking to that woman in the salon."

But she did talk to her. The stone plaque at my bedside with an engraved message is proof.

Later that day while lying in bed, Mom returned and with hair coiffed she told me about a conversation she had had at the salon with a complete stranger. "I have no idea why, but I… I just opened up to her. Not sure why, but I did. I had no reason to tell her why I was here in Richmond, but I did. For some reason, I told her about your accident… And guess what?"

"What?"

"Her husband is a former Navy SEAL!"

I perked up. "Wait, what? Really??"

She nodded. "Uh huh. And she actually spoke to him while I was there." She paused. "He wants to come here, to meet you."

"No way!"

The next day a SEAL showed up with a knock at my door. I called out from the bed and welcomed him in then greeted him with as firm a handshake as I could muster, profusely thanking him for coming.

"Of course, of course. It's my pleasure." He slid one of the room's extra chairs next to the bed, took a seat, and placed what looked like a picture frame on his lap without a word about it. I studied him as he settled down.

I had been all set to join the Marines until those bricks broke free. But the fall didn't damage my desires or curb my interest, and now, in this very room, sitting next to me, there wasn't just a soldier, there was the ultimate soldier: a hardcore, one-of-a-kind Tier One Navy SEAL. And he was talking—to me.

I had never met an active duty or former SEAL before, so naturally I was curious and infatuated with the man before me.

From the looks of him you would never guess he was once a member of the warrior elite. He was fit and trim, yes, but his frame was altogether unassuming. The threads of his shirt weren't about to burst from bulging muscles and he wore no scowl or scar upon his face. He didn't have any signs one might expect if they came across a black ops operator from their movies or minds.

Rather, the man before me was just that—a man. I sized him up.

His humility was captivating. I wanted nothing more than to pick his brain and shower him with questions, the way a curious child might nag a parent over something new, tempting or mysterious.

After a few niceties for introduction, he questioned me and made it clear that his intentions were not about him but about me, and how he could help. "So, what's goin' on?" He asked, diving directly into the heart of the matter. "I heard what happened. How you holdin' up?"

"Well…" I broke eye contact to survey and consider the broken body lying motionless beneath fresh linens. I looked up. "Well…to be honest, surprisingly well. Given the circumstance."

He nodded silently, holding my gaze. I sensed he wanted more and obliged.

"I've always been a pretty upbeat and positive person. It's definitely helped." I cut myself off and let my eye walk around the room slowly, as if taking it all in for the first time. "Not to mention, it's tough to get sad and depressed with the incredible amount of love and support I've had around here. A family member is always here. My friends come down, too. I go to Randolph-Macon, just up the road…"

He made a knowing gesture.

"There's always visitors here, too, coming and going. There's not a lot of time to dwell on the sad stuff, really. I guess I'm lucky in that. They even had to move me to a separate room when I got here. They were clogging the ICU halls. But yeah, I guess I'm lucky."

I stopped again. I was rambling.

I felt self-conscious and looked at him, hoping he'd take the mantle and say something. He had leaned forward during my monologue and was listening, looking patiently like an old friend lending an ear. His eyes and body language told me he was actually interested and engaged.

He had come to my side at the behest of his wife, but I could see that now he was here, he was staying for more than just brownie points with the misses.

Like I'd hoped, he took the mantel on cue and I no longer felt embarrassed for my rambling. In fact, talking about it was therapeutic, and it only got better as we continued to talk.

"You certainly are lucky in that indeed." Said the SEAL. "It's good to hear you haven't gone belly-up. Hospital stays can be tough, tricky things. Not everyone handles it the same. Not everyone can handle it. Especially not the way you seem to be. You should be proud of that."

I allowed myself a self-indulgent smile. This was high praise coming from anyone, but this was a friggin' SEAL. "That means a lot," I said. 'It's not always this easy though. It seems like every half hour there's another thing to deal with, some challenge. The pain doesn't help either."

I suddenly missed the morphine all over again and remembered the long night and my fortunate misfortune. The thought of it sent a chill through me.

"Such is life." Said the SEAL. "Things can be goin' good, goin' good, and then…*BAM!* And before you know it, you and everything around you is covered in crap." He gave a look of disgust.

"Yup. Sounds about right. One minute I'm hangin' out with friends after a killer 80's party and the next I'm cursing the paramedics in the back of a speeding ambulance." I shook my head slowly and dropped my eyes, out of sheer stupidity and dumb luck, not depression. "Funny how things work out."

There was a short silence. Our chat had taken a heavy turn. The SEAL ran with it.

"I have something here for you," he said, scooping up the object on his lap, studying it.

He held it with precious reverence and read the words before showing it to me and spoke it a second time.

"Never. Never. *Never*...give up." He stated, then in a softer tone adding, "Churchill said it. During World War II, long time ago. It was his message to the people during Hitler's bombing runs over Britain. This was the mantra he wanted them to live by during some seriously tough times." He looked up at me and cocked an eyebrow.

The corner of his mouth twitched; a contagious smile sprouted.

"Never give up." I repeated, slow and measured.

"That's right, Mike." He handed me the gift. "Never give up. Never, never, never give up."

The weight of it surprised me. It looked like a picture frame and about the same size, but it was entirely made of stone. I ran my fingers across it. It had a nice balance of smooth and rough, the way processed stone would. I guessed marble and traced the grooves forming this simple but powerful phrase that once galvanized a country.

Since then, its universal message—particularly in the online viral age—has continued to empower thousands upon thousands, if not millions, in their time of need.

The SEAL continued. "I know you're handling all this like a true warrior would, but it won't always be easy. It won't always be sunshine and rainbows." I nodded vigorously. "Exactly. At some point things will stop being easy. Sooner or later that sunshine and those rainbows will become thunderstorms and shadows." I chuckled. "And when it does you'll have to respond...mentally and physically."

He stopped, letting his words sink in. I had told him about my hopes of becoming a Marine officer, so he turned military to drive his message home.

"There's a saying in BUD/S..." He paused. "It's what all of us lived by when the instructors were repeatedly feeding the fans with crap, crap, and more crap, day and night. For six months. It said that 'The only easy day was yesterday'."

I knew the saying. But now that it came from the mouth of an actual SEAL, it was like hearing it for the first time.

The SEAL adopted a more serious tone, returned to the edge of his seat, and leaned in.

"Everything that happened in the past is simple, easy." He revealed. "Over and done with. The hard stuff is always ahead, either hiding in ambush or waiting for you in plain sight. You have to be ready for it. You have to be ready and willing to respond to it body and mind. Mentally. Physically. You have to have the right attitude when the thunderstorm and shadows roll in. You have to have the right attitude and you have to put forth the right effort, just like you've been doing."

He looked me square in the eyes.

"But you have to keep doing that." The SEAL challenged. "You have to keep going. You have to refuse to quit. You have to defy defeat. You have to never, never…NEVER give up. You got me?"

I felt a surging pride. The hairs on my neck stood tall at attention. "I got you. Sir."

Something stirred inside me. The Sir I added was a reflex that came without meaning it. It triggered a second wave of pride-infused chills. I imagined myself in dress blues, the Eagle Globe and Anchor emblazoned on my chest.

As I hung on his every word and devoured his thoughtful gift that was more than just the five words engraved in stone, I found new purpose, passion, and motivation listening to him speak about his days in BUD/S, and beyond.

Fires ignited in my soul hearing about his grueling time spent in the sand and surf of Coronado Beach, battling frigid waters, weathering barking instructors and chaffing sand, hardening resolve and mental fortitude for half a year as they defied constant impulses to quit, ring the famous bell, and add their helmets to the lineup of others who chose the easy out.

But the man sitting inches from my hospital bed never rang the bell. The man sitting beside me never, ever quit. And I wasn't about to either.

Over twelve years have passed since the SEAL met with me. Since then, his gift has graced every bedside table of mine and forever follows me, the message burning in my heart.

Never Never Never Give Up.

I didn't then. I haven't now.

Epilogue
RETURNING RESILIENT

"PTG describes the experience of individuals whose development, at least in some areas, has surpassed what was present before the struggle with crisis occurred.

The individual has not only survived, but has experienced changes which are viewed as important, and that go beyond what was the previous status quo.

PTG is not simply a return to baseline—it is an experience of improvement that for some persons is deeply profound."[59]
—Tedeschi and Moore, *The PTG Workbook*

Late-August, 2007. Randolph-Macon College. Ashland, VA.

That first weekend back before Monday classes was nuts. There were tons of parties and lots of drinking, something I missed. It was quite the shock to my bladder, though.

My first party in a wheelchair was at Kappa Alpha.

Come Saturday night the house was packed; music blaring, people raging, and friends reunited. The semester had officially begun. Like I'd do many times to come, I entered through the back of the house after a brother unlocked the entrance gate in the fence. From there I proceeded to party like I hadn't missed a step.

To my surprise though, I soon realized that my presence, not just there in the house, but campus altogether, was a bigger deal than I'd thought.

I was the center of attention.

Everyone seemed so eager to say hi and welcome me back and give me huge hugs and fresh drinks— It was almost overwhelming.

For no less than 90% of the students at KA, this was their first time seeing me since my accident. People showed up to the hospital in droves, sure, but what happened to me had a ripple effect campus-wide, and at such a small school you have connections to almost everyone, so obviously not everyone could come down to visit.

But that was months ago. And just like rumors among a student body only 1,200 strong, word of my return spread like wildfire. It almost seemed like many of them came to KA that night specifically to share their love and support.

As the night wore on, it became apparent that little had changed. Eventually Campus Security wandered over to close the party.

Luckily, according to a loophole in the by-laws of Macon, or something like that, Campus Security was confined to the first floor when closing a party. Upstairs was off-limits. So, upstairs was where everyone typically fled to when a party was formally closed but the partying continued. It was nothing new.

Now, as the warning spread, I watched the party migrate up the central plantation-style staircase off of the living room. I was lost. I didn't know what to do.

Thwarted by my arch-nemesis—the stair—I was anxious and worried about getting left behind. I didn't know what to do.

The party had almost entirely moved to the second floor, the once-packed living room dance floor now empty, and me lost and confused. I looked around frantically—then it hit me.

I decided to fake like I was headed for the bathroom, an easy out so I didn't look stupid all by myself… And that's when two KA brothers nonchalantly came to my rescue, there at the bottom of the grand staircase.

"Ok, how do we get you up?" One asked coolly, like it was no big deal.

But it was. To me it was a huge deal, a simple question that spared me the embarrassment of being left behind, alone.

"Easy." I fired back, concealing my angst. "I'll show you."

Like I learned at NRH, I swung round, backed up snug against the first step, and before popping that initial wheelie, I gave a quick thirty-second tutorial with a comfortable confidence that comes from months of wheelchair boot camp.

Adopting a more serious tone to ensure cooperation, I said, "Okay, you in front. You behind. Hold on here, here…and back here." I half turned to the guy pulling in back. "We'll go at your pace. Nice n' easy. Watch your feet so you don't trip up. I'll give a 3-2-1 count for each step so we're on the same page. Cool?"

He nodded.

I turned back to the other volunteer in front, looked him in the eye. "I'm gonna pop a wheelie first to get into position. Your job is to keep me level as we go, so I don't tip forward." He nodded. "And you're not *lifting* so much as you are *pushing*," I clarified adding hand gestures, "to keep my wheels flush against the stairs. Got it? …Good."

I gripped the rims, shifted my weight, popped the wheelie, and the two simultaneously took hold where I'd indicated. One on the frame's two bars beside my calves, the other the horizontal bar at my back.

"On my count…" I announced firmly. "3…2…" On "1" they pushed and pulled. My wheels turned. Up I went. "3…2…1…up." Reset. "3…2…1 up." Reset…

We steadily inched our way up the grand staircase. Start. Reset. Start. Reset. I quickly picked up the cadence as the three of us found our rhythm. "3, 2, 1 up. 3, 2, 1, up. 3, 2, 1, up."

Step after step after step; one pulling, one pushing, me yanking backwards on my rims, helping as best I could. We were in a zone. When I happened to steal a glance upwards, I saw something and was completely taken aback. Stunned.

The wrap-around balcony overlooking the stairs was packed with students all crowding around close, hanging over the railing to watch. I hadn't noticed, nor even considered it. I thought the party was still raging on upstairs, room to room. I was wrong.

I continued to bark out the steady three-count, only this time it came with an added twinge of pride.

I'd come a long way since April.

It buoyed my spirits, in fact. In my nearly twenty-two years, I'd never been stronger than I was now. After playfully grabbing his arm one day, even Kyle was admittedly shocked at my newfound strength.

I was proud of all I had accomplished. And it was on display as the KA brothers took me up the final steps.

I doubt that anybody watching had ever considered what occurs in rehab when someone lands themselves in a wheelchair. Whatever it is, if anything, I'm sure the how-to's involving a flight of stairs didn't cross their mind, so I'm sure seeing this caught a few by surprise.

To my own surprise, when we reached the top, and my four wheels set down on the small landing before a shorter, second flight of about half a dozen steps, the crowd erupted in a great cheer.

Screams, whistles, and feverish applause echoed off the walls and through the house. I tried to suppress a huge budding smile to no avail. I looked up, saw my fellow classmates, and gave a small wave of appreciation.

Many I knew well, others less so, but we were all Yellow Jackets at Randolph-Macon. We'd been through a lot in these last three years, and as some would come to tell me in time, my accident had a profound impact on our quaint little campus.

Amidst the raucous applause I thanked my two helpers and then positioned my chair for the final steps leading to the main hall.

"Just like before." I said over the noise. They nodded. "Okay…3, 2, 1 up!"

This time, the crowd joined in, having picked up on my technique. "3, 2, 1, UP! 3, 2, 1, UP!" they sang harmoniously.

The energy goaded my team on. Faster and faster we moved. Yet the two saviors managed to maintain control and hold their footing until the final step was conquered and the second floor reached.

Our summit was again met with cheers all around. I gave a humble wave to the surging crowd and then quickly directed everyone's attention to the two-man team busy catching their breath beside me, hoping the crowd recognized their service and sacrifice as much as I had.

Everyone roared.

ACKNOWLEDGMENTS

This book has been possible because of the countless people who have worked together to get me to where I am today and tomorrow. With the limited space available, though, I must acknowledge some.

First and foremost, the love of my life and my best friend: Casey. Since 2012 I've grown into a better human being because of you. Your work ethic and drive has motivated me more than you can ever know. I love you fiercely as my wife, but even more as the beautiful mother of our sweet little dude, Dylan, and our fur baby, Gunner.

Second only to Casey is, of course, my family: Mommom and Poppy, Grandmother Murphy and Granddaddy Murphy, Mom and Dad, Frank, Cristina, Olivia and John, Meredith, Eric, Claire, Everly, and Jack, Melanie, Jeffrey, and Scott, Aunt Paige and Steve, Uncle Paul and his brood of Duane, Rachael, Leah and Evelyn, and all others in the Murphy-Gardner Clan. If I could, I'd dedicate a full page of appreciation to each one of you.

I'd happily list all of the members of my wife's Aber-McInerny-Groff Clan that I've been pulled into with open, loving arms, but that would eat up at least a dozen extra pages. There's too many. But you know who you are, so know that I'm proud to be legally tied to you people—whether I like it or not. But to Pam and "TM"—thanks again for letting me marry your daughter.

Next is everyone I've called a friend and done dumb stuff with:

Thank you for all the good times past and all the better times future. Thank you for the laughs, the support, the smack talk, the advice, the camaraderie, the teamwork, the late nights, early mornings, and all the memorable hijinks as high schoolers, collegiate adults, 20-something semi-adults, and now as a bunch of 30-something-year-olds with wives and husbands and kids who keep us in check. You know who you are.

Because of the central role academics has played in my life, both good and bad, I'd be remiss if I didn't acknowledge my teachers.

From Potomac to Randolph-Macon to George Mason, for years, through good grades and bad, you poked, prodded, and pushed me to my intellectual limits. At times I despised you, cursed your assignments and expectations and at times I loved you. At times I smiled and was thankful and told funny stories about what this teacher did or how that teacher saved me.

My journey from classroom to classroom was a weird one. It has helped make me who I am. YOU have helped make me who I am. Thank you.

Next, I must tilt my cap to all my coaches. You too know who you are. From Little League Tee-ball to high school varsity, the D3 arena after, and the world of adaptive sports after that—you've kept me humble, hungry, and constantly competitive.

You expected the best and then some from me. You held me to a standard that, at times, I didn't think capable and it forged me into a competitor that I hope made you proud. You helped foster environments for me to live out my love for winning. You taught me about life. You taught me about teamwork. You taught me how to have fun. And for that I'm eternally grateful. Thank you.

To my supporters in general: You have been the army behind me and beside me for all my days. You are constantly in my thoughts in everything I do. You inspire me to do right and to habitually set the example and be the example. Thank you.

Finally, I must recognize a handful of people who have been instrumental in helping me with all things Michael Murphy Speaks LLC related—namely, public speaking and the creation of this book and those still to follow.

To Bernie and Paula Swain. You've been wonderful friends of the family for as long as I can recall. The support you've showered over me post-accident and then with the start of my business is too much to properly repay or put into words. Thank you.

A huge shout out must go to my editor with that awesome English accent— Virginia Seatherton.

I can't thank you enough—but through the currency of "boxes of wine," I hope I did my best. You were the variable that made this book into what I always knew it could be. Through brutal honesty and hilarious commentary, you helped whittle away the excess crud that my book had been stuck in. Even though we "knew" each other while not really "knowing" each other in college, I cherish the friendship we've created through texts, emails, and phone calls these last few years. You're the best! Thank you.

To Meredith. My junior editor/sister/fact-checker. You said that editing and fact checking brings you "joy"... Therefore, I'm glad to have given you this joyful opportunity. You're welcome. (But really. Thanks, Dingus!)

To Kristin Beale. The advice you gave me during the book writing process has been invaluable. By vouching for me and presenting my work to the Morgan James family, you have changed my life in profound ways. Nicely done. Keep it up! And, thank you.

To everyone at Morgan James Publishing. Thank you for saying yes and giving my message a chance. Thank you, thank you, thank you. I am eternally grateful.

To Jovanna Suarez, the mastermind behind my website beginning in 2015. You created an amazing vision for what my website could be and how it could stand out, and you delivered. Please accept my deepest gratitude.

And to Derek Thompson, long-time friend, classmate, and academic motivator. Without your expert advice and assistance, I still probably would have never heard of Posttraumatic Growth even as I continue to live life with it. Your recommendations and input surrounding PTG has unquestionably elevated this story. Thank you for helping me in my ongoing quest of helping others.

A NOTE ON RESOURCES

PTG is a new field. It is best known and understood by psychologists, clinicians, and scientists closely associated with its development and research—and by those, like me, who enjoy chasing footnotes in a quiet university library. It is safe to suggest, then, that the general public is largely in the dark about PTG. I know I was.

Therefore, I think it will be helpful to include an explanation about my research, source material, and use of those sources to clarify this theme in my stories.

For this PTG thread, I decided to focus on a few select works to maintain some semblance of continuity throughout and avoid information overload.

Dr. Haas' *Bouncing Forward*, Dr. Joseph's *What Doesn't Kill Us*, and, finally, *The Posttraumatic Growth Workbook* by Drs. Tedeschi and Moore. These three, to me, stand out among the field not only for their lucid, succinct summaries and analysis of PTG, but also for their target audiences: the survivor and the survivors' loved ones.

Countless other resources have been combed through to supplement the context of these works, but these three represent a solid, almost-all-encompassing cross-section of the field from the last decade.

And that they have also been featured regularly in bibliographies of their peers speaks to their influence and importance.

Please note that I do not pretend nor claim to be an expert in this field. I have not done the leg work that these professionals have. But I do have a couple of degrees. I (humbly) know how to research, read, and critically analyze a scholarly topic as well as how to breakdown the historiography within the published academia from its inception to the present day.

Historiography is the history of the history.

For instance, the historiography of D-Day wouldn't focus on the events of June 1944, it would focus on the arguments of historians in the decades since, tracing things like, say, how a new cache of declassified material 40 years later proves or disproves a long-held line of thinking accepted by historians. This is the history of the history.

So, when it comes to PTG, I'm able to take this information and boil it down into a lucid, relatable story that's comprehensible for readers to easily digest. Because this is something readers, I feel, should—and need to—hear. Because I've lived it.

I have spent endless hours with my nose in the world of PTG psychology. I have consulted books, memoirs, clinical studies, online resources, and articles from respected academic journals from the past 30 years. I have chased footnotes and endnotes and browsed bibliographies and *Works Cited* sections to trace the historiographical breadcrumbs of Posttraumatic Growth.

I have done this to bring awareness to this growing idea and to add an important extra element that hopefully helps those who need it.

I don't pretend to be something I'm not—a psychologist. Or even a professional academic with degrees beyond that of my Masters or decades worth of field experience to qualify myself as a voice of authority. Instead, I have let the real voices of authority speak for themselves.

SUGGESTED READINGS AND RESOURCES

For anyone in need of more information and resources:

Dr. Haas has done her due diligence by researching and understanding this field, but she's also done her own leg work. As a result, *Bouncing Forward* is a well-written, well-researched How-To book with powerful vignettes and words of wisdom.

The book represents a critical step in bringing this important topic to the mainstream masses where the average person can learn about PTG and understand precisely how to experience it for themselves, if they haven't already. The hope is that my book adds to Dr. Haas' mission.

For quick links and easily accessible data and information, Dr. Haas has a great website that was instrumental in the early stages of my own PTG research:

See www.WhenIFell.com for link.

Here you will find a reading list featuring inspiring PTG testimonials, lifeline phone numbers for those in need, links about Buddhist wisdom and lists featuring books specifically by psychologists. There's even a "Bouncing Forward Playlist" YouTube link with Dr. Haas' personal go-to music set to inspirational lyrics.

For the more academic-type, UNC Charlotte's Psychology Department has an entire site dedicated to the ground-breaking work spurred by Drs. Tedeschi and Calhoun:

See www.WhenIFell.com for link.

The website has not been updated in years; however, it is a great place for both intro-level information and more in-depth material for researchers. Here you will find an exhaustive list of some of the most instrumental publications (books, articles, book chapters) in the field.

Dr. Joseph's *What Doesn't Kill Us* is another valuable tool beyond its main text.

This book concludes with his own six steps to facilitate posttraumatic growth, "designed to offer readers guidance in managing their emotions and taking the first steps toward seeking growth". It includes "common reactions to trauma… changes that people might experience, and exercises that might be helpful along the way."[60]

Similarly, *The Posttraumatic Growth Workbook* also offers exercises, but on an entirely deeper level that challenges the reader to confront themselves and answer tough, brutally honest questions intended to cut to the core of the individual and reveal the nature of the issues or problems (either made up or real) that's holding them back and preventing growth.

This too has a solid, but not overwhelming, list of references and resources at the end that's worth consulting. But for this book it is the main, exercise-driven text as a whole that's truly worth noting.

Of course, there's much, much more out there. Perhaps too much. But for those new to PTG, like I recently was, these are great launching spots.

Additionally, a list of resources and foundations that have helped Michael can be found and accessed on the Resources page of this books' website along with the previously mentioned website above:

www.WhenIFell.com.

ABOUT THE AUTHOR

Michael is an 11-time marathoner with Top 5 finishes in New York and Boston. He is a Tough Mudder adaptive athlete finisher.

He received his B.A. in History from Randolph-Macon College, with a double Minor in Classical Studies and Art History, and his M.A. in American Military History from George Mason University. He launched Michael Murphy Speaks LLC in 2015 to speak about and write his story.

Originally from McLean, Virginia, Michael resides in Denver, Colorado, with wife Casey, German Shepherd, Gunner, and new baby, Dylan. He is now a sit-ski racer pursuing his Paralympic dream for Team USA.

REFERENCES AND WORKS CITED

Calhoun, Lawrence G. and Richard G. Tedeschi. "The Foundations of Posttraumatic Growth: New Considerations." *Psychological Inquiry* 15, no. 1 (2004): 93-102.

Calhoun, Lawrence G. and Richard G. Tedeschi. "PTG: Conceptual Foundations and Empirical Evidence." *Psychological Inquiry* 15, no.1 (2004): 1-18.

Carver, Charles S. "Resilience and Thriving: Issues, Models, and Linkages." *Journal of Social Issues* 54, no. 2 (Summer 1998): 245-266, https://spssi. onlinelibrary.wiley.com/doi/abs/10.1111/j.1540-4560.1998.tb01217.x.

Collier, Lorna. "Growth After Trauma." *American Psychological Association* 47, no. 10 (November 2016): 48, https://www.apa.org/monitor/2016/11/ growth-trauma.

Duggan, Colette, PhD, Catherine Wilson, PsyD, Lisa DiPonio, MD, Brad Trumpower, MS, and Michelle A. Meade, PhD. "Resilience and Happiness After Spinal Cord Injury: A Qualitative Study." *Topics in Spinal Cord Injury Rehabilitation* 22, no. 2 (Spring 2016): 99-110, https://www.ncbi.nlm.nih.gov/ pmc/articles/PMC4896325/.

Groleau, Jessica M., Lawrence G. Calhoun, Arnie Cann, and Richard G. Tedeschi. "The Role of Centrality of Events in Posttraumatic Distress and Posttraumatic Growth." *American Psychological Association* 5, no. 5 (2013): 477-483. Psychological Trauma: Theory, Research, Practice, and Policy.

Haas, Michaela, PhD. *Bouncing Forward: Transforming Bad Breaks into Breakthroughs.* New York: Atria/Enliven Books, 2016.

Haas, Michaela, PhD. "What is Posttraumatic Growth?" Accessed May-July 2019. https://www.michaelahaas.com/what-is-posttraumatic-growth.

Holy Bible, New International Version, NIV, Biblica Inc. 2011

Joseph, Stephen, PhD. *What Doesn't Kill Us: The New Psychology of Posttraumatic Growth.* New York: Basic Books, 2011.

Kennedy, P., P. Lude, M. L. Elfstrom, and A. Cox. "Perceptions of Gain Following Spinal Cord Injury: A Qualitative Analysis." *Topics in Spinal Cord Injury Rehabilitation* 19, no. 3 (Summer 2013): 202-210, https://www.ncbi.nlm.nih.gov/pubmed/23960704.

Mullins, Aimee. "The Opportunity of Adversity." Filmed October 2009 at TEDMED, San Diego, CA. Video, 21:43. https://www.ted.com/talks/aimee_mullins_the_opportunity_of_adversity.

PTSInjury. "Background Of The Debate." Accessed May 2019. https://www.posttraumaticstressinjury.org/.

Proffitt, Deborah, Arnie Cann, Lawrence G. Calhoun, and Richard G. Tedeschi. "Judeo-Christian Clergy and Personal Crisis: Religion, Posttraumatic Growth and Well Being." *Journal of Religion and Health* 46, no. 2 (June 2007): 219-231, https://sites.uncc.edu/ptgi/wp-content/uploads/sites/9/2015/01/Judeo-Christian-clergy-and-personal-crisis.pdf.

Rendon, Jim. *Upside: The New Science of Post-Traumatic Growth.* New York: Touchstone, 2015.

Sundquist, Josh. *Just Don't Fall: A Hilariously True Story of Childhood, Cancer, Amputation, Romantic Yearning, Truth, and Olympic Greatness.* New York: Viking Penguin, 2010.

Tedeschi, Richard G. "Posttraumatic Growth in Combat Veterans." *Journal of Clinical Psychology in Medical Settings* 18 (May 2011): 137-144, https://ptgi.uncc.edu/wp-content/uploads/sites/9/2015/01/Posttraumatic-growth-in-combat-veterans.pdf.

Tedeschi, Richard G. and Lawrence G. Calhoun. "The Posttraumatic Growth Inventory: Measuring the Positive Legacy of Trauma." *Journal of Traumatic Stress* 9, no. 3 (1996): 455-471, https://sites.uncc.edu/ptgi/wp-content/uploads/sites/9/2015/01/The-Posttraumatic-Growth-Inventory-Measuring-the-positive-legacy-of-trauma.pdf.

Tedeschi, Richard G. and Bret A. Moore. *The Posttraumatic Growth Workbook: Coming Through Trauma Wiser, Stronger, and More Resilient.* Oakland: New Harbinger Publications, Inc., 2016.

UNC Charlotte Posttraumatic Growth Research Group. "What is PTG?" Accessed April 17, 2019. https://ptgi.uncc.edu/what-is-ptg/.

Wikipedia. "Posttraumatic growth." Accessed April-September 2019. https://en.wikipedia.org/wiki/Posttraumatic_growth.

Zupan, Mark and Tim Swanson. *Gimp*. New York: HarperCollins Publishers, 2006.

ENDNOTES

1   Richard Tedeschi and Bret Moore, *The Posttraumatic Growth Workbook: Coming Through Trauma Wiser, Stronger, and More Resilient* (Oakland: New Harbinger Publications, Inc, 2016), 67.

2   "What is PTG?," UNC Charlotte Posttraumatic Growth Research Group, accessed April 17, 2019, https://ptgi.uncc.edu/what-is-ptg/.

3   "What is PTG?"

4   Michaela Haas, *Bouncing Forward: The Art and Science of Cultivating Resilience* (New York: Atria/Enliven Books, 2016), 3.

5   Haas, *Bouncing Forward*, 3.

6   Ibid., 4.

7   Ibid., 9.

8   Ibid., 3.

9   Dr. Stephen Joseph, *What Doesn't Kill Us: The New Psychology of Posttraumatic Growth* (New York: Basic Books, 2011), xiv.

10 Joseph, *What Doesn't Kill Us*, xiii.

11 Ibid., xvii.

12 Ibid., 117.

13 Ibid., 121.

14 Ibid., xiv.

15 Lawrence G Calhoun. and Richard G. Tedeschi. "PTG: Conceptual Foundations and Empirical Evidence," *Psychological Inquiry* 15, no.1 (2004): 1.

16 Tedeschi and Moore, *The Workbook*, 5.

17 Tedeschi and Moore, *The Workbook*, 47.

18 Ibid., 47.

19 Joseph, *What Doesn't Kill Us,* xiv.

20 Ibid., xiii.

21 Ibid., 129.

22 Ibid., 127.

23 Ibid., 128.

24 Ibid., 126.

25 Ibid., 127.

26 Richard Tedeschi quoted in Lorna Collier, "Growth After Trauma," *American Psychological Association* 47, no. 10 (November 2016), 48, https://www.apa.org/monitor/2016/11/growth-trauma.

27 Haas, *Bouncing Forward*, 3.

28 Tedeschi and Moore, *The Workbook,* 46-49.

29 Ibid., 49.

30 Ibid., 72.

31 Colette Duggan, Catherine Wilson, Lisa DiPonio, Brad Trumpower, and Michelle A. Meade, "Resilience and Happiness After Spinal Cord Injury: A Qualitative Study," *Topics in Spinal Cord Injury Rehabilitation* 22, no. 2 (Spring 2016): 107, https://www.ncbi.nlm.nih.gov/pmc/articles/PMC4896325/.

32 Haas, *Bouncing Forward,* 318.

33 Tedeschi and Moore, *The Workbook,* 84.

34 Tedeschi and Moore, *The Workbook,* 4-5.

35 Joseph, *What Doesn't Kill Us,* 122.

36 Haas, *Bouncing Forward,* 385.

37 Ibid., 383.

38 Joseph, *What Doesn't Kill Us,* 122.

39 Haas, *Bouncing Forward,* 383.

40 Tedeschi and Moore, *The Workbook,* 84.

41 Tedeschi and Moore, *The Workbook,* 84.

42 Ibid., 84.

43 Joseph, *What Doesn't Kill Us,* 124-125.

44 "Ecstasy," Dictionary.com, accessed February 20, 2020, https://www.dictionary.com/browse/ecstasy?s=t.

45 Tedeschi and Moore, *The Workbook,* 105.

46 Tedeschi and Moore, *The Workbook,* 75.

47 Ibid., 105.

48 Ibid., 107.
49 Haas, *Bouncing Forward,* 60.
50 Joseph, *What Doesn't Kill Us,* xv.
51 Tedeschi and Moore, *The Workbook,* 6.
52 Tedeschi and Moore, *The Workbook,* 78
53 Tedeschi and Moore, *The Workbook,* 78.
54 Ibid., 78.
55 Tedeschi and Moore, *The Workbook,* 72.
56 Tedeschi and Moore, *The Workbook,* 72.
57 Ibid., 72.
58 Ibid., 73.
59 Tedeschi and Moore, *The Workbook,* 4.
60 Joseph, *What Doesn't Kill Us,* 171.

CPSIA information can be obtained
at www.ICGtesting.com
Printed in the USA
JSHW041239230321
12824JS00002B/80